1 MONTH OF FREE READING

at
www.ForgottenBooks.com

By purchasing this book you are eligible for one month membership to ForgottenBooks.com, giving you unlimited access to our entire collection of over 1,000,000 titles via our web site and mobile apps.

To claim your free month visit:
www.forgottenbooks.com/free71480

* Offer is valid for 45 days from date of purchase. Terms and conditions apply.

ISBN 978-0-484-60143-6
PIBN 10071480

This book is a reproduction of an important historical work. Forgotten Books uses state-of-the-art technology to digitally reconstruct the work, preserving the original format whilst repairing imperfections present in the aged copy. In rare cases, an imperfection in the original, such as a blemish or missing page, may be replicated in our edition. We do, however, repair the vast majority of imperfections successfully; any imperfections that remain are intentionally left to preserve the state of such historical works.

Forgotten Books is a registered trademark of FB &c Ltd.
Copyright © 2018 FB &c Ltd.
FB &c Ltd, Dalton House, 60 Windsor Avenue, London, SW19 2RR.
Company number 08720141. Registered in England and Wales.

For support please visit www.forgottenbooks.com

ORY OF ST MARY'S EY OF BUCKFAST

IN THE COUNTY OF DEVON)

A.D. 760—1906

ADAM HAMILTON, O.S.B.

SOLD BY THE PROCURATOR

AST ABBEY, BUCKFASTLEIGH
DEVON

HISTORY OF ST MARY'S ABBEY OF BUCKFAST

(IN THE COUNTY OF DEVON)

A.D. 760—1906

BY

DOM ADAM HAMILTON, O.S.B.

SOLD BY THE PROCURATOR
AT
BUCKFAST ABBEY, BUCKFASTLEIGH
DEVON

TO THE
RIGHT REVEREND FATHER ABBOT
DOM ANSCAR VONIER, O.S.B.
AND THE
MONKS OF BUCKFAST ABBEY
THE HISTORY OF OUR DEAR MONASTIC HOME IS
REVERENTLY AND AFFECTIONATELY
DEDICATED

PREFACE

THIS history has been written primarily for the monks of St Mary's venerable Abbey at Buckfast, and, in the second place, for Devonshire men.

Their love for our county will make them readily understand that the writer could not but delight in a tale of "Fair Devon." He could never see from the railway the towers of Exeter Cathedral without emotions of pleasure and affection at the thought that in that dear old city his mother was born.

One hundred years ago, in 1806, the walls of our Abbey Church, which for two hundred and sixty-seven years had been left to ruin and decay, were finally levelled, the materials sold or employed in building a mansion on the site of the former guest-house, and every trace of the sacred edifice effaced. Nothing was left when the monks took possession of the Abbey in 1882 to tell them that under the turf of the meadow that adjoined the mansion at its north-east corner, they would find the buried foundations of St Mary's Abbey Church.

Now, in 1906, its walls are being reared anew, by the labour of the monks, on those twelfth-century foundations, which rest in part on earlier masonry of Saxon days, dating perhaps from the Heptarchy. The centenary year from the final effacement of the consecrated fabric marks the beginning of the joyous work of building up again what had been in days of infinite sadness laid low.

But not to Devonshire men alone, we may hope, will the story of the monastery on the Dart be of interest. Only in its almost unbroken tranquillity did the mission of the children of St Benedict at Buckfast differ from their work in other parts of England, and their part in forming the English nation may be here studied with advantage. How they first formed agricultural and pastoral settlements, created villages round a parish church, obtained royal grants for these colonies of husbandmen, till they grew into flourishing market towns under the sway of the Abbot's crozier, and educated them in the Christian Faith and the arts of civilisation, is well illustrated in our history. Some perhaps, like the writer himself, will find greater pleasure in the little incidents of social life contained in what has survived to us of our records. The spirit of the Ages of Faith gives them a charm in which later times are sadly lacking.

It would be idle to hope that no errors will be found in the course of the volume. These will be corrected, and ampler materials brought to light, no doubt, by the researches of future writers.

It may appear to some that a mythical antiquity has been claimed for our monastery. But in reality there is no getting away from the fact, certified in Domesday Book, that none of the Kings of Wessex or of England before the Conquest ever ventured to assess the little manor on which our Abbey was situated, while every acre besides in the county was rigorously assessed. So remote is its antiquity, that no memory of its founder is to be discovered in the most ancient records.

The historic names of Denys Petre, Drake, D'Oyley, Rolle, Clinton, Mainwaring, and Baker would have given interest to an account of the lay possessors of the Abbey and its estates since 1539, but it has not been found practicable in this edition.

Among the authorities that have been the bistorical sources of the narrative, three living Devonshire historians have been chiefly followed. The first place is due to Mr J. Brooking Rowe, in his most valuable work on the Cistercian Houses of Devon. The Rev. Oswald Reichel, than whom no man living is better versed in the *gesta* of Anglo-Saxons in the West, in his contributions to the *Transactions of the Devonshire Association*, and the Rev. Prebendary Hingeston-Randolph in his colossal labour of editing the *Episcopal Registers of the Exeter Diocese*, come next in order. The late Mr Davidson's *Saxon Conquest of Devon*, Dr Oliver's *Monasticon of the Exeter Diocese*, and Mr Charles Worthy's books on Devonshire have helped to clear up many obscure points in our history and add names to the list of our Abbots. The neglect of civil and ecclesiastical records between 1450 and 1500 leaves that period a very dark one.

Besides those Devonshire antiquaries mentioned above, who are still happily with us, I owe a debt of gratitude to Mr F. Walters, the architect of the restoration, for several illustrations; to the Chi-

PREFACE

chester family of Calverleigh, for their pedigrees of Chichester and Beaumont; to Dom Norbert Birt, O.S.B., Miss Henrietta Walton, the Rev. Canon Edmonds, librarian of Exeter Cathedral, Mr H. Hems, and others, for much valuable help.

The circumstances attending the death of Abbot Boniface Natter in the wreck of the *Sirio* on the 4th August in this year, and the election of his successor, Abbot Anscar Vonier, necessitated the addition of two chapters. Both these prelates were "children of the Abbey," and grew up from boyhood within its walls. On both the nameless charm of Devon cast its spell, and made them fervent lovers of their monastic home, and their names will be chronicled by some future annalist as worthy successors of Abbots Ælfwyne and Eustace, Philip Beaumont, William Slade, and John Rede.

BUCKFAST ABBEY,
Feast of All Saints of the Order of St Benedict,
13th November 1906.

CONTENTS

CHAPTER I

"Bucfaesten," the stag's fastness. The Kingdom of Wessex, A.D. 760. King Cynewulf and Bishop Ethelmode. The Saxon conquest of Devon. Battles round Hembury Fort. The Manor that "never paid the geld." The Saxon Monastery. Antiquity of St Mary's Abbey. The Lady Beornwyn. St Petrock's territory 1

CHAPTER II

The earliest home of the monks; its surroundings. The great moor. The Dart. The Holy Brook. Buckfast and Buckfastleigh. Existing portions of the old Abbey. Children of the Abbey. Its dependent oratories. Festivals at Buckfast in Saxon days. Abbots Ælfsige and Ælfwine . 11

CHAPTER III

The Northmen in Devon. Tavistock Abbey destroyed. Abbot Ælfwine. A meeting of the Shire-mote; its members. Earl Godwin. The Bishops of Crediton and Sherburne. The Abbots of Buckfast and Tavistock. Other thanes. A legend of Earl Ordulf 18

CHAPTER IV

A Journey from Buckfast to Exeter in the Reign of the Confessor. Bishop Leofric of Crediton installed by the King in his new Cathedral of Exeter. The Abbots of Buckfast and Tavistock in the Confessor's Reign at the Exeter Shire-mote. The Norman Conquest. St Mary's Abbey not disturbed. Domesday Book and the estates of Buckfast Abbey. Serfdom in Anglo-Saxon times . . 25

CHAPTER V

Lands of St Mary's Abbey in the reign of Edward the Confessor. The South Devon estates. Brent, Ash, Heathfield, Churchstow, Kingsbridge. Dodbrooke and the Lady Godeva. Trusham near Chudleigh. Zeal Monachorum. Down St Mary and Petrockstow in North Devon . . . 32

CONTENTS

CHAPTER VI

The earliest of our extant charters. A deed in the reign of Henry I., now in the possession of the Abbey. Judhel the son of Alured the Giant. Sir Roger de Nnuant and his family. The "Mary Mass." The wood and meadow on the banks of the North Brook. "Priestaford." The knightly witnesses to the charter. The Earl of Totnes. The arms of Buckfast. **37**

CHAPTER VII

The religious revival in England in the reign of Henry I. His charter granted to St Mary's Abbey. Extinction of the Saxon community. The Grey Monks at Buckfast. Robert de Mortaigne and Ralph de Fougères. Ipplepen. Blessed Vitalis and the Order of Savigny. The Synod of London in 1102. Norman monks introduced at Buckfast about 1105 Death of Blessed Vitalis of Savigny . . . **45**

CHAPTER VIII

Buckfast Abbey a Cistercian house. The General Chapter of Citeaux, 1148. Blessed Eugene III. The English monasteries of the Savigny Congregation hesitate to become Cistercians. Charter of Henry II. St Thomas of Canterbury. The Tracys of Devonshire. Foundation of Torre Abbey **57**

CHAPTER IX

Sufferings of the Monks in the reign of King John. The Interdict of Innocent III. The holders of the Baronies of Totnes and Harberton. Peace restored. The Cistercian Abbeys of Buckland, Newenham, Dunkeswell, and Ford, in Devon **66**

CHAPTER X

Growing prosperity. Cistercian lay-brothers. The out-lying possessions of the monks on Dartmoor. Buckfast Moor. Agricultural labourers in the thirteenth century. Abbot Nicholas sells houses at Exeter. Abbot Michael. Architectural remains of the Abbey at the present day . . **72**

CONTENTS

CHAPTER XI

Sir Robert de Helion's kindness to the monks of Buckfast. A distinguished company assembled in the chapter-house. Sir William Hamelin of Deandon. Sir Reginald de Valletort's land. A bad bargain. Trouble about the pigs. Sir Stephen de Bauceyn. Everything now as in days of yore. Abbots of Buckfast from 1142 to 1272 . 82

CHAPTER XII

Sir Stephen de Bauceyn slain in battle by Rees Vaughan. His land at Holne, now called "Bozon's Farm." Sir Richard de Bauceyn. Faith and chivalry in the thirteenth century. The Chronicle of Newenham Abbey in Devon. The holy death of Sir Reginald de Mohun 90

CHAPTER XIII

Tranquillity of Devonshire during the War of the Barons in the reign of Henry III. Durand and Henry, Abbots of Buckfast (1253-1272). Walter Bronescombe, Bishop of Exeter. The Bishop holds his court in the chapter-house of the Abbey (1259). His zeal and activity. Social changes in Devon. Bondmen become wealthy landowners. Richard Tyulla. The hospital of the poor at Buckfast Abbey. Bishop Bronescombe a friend to the community. Priory of St Nicholas 97

CHAPTER XIV

Abbot Simon, 1272. Amicia, Countess of Devon, founds Buckland Abbey. A dispute between the Bishop of Exeter and the Buckland monks. Abbot Robert, 1280. Defence of his rights against the crown. Baronial rights of the Abbot in the reign of Edward I. A question concerning pasturage on Dartmoor. The perambulation of Dartmoor in 1240. A delightful summer ride. The Abbey moors no part of the Forest of Dartmoor 105

CHAPTER XV

The new order of things in England. Cistercian decline. Parliament at Exeter in 1285. The Exeter Synod of 1287. Death of Abbot Robert. Extracts from the Buckfast cartulary. Edward I. visits the Abbey. Abbot Peter II. Distress of the monastic houses in the reign of Edward I. Abbot Robert II. 115

CONTENTS

CHAPTER XVI

Enthronement of Bishop de Stapeldon. Sir Hugh Courtenay as seneschal. Ordinations. Names of the monks. The language spoken by the community at the opening of the fourteenth century. Ashburton; its wollen trade and the monks of Buckfast. The chapel of St Lawrence. The service-books written by the monks. The Bishop's last visit. A manumission. Bishop Stapeldon murdered, 15th Oct. 1316 122

CHAPTER XVII

Bishops of Exeter. James de Berkeley. John de Grandisson. Installation of Abbot Stephen, 1327. He reconciles Thurlestone Church. Bishop Grandisson at Buckfast Abbey. Abbot Stephen at the Council of London, 1329. The statue of our Lady of Buckfast. Abbot John of Churchstow, 1332. Abbot Gifford, 1333. The Devonshire Giffords. Abbot Stephen of Cornwall, 1348 132

CHAPTER XVIII

The Black Death; its ravages in Devonshire. Abbot Stephen of Cornwall, 1349. Abbot Philip Beaumont, 1349. Abbot Robert Simons. Bishop Ware's grave at Buckfast; his ring. The Beaumonts of Sherwell. Sherwell and Youlston. Chichesters of Raleigh. Chichesters of Calverleigh . . 140

CHAPTER XIX

Wyclif and the Lollards. Troubles in Devonshire. Bishops Brantingham and Stafford. Abbot William Paderstow. Brothers William Stele and John Stourton. Abbot William Slade; his education at Exeter and Oxford; his reputation for learning 150

CHAPTER XX

Churchstow, "the place of the church." The town of Kingsbridge. St Edmund the Martyr's Church. The monks build a new church at Kingsbridge. Monastic remains. Leigh Barton. Cistercian wood-carving. Death of Abbot Slade. The blind Earl of Devon. A Tiverton legend. Boys educated for the Church at our Abbey . . 158

CHAPTER XXI

Abbot William Beaghe. Loyalty of the monks. A domestic incident. Abbots Rogger and Ffytchett. Abbot John Matthew, 1449. The Matthews of Glamorgan. Three of the Abbey settlements developed into flourishing market towns. Was Bishop Bothe of Exeter Abbot of Buckfast? Abbot King and his restoration work. A Buckfast monk Prior of St Bernard's College, Oxford. Abbots Rede, Pomeroy, and Gyll 170

CHAPTER XXII

The last Abbot before the Dissolution. Dearth of records. Isolation of the Abbot. The Convocation of 1531. The Act of Succession. The Oath of Supremacy; was it taken by the monks of Buckfast? Abbot Rede's integrity. Prior Arnold Gye 187

CHAPTER XXIII

Gabriel Donne. Abbot Rede's last act. The Cistercian house of Stratford Langthorne. Donne's earlier career. "The wolf rampant." Surrenders of Devonshire monasteries in 1539. Canonsleigh, Hartland, and Torre. The Eve of St Matthias, 1539. A strange coincidence. Sir William Petre . . 196

CHAPTER XXIV

Haste of the Royal Commissioners. Hostile attitude of the people. Arrival of Petre and his company at Buckfast. The last scene in the chapter-house. Names of the monks. Dismantling of the Abbey after the expulsion of the community . 206

CHAPTER XXV

Buckfast Abbey after the Dissolution; its lay impropriators. Sir Thomas Denys; providential consequences of his purchase of the Abbey. The Catholic insurrection of 1549. Descendants of Sir Thomas Denys. The Rolle family. The building levelled in 1806 212

CHAPTER XXVI

St Mary's Fountain in the forest. Père Muard. Arrival of the monks at Buckfast in 1882. The first mass. The temporary church. The Feast of St Robert, 1886. Excavations. Autonomy granted to the community . . 221

CHAPTER XXVII

The election of Abbot Boniface Natter, 19th November 1902; his blessing and enthronement, 24th March 1903. The ancient statue of our Lady of Buckfast. The west front of the Abbey completed. Abbot Boniface and Dom Anscar embark on the *Sirio* 229

CHAPTER XXVIII

The wreck of the *Sirio*, 4th August 1906. Death of Abbot Boniface. Election of Abbot Anscar Vonier; his blessing and enthronement by the Bishop of Plymouth, 18th October 1906 245

APPENDIX—Historical Notes 255

INDEX OF NAMES OF PERSONS (chiefly with reference to times prior to A.D. 1539) 266

LIST OF ILLUSTRATIONS

Ruins of Buckfast Abbey in the Eighteenth Century	*Face title-page*	
Our Lady of Buckfast	*Face p.*	1.
River Dart, Buckfast	,,	11.
Arms of Buckfast Abbey, impaled with Arms of Clifford of Chudleigh	,,	37.
Buckfast Abbey: Plan of Ancient Foundations	,,	57.
Buckfast Abbey: The Cloister	,,	72.
Specimens of Thirteenth-Century Flooring Tiles	,,	80.
St Mary's Abbey, Buckfast (view from north-west)	,,	97
Buckfast Abbey: Remains of North Gate	,,	121.
St Mary's Abbey, Buckfast (view from north-east)	,,	150
Buckfast Abbey: Refectory rebuilt on old Foundations	,,	170.
Door of a Thirteenth-Century Enamelled and Gilded Brass Limoges Work Chasse or Shrine	,,	187
Buckfast Abbey: First founded in Eighth Century	,,	206
The Right Reverend Dom Boniface Natter, O.S.B., Abbot of Buckfast	,,	229
Right Reverend Dom Anscar Vonier, O.S.B., Abbot of Buckfast	,,	245
Sink Stone of Large Piscina	,,	254

CORRIGENDA

Page 65, line 2, "thus" should be "then."
 „   93, „   3, "Turkasia" should be "Turkesia."
 „   135, „   26, "Nather" should be "Natter."
 „   178, „   14, "accorded" should be "according."
 „   190, „   17, "1333" should be "1533."
 „   230, „   9, "typographical" should be "topographical."
 „   256, „   20, "dignity" should be "dignitary."
 „   263, „   20, "found" should be "formed."

In the inscription at foot of illustration facing p. 121, "1st April" should be "8th April."

OUR LADY OF BUCKFAST. Restored Fourteenth Century Statue.

[*To face page* 1.

HISTORY OF BUCKFAST ABBEY

CHAPTER I

"Bucfaesten," the stag's fastness. The Kingdom of Wessex, 760 A.D. King Cynewulf and Bishop Ethelmode. The Saxon conquest of Devon. Battles round Hembury Fort. The Manor that "never paid the geld." The Saxon Monastery. Antiquity of St Mary's Abbey. The Lady Beornwyn. St Petrock's territory.

MY story begins, as nearly as dates can be fixed, in the year 760. At the south-east corner of the wild upland known as Dartmoor, on the right bank of the Dart there was a dense forest, stretching along the riverside. The portion of this forest that lay at the foot of the steep hill of Hembury, whose summit was crowned by the still clearly traceable Hembury Fort, was frequented by the herds of red deer that roamed over Dartmoor, and came down to drink at the waters of Dart, at a spot now occupied by the Abbey meadows. Hence the English settlers of this part of the country give it the name of "Bucfaesten," the stag's fastness, and the Norman abbots who succeeded them, learning from the Saxons the name of the place and its meaning, chose a stag's head caboshed, for the armorial bearings of St Mary's Abbey of Buckfast.

The history of Buckfast Abbey, which I am writing

within its walls, begins, according to the most learned and critical of our Devonshire historians, whose conclusions I am fain to adopt, from the year 760 or thereabouts, as I have just said. Cynewulf was then reigning over the kingdom of Wessex, that is to say, over the counties of Surrey, Hampshire, Berkshire, Wiltshire, Dorset, Somerset, and Devon. To the "royal wolf," for such is the meaning of his name, the foundation of St Mary's Abbey is probably due. Half a century before, this western part of the kingdom of Wessex had been severed from the bishopric of Winchester, and was thenceforward governed by the Bishop of Sherburne, who in 760 was the monk Ethelnold or Ethelmode, the fourth bishop of that see.

Ethelmode must then be accounted our first bishop. St Mary's Abbey and the faithful of the county of Devon have been governed successively by the Bishops of Sherburne, Crediton, Exeter, and Plymouth. It was Cynewulf's conquest of this part of Devon from the British that added the territory on the banks of the Dart[1] to the diocese of Sherburne. For, by a system certainly not contemplated when St Gregory the Great sent St Augustine and his fellow-monks to England, the Anglo-Saxon bishops had become to a great extent tribal rather than territorial. Hence it is that at the Council of Clovesho in 747, we find them designated as "these prelates of the churches of Christ, beloved of God ... the most reverend Bishops of the Mercians ... the most approved Bishops of the West Saxons ... the

[1] Davidson, "The Saxon Conquest of Devon," *Dev. Soc. Trans.*, 1877-78.

venerable Bishops of the East Anglians," and so on.[1] If not approved, the practice was at least tolerated by the Holy See, and Bishop Ethelmode is rightly to be numbered among the legitimate predecessors of the Right Rev. Charles Graham, Bishop of Plymouth, whom God long preserve.

Cynewulf's final conquest of Devon was in all likelihood the occasion of the foundation of our monastery. The work of driving the British across the Tamar into Cornwall was only accomplished after a long and desperate struggle. "A sharp and severe contest would have to be waged by the invader of a thickly-wooded region like Devonshire, intersected by many streams, almost all flowing north and south, and each presenting a fresh barrier to the advance of an armed force. Many a desperate encounter must have been fought out among the tangled thickets that line the banks of the Exe, Teign, and Dart; and the rocky fastnesses of Dartmoor would probably remain unsubdued to the last."[2] Nowhere would the fierce Saxons find a more formidable obstacle to their arms than where their heroic foes had to be driven from the fortified camp on Hembury. From those ancient entrenchments the view over the vale of the Dart is one of matchless beauty, but the eye of the beholder rests with singular interest on the venerable abbey. For there can be little doubt that Hembury Fort and St Mary's Abbey are historically linked together, and while recalling the scenes of slaughter,

"When all day long the tide of battle rolled,"

---

[1] Rev. O. Reichel, "The 'Domesday' Churches of Devon," *Dev. Soc. Trans.*, 1898.

[2] Davidson, "Saxon Conquest of Devon," *Dev. Soc. Trans.*

it is with softened feelings towards the conquerors that one looks down on the sacred pile whose walls were first reared that Mass might be said and prayers offered up for ages to come for the souls of the slain, and the welfare of the new nation, in which Saxon and Briton were to be henceforward blended into one imperial race.

For indeed, as far as the keenest students of our history have been able to scan those dim and distant times, this was the origin of Buckfast Abbey. If in Cynewulf we do not find the gentle piety of Ine, yet he none the less followed the maxim of the kings of the Heptarchy, to wit, that his newly-conquered domains could only be civilised and cultivated by the foundation of monasteries; and we know that towards the end of his life he sought to make atonement for the guilt of his sanguinary wars by the endowment of these homes of labour, study, and prayer.

"Mr Brooking Rowe has suggested," writes the Rev. Oswald Reichel, "that Buckfast Abbey probably existed before the coming of the Northmen; that would be before 787 A.D. It may be so; but at least it must be grouped with Bodmin and Glastonbury Abbey as one of a trio of monastic churches which had property in Devon before King Edgar's time, and is probably, with the exception of Exeter, the only monastery before that time existing in the country. *Its extreme antiquity may be inferred from the fact that Bucfestre* (Bucfaesten, the original manor on which the abbey is built) *never was assessed.* The bulk of its property was, however, probably given by Æthalstan and Cnut. Considering its close proximity to Stock in Holne and

Hembury Castle, its foundation may be due to the desire of relatives to procure the prayers of holy men for those who had fallen in defending these fortified positions against the West Weala."

As the Saxons were the invaders, I have ventured to put it that their work lay rather in driving the British from their strongholds. But no man living is more at home than Mr Reichel, to whose kindness I am deeply indebted, in the history of the Anglo-Saxons in Devon.

As I hold in abhorrence the putting forward claims to a mythical antiquity, I will tax the patience of the reader that I may set forth the strength of the Rev. Mr Reichel's reasoning, which is really overwhelming. Until the Conquest, the little manor of Buckfaesten, on which the abbey is built, and which was never confused with its other possessions was never assessed, even to the value of one penny. The statement in Domesday to this effect is explicit: "Bucfestre is the head of the abbacy. It never paid geld."

In the whole of the vast county of Devon there is no second example of such an exemption; Bucfaesten stands alone. So far, there is no dispute, although towards the end of Saxon times it was a rich abbey, and it had always paid the geld for all the other manors which it possessed.

Now, as Mr Reichel writes me, the assessment of estates was made in Alfred's time, and if the manor had been given to the Church after the assessment, that assessment would have been most carefully noted in Domesday, as is the case with every church-land in the county except Bucfaesten. So the foundation was before the reign of Alfred (871). For the moment, this is all I assume as historically certain. True, there were in Devon the four exempt royal estates, Axminster, Axmouth, Silverton, and Bampton, but there is not the slightest indication that Buckfast was ever dependent on any one of these four.

If I have ventured to put the beginning of St Mary's a century earlier than Alfred, I of course do not claim for such an antiquity the same certainty, but have followed the writers just quoted (who do not allege it as more than probable), as I find their reasons worthy of their critical acumen, and of their freedom from any tendency to exaggerate. To the reasons already given for this assumed antiquity may well be added the total absence of any real or pretended charter of foundation, or even a tradition of the name of a real or supposed founder, which omission would have been well-nigh impossible in the case of a monastery founded later than 800 A.D.

Concerning Mr Baring-Gould's suggestion, that before Saxon times there was at Buckfast (whatever name the place then bore) a centre of British monachism, dating from about 500 A.D., and that the title was changed by the Benedictines from St Petrock to St Mary, I shall have something to say further on.

To people the new foundation, a colony of Benedictine monks would have to be brought from one of the already existing monasteries in the kingdom of Wessex. There was, of course, the great Abbey of Glastonbury, in the neighbouring county of Somerset which the holy King Ine, before he abdicated and journeyed to Rome (to live and die there in poverty and humility, maintaining himself by the work of his hands) had rebuilt with regal munificence, his donations amounting to two thousand nine hundred pounds of silver and three hundred and fifty pounds of gold. But I incline to think that Buckfast was colonised from Sherburne; for, while Glastonbury owned little in Devon, if anything, beyond Uplyme in its south-eastern corner, near Axminster, Sherburne possessed lands at Abbotskerswell, only eight miles from Buckfast (Abbotskerswell took its name from the Abbot of Sherburne), as well as at Littleham, Exmouth, and elsewhere in South Devon.

As in the case of other monastic foundations of such remote antiquity, the names of its first abbots are unknown to us. At Sherburne itself, though the bishop had transferred his see to Old Sarum in 1076, our list of known abbots only begins with Thurstan in 1122. The first Abbot of Buckfast known to us by name is Ælfwine in the reign of Canute, a century earlier. Canute granted to the Abbey of St Mary the distant manor of Zeal Monachorum. But from Cynewulf to Canute no record of its vicissitudes has survived, though from our clear and minute knowledge of Benedictine usages it is easy to draw a picture of daily life at Buckfast on no uncertain lines.

One mute witness of those olden days has been brought to light within these last few years, when in excavating the foundations for rebuilding, we have now and then come upon the massive Saxon foundations underlying the Norman masonry of the twelfth century.

> "In Saxon strength that abbey frowned,
>   With massive arches, broad and round . ..
>   On ponderous columns, short and low,
>   Built ere the art was known
>   By pointed aisle and shafted stalk,
>   The arcades of an alleyed walk,
>   To emulate in stone."

Such was the aspect of our beloved abbey when in 833, some seventy years after it was built, the Lady Beornwyn, a noble Saxon heiress, chose to give up her share of the paternal estate at Almer, in Dorset, in exchange for the manor of Dartington, some three miles from St Mary's, which she no doubt would visit on high festivals, as was then the universal custom. She would perhaps find a homestead near the Abbey, so as to be able to carry out the usage sanctioned at a later date by Archbishop Ælfric: "Let every Christian that can do it, come to the church on Saturday, and bring a light with him, and there hear evensong and nocturns at their proper hour, and come in the morning with an offering to High Mass." The chant of the monks was the delight of thane and peasant alike, and we have all read Canute's own verses, which I may give in modernised English:

> "Merrily sang the monks within Ely
>   When that Cnut King rowed thereby;
>   'Row, men, row near the land,
>   And hear we those monks sing.'"

The Lady Beornwyn's coming to Dartington (which has long been the home of the Champernownes) is the first known instance of a Saxon settlement in Devon.[1] Until the day when the enormous growth of royal power was able—in the reign of Henry VIII.—to trample on the liberties of Englishmen, and when his tyranny forced "fierce men into treason and thoughtful men into disobedience," the monastic garb and tonsure were as familiar a sight in the valley of the Dart as now in the reign of King Edward the Seventh.

I may be allowed to close this chapter by noticing what the Rev. S. Baring-Gould writes on the origin of St Mary's Abbey in his charming volumes on Devon and Dartmoor. Without definitely adopting his opinion, we cannot absolutely reject it. He thinks it probable that the original founder and patron saint of our Abbey was St Petrock. If this were so, then the Saxon monarch would have established and endowed a Saxon colony on a site which up to that date had been tenanted by British monks. Let us examine Mr Baring-Gould's reasons.

St Petrock, one of the most celebrated British saints, was a native of Monmouthshire, who settled at Bodmin, made many excursions into Devon, and died in 564. His relics were kept in a beautiful shrine before Our Lady's altar at Bodmin, and we learn from Mr Baring-Gould that the ivory reliquary which contained them is now in the possession of the Bodmin municipality. His feast was kept, as it is to this day in Brittany, on the 4th of June.

Now it was a noted peculiarity of the British that they invariably honoured the memory of their saints in the places where they had preached and laboured, so that we can to some extent trace the course of the

[1] Davidson, "Saxon Conquest of Devon," *Dev. Soc. Trans.*

saint's apostolic career by the churches which bore his name. These were numerous in Devon, but in the neighbourhood of Dartmoor, or along the Dart, they are clustered together as there are nowhere else. Thus we have St Petrock's of Lydford, St Petrock's of Brent, St Petrock's of Dartmouth, St Petrock's of Harford, St Petrock's of Clannaborough. Moreover, two of the six earliest dependent churches on our Abbey were dedicated to St Petrock, though the saint was not in the Saxon calendar, and Saxon ecclesiastics were by no means given to choosing British patrons for their churches.

Of course they found the cultus of the saint already established among the people. But Mr Baring-Gould suspects that the original abbey was one of St Petrock's monastic foundations, though the monks re-dedicated it to our Blessed Lady. This establishing of Saxon communities on existing British foundations was common enough, but until further evidence is forthcoming we cannot claim for certain the great British missionary as a saint of Buckfast, though St Mary's is undoubtedly within St Petrock's territory.

If Mr Baring-Gould's theory is correct, the earliest foundation of the Abbey would date from about A.D. 550 and it would share with Glastonbury the distinction of having been a centre, first of Celtic and then of Benedictine monastic life.

RIVER DART, BUCKFAST.

[To face page 11.

CHAPTER II

The earliest home of the monks; its surroundings. The great moor. The Dart. The Holy Brook. Buckfast and Buckfastleigh. Existing portions of the old Abbey. Children of the Abbey. Its dependent oratories. Festivals at Buckfast in Saxon days. Abbots Ælfsige and Ælfwine.

THE halidome of St Mary's, our Abbey's earliest patrimony, the *caput abbatiæ* of Domesday, that royal gift so revered by our Saxon monarchs that it alone was exempt from the *geld* paid by every churchland in Devon, now claims our attention.

Only its northernmost corner, seventeen acres in extent, is now occupied by the monks. But this is the most hallowed part of our Ladye's domain, for on this portion our forefathers built the church, the cloister with the chapter-house, and the other conventual buildings. It is also the fairest, and its meadows, sloping down to the river, are the richest and most beautiful of our ancient inheritance. Abbot Anscar at the present day holds rule where Ælfwine the Saxon and Eustace the Norman swayed the crozier of Bucfaesten in the days of old. But I must, however briefly, describe our surroundings.

The treeless "Forest of Dartmoor" dominates the region. Buckfast is two miles distant from the south-east extremity of this wild granite range. High up on the bleak table-land, which varies in height from 1200 to upwards of 2000 feet, and measures twenty-two miles by eighteen, is Cranmere Pool. "The intense desolation of the spot is impressive. On such solitary stretches, where not a sound of life, not the cry of a curlew, nor the hum of an insect is heard, I have known a horse stand still and tremble and sweat with fear."[1]

Within a radius of two miles from Cranmere, four Devonshire streams take their rise, flowing in different directions: the Taw, the Teign, the Tavy, and, most beautiful of all, the Dart. Its infant course is through the most rugged part of the stern wilderness of Dartmoor, but as it nears the monastery it flows between banks thickly wooded with oak copse. At eighteen miles from its source, it receives on the right, just above Buckfast Weir, a lovely little stream, which for the last few centuries has been called by the name of the Holy Brook. Our Saxon fathers, because it formed, as it does now, the northern limit of St Mary's patrimony, chose to call it "Northbroc," the North Brook; just as the copse on its banks has been called Northwood from the days of Edward the Confessor at least, the Abbey being the centre to which everything in the neighbourhood converges.

Holy Brook, after flowing round Hembury Hill, runs due east, and from its outfall into Dart to the site of the ancient church is only the distance of a few hundred yards across the Abbey meadows. From the weir the eye of the beholder does not now

[1] Baring-Gould, *A Book of the West.*

rest on the stately church whose massive foundations have been laid bare, but on the Abbey itself.

Dart itself formed the boundary of the manor from north to south, for a mile and a half, as far as the broad pasture-lands on the banks of the rivulet called the Mardle, which at the present day flows through the large village of Buckfastleigh. Here, for convenience of pasturage, the herdsmen and shepherds of St Mary's formed their settlement, for whose benefit Abbot Philip in 1340 obtained from the king a weekly market at Buckfastleigh and a yearly fair at Brent. The relative position of Buckfast and Buckfastleigh is expressed in the old couplet, which was repeated to me by a Buckfast villager:

"Buckfast Abbey was a borough town
When Buckfastleigh was a furzy down."

How far back from the riverside the Abbey manor extended in width is not accurately known, and the Rev. O. Reichel, while giving the exact extent of the other Devon churchlands, was only able to say: "Area unknown: was never assessed." To myself, from a comparison of charters, it seems clear that it nowhere exceeded about half a mile in breadth, and was perhaps bounded by what was called in early Norman charters, "the *old* road to Northbrook," meaning a road that had existed in Saxon days.

To this dry description I need only add that the Norman arch of what is still rightly called the North Gate, remains to the present day, with the buildings on either side, which, formerly the porter's lodge and chapel, are now converted into cottages and are the property of the monks, as well as the South Gate, of which only the original piers remain. The handsome tower which adjoined the *cellarium* or quarters of the lay brothers, is perfect. A large part of the *cellarium* still remains, built into the existing edifice, and the fine twelfth-century foundations have served to support the walls that have once more been reared, to the honour of God and our Blessed Lady, on their ancient site.

Benedictine life in the days of St Aldhelm or St Dunstan is too accurately known to need description here. A Saxon monastery always attracted thane and franklin to settle near it. "The religious habit," wrote Venerable Bede, "was in great veneration, so that wheresoever a priest or monk happened to come, he was joyfully welcomed by all as a servant of God. And if they chanced to meet him on the way, they ran to him, and, bowing down, were glad to be signed with his hand or blessed from his mouth. Great attention was paid to his exhortations, and on Sundays people flocked eagerly to the church or the monastery, not to feed their bodies, but to hear the word of God." St Mary's necessarily had its school. It was a rule that no recompense for teaching should be asked of parents, nor any received save what they gave of their own free will. Exactly as now, boyish voices at play enlivened the woods and meadows around, and the children of the Abbey rambled along North Brook and climbed to the top of Hembury. In due time, many of the boys would chant their *Suscipe* and make their profession in the Abbey Church.

To clear the forests and till the ground, to bridge the streams and make roads, was a great part of the work of the monks. The "Abbots' Way" across the desolate moor from Buckfast to Tavistock and Plympton, an object of wonderful interest to antiquarians, is marked by a succession of low stone crosses at intervals, of which many still remain.[1] In the wildest part of Dartmoor, at Huntington Cross, "where the only signs of life are the furry inhabitants of the warren, and, perchance, a herd of Dartmoor ponies, as wild as the country over which they roam ... the Abbot's Way is distinctly seen ascending the left bank of the river as it makes for the enclosed country above Dean Burn."

Outlying oratories were of course established and served from the Abbey, which oratories afterwards became noble churches. Those referred by Reichel to Saxon times were the following: Petrockstow, Zeal Monachorum, Down St Mary, Trusham, Church Stow, and South Brent. Trusham Church is two miles from Chudleigh amid beautiful surroundings. It was rebuilt in 1259, each of its pillars being a monolith of granite. It is interesting to note the dedications of the churches. With our Blessed Lady, St Michael, and St Peter, we find two dedicated to the British St Petrock. These, unlikely to have been first so named by Saxon ecclesiastics, are relics of the piety of the conquered race. But the title was preserved by the monks of Buckfaesten. The Faith of Christ had tamed the fierce Saxon, and the sword of extermination was no longer, as in the days of Hengest, or in those of Penda, heathendom's last champion, the doom of the vanquished. The British

[1] W. Crossing, *Ancient Crosses of Dartmoor*, 1887; *Crosses of the Dartmoor Borders*, 1892.

lived on in the vale of Dart; they gathered round the sanctuaries of the saints of their own race and tongue, and the Saxon monks ministered to Saxon and Briton alike, and the memory of the great British saint came to be in veneration among those who had brought his people under their sway. But when on Christmas or Easter, or the Feast of our Lady's Assumption, Briton and Saxon alike flocked to St Mary's for High Mass, it seemed to them a glimpse of Paradise. It is marvellous to read what Anglo-Saxon writers tell of the splendour of divine worship in their times; of the countless waxlights that made night as bright as day; of the sacred vestments, sparkling with gold and precious stones; of the voices of the singers in choir, accompanied by musical instruments; of the clouds of incense, and the great censer, filled with aromatic gums, that hung from the roof and was kept burning during the sacred rites. From infancy they were taught that this outward splendour was but a fit surrounding for "the renewal of the Passion and Death of the Lamb, the sacrifice of the Body and Blood of Christ."[1] That they might be better prepared, and have time for confession, the laws of Edgar and Canute ordained: "Let men keep every Sunday's freedom [from work] from noon-tide [3 P.M.] of Saturday till the dawn of light on Monday." But I must not here repeat at length what is to be found in all writers on Anglo-Saxon history. I have said above that Ælfwine is the earliest Abbot of Buckfast known to us by name. This by no means signifies that the names of his predecessors are not to be found in our Saxon deeds and charters. But as in

[1] Lingard, *Antiquities of the Anglo-Saxon Church.*

signing these documents it was customary for the abbots to add simply the title *abbas*, without designating the monastery each one governed, they are not easily identified, though from other indications it is possible to do so in some instances.

Abbot Ælfwine, indeed, is expressly designated as Abbot of Buckfast. He flourished in the reign of the Confessor, and probably was already in office under Canute. Leaving to our next chapter what is to be said concerning Ælfwine and his times, I shall give my reasons for assigning Ælfsige as probably his immediate predecessor.

In those Saxon times, when monastic communities enjoyed no exemption from Episcopal jurisdiction, each bishop, when invited to assist, for example, at the foundation of a new monastery, brought with him the abbots of his diocese, whose signatures, after those of the bishops, are appended to the act of foundation. From 994 to 1002, during which time Alfwold and Ednoth were Bishops of Crediton, in which diocese Buckfast was situated, we find that whenever the Bishop of Crediton appears, there is always an Abbot Ælfsige among the signatures. He was not Abbot of Exeter or Tavistock, whose lists we possess, and he disappears when Abbot Ælfwine comes on the scene. It is true that on one occasion we find at Shaftesbury in 1001 two Ælfsiges among the abbots, and I cannot affirm my theory with certainty; but as the abbey was certainly in existence, and its abbot would almost necessarily be present on such occasions, there is a valid presumption that Ælfsige was the name of Abbot Ælfwine's immediate predecessor.

B

CHAPTER III

The Northmen in Devon. Tavistock Abbey destroyed. Abbot Ælfwine. A meeting of the Shire-mote; its members. Earl Godwin. The Bishops of Crediton and Sherburne. The Abbots of Buckfast and Tavistock. Other thanes. A legend of Earl Ordulf.

THE summer of the year 997 was a time of incessant alarms for our monks at Buckfast, for every messenger from Exeter or Totnes brought tidings of the havoc wrought by the Danish hordes in Devonshire. Four or five times already they had laid waste the county. But in this year Lydford and Tavistock Abbey were burnt to the ground. Abbot Aylmer of Tavistock, whose abundant charity had never failed the homeless peasants whose homesteads had been fired by the invaders, had been forced to fly. The great moor lay between Tavistock and Buckfast, and the natural course for him and his monks was to cross it by the Abbot's Way, and take refuge with their brethren at St Mary's.

The Saxon Chronicle usually describes the route taken by the Danes with sufficient detail, and it does not seem that they ever reached Ashburton or Buckfast. Our abbey lay too much out of their way to Exeter, where they might look for plunder, and they seem never to have got nearer than Totnes. The men of Devon were stout warriors; and for the Danes to have entangled themselves among the thickly-wooded hills was unsafe; and it was in Devon that they had met with a bad reverse, when their leader was slain and the Raven standard lost. When the long struggle was over, and "Woden had yielded to Christ," a Danish monarch of England became one of our greatest benefactors; and the Devonshire family of Denys has ever been proud of its Danish origin. The earliest of our extant abbey charters is signed by their ancestor "William the Dane." Before his time, however, Danes and Saxons had been united into one nation of Englishmen, and King Knut, or Canute, who granted to our abbey the manor of Zeal Monachorum, had surely a loyal subject in the Abbot of Buckfast, Ælfwine the Saxon. (1035-1066 *circ.*)

Abbot Ælfwine figures in more than one charter in the days of Canute and Edward the Confessor. Like the other great landowners, he had a seat in the Shire-mote, or council of the county, which was presided over by the Bishop with the Earl or Ealdorman, in which the abbots, as principal mass-thanes, usually signed their names before the lesser thanes. Two of these great meetings, at which Abbot Ælfwine was present, deserve a special record. But we must first note that the arrangement of dioceses was no longer what it had been in the days of Bishop Ethelmode. Devon and Cornwall now formed the diocese of Crediton, shortly to become the diocese of Exeter. It was governed by Bishop Lyfing, formerly Abbot of Tavistock, by whom Abbot Ælfwine had himself been confirmed in office after his election by the monks of St Mary's. Lyfing succeeded Ednoth as Bishop of Crediton about 1032. Dorset now formed the Diocese of Sherburne. Here we may also note that Abbot Ælfwine's reign at Buckfast was a very long one. He survived the Norman Conquest, and is mentioned in the Exeter Domesday under the heading, "The Land of the Church of the Abbot of Bucfestre in Devonshire," as follows: "The Abbot has a manor which is called Brent which the Abbot Alwin (the Norman form of *Ælfwine*) held on that day on which King Edward was alive and dead." Now let us return to our story.

We are in the great hall of the Shire-mote at Exeter, and can look round as spectators at the personages there assembled. The renowned Earl Godwin, father of the unfortunate King Harold, fills the chair of state. He is seated between the Bishops of Crediton and Sherburne. Bishop Alfwold of Sherburne, sometime monk of Winchester, lives as austere a life on the Episcopal throne as he did in his cell. "Amid the sumptuous feasting of the Danes he was wont to eat his unseasoned herbs out of his wooden platter, mingling his drink with water till it had no taste of ale," writes William of Malmesbury. Better accustomed to the atmosphere of the Court, but still a zealous Bishop, Lyfing of Crediton, learned and eloquent, sits on the right hand of Godwin. Both the great prelates wear their Benedictine habit.

Next in rank and order come the two Abbots, Ælfwine of Buckfast, and Sihtric of Tavistock, their dark cowls and shaven crowns making them conspicuous among the thanes in martial garb and short Saxon tunic, by whom they are surrounded.

Many of these are men of note. There are the two noble brothers, Odda and Ælfric, kinsmen of St Edward the Confessor. After the disgrace of Godwin, Odda was created Earl of Devon, Somerset, and Dorset. "A good man he was, and right noble, and he was professed a monk before his end," says the Saxon chronicler, "and he died on the 2nd before the Kalends of September (1056)." Both the brothers were professed at Deerhurst, Ælfric dying there three years before his brother. Odda's biographers all extol his virginal purity. His body was laid to rest at Pershore, where it was discovered in 1259, in a leaden coffin with this inscription: "Sit ei gaudium in pace cum Christo Deo. Amen." (May he rejoice in peace with Christ our God. Amen.)

Among the other noble thanes present is Æthelmaer, whose father Cola fell at the dreadful battle of Pinhoe that "raged from early morn till eventide," when the army of the English was defeated by Sweyn of the forked beard, the father of King Cnut. Here, too, is Leofwin of Exeter; and Godman the priest, who owned the church of St Petrock at Clannaborough; and Dodda *Child* (a Saxon title of rank); and Wiking, Lord of Heavitree and Exminster, with others less easy to identify.

One group of brothers may not be passed over. Immediately below Odda and Ælfric, and even before Dodda Child, are the three brothers Ordgar, Ælfgar, and Eschbern. That they are powerful thanes is clear from the fact that the names of Ordgar and Ælfgar will appear as the first of the nobles in the royal grant of Holcombe in Dawlish to Leofric the King's chaplain, afterwards Bishop of Exeter.

The date of this meeting of the Shire-mote is unknown. Thorpe assigns it[1] to 1040, others to even an earlier date. Of its deliberations nothing is known save what is contained in the single charter given at the end of this book, being a transfer of land at Holcombe (not the Holcombe mentioned above), to the monastery of Sherborne. If held in 1040, it would certainly have been occupied with preparations for the accession of Hardecanute, to whom Godwin made his magnificent present of a ship whose stern was covered with plates of gold, carrying eighty of Godwin's retainers, whose splendid armour glistened with decorations of gold and silver. As Earl of Devon, Godwin would of course have to assemble the chief landowners on behalf of Hardecanute.

We would fain linger awhile on these old Saxon days, when king, earl, and abbot seem to have lived on very familiar terms. Only a generation had passed since Tavistock Abbey had been founded by Ordgar, and completed by his son, the giant Earl Ordulf. Ordulf was almost revered as a saint, and his colossal tomb was shewn for centuries at Tavistock. Many a Devonshire legend was told of his herculean strength. I may be allowed to give one from William of Malmesbury. He was riding from Tavistock to Exeter with King Edgar, his brother-in-law. They loitered on the way, and when they reached Exeter, the city gate was barred and bolted, and the porter absent; their arrival not being

[1] *Diplomatarium Anglicum Ævi Saxonici.*

expected. The Earl dismounted, grasped the gate-posts, and tore them up, bringing down a part of the wall with them, completing the work with a tremendous kick, and king and earl rode into the city. The bystanders exclaimed at his marvellous strength; King Edgar jestingly said it was the work of the devil. Earl Ordulf founded also the abbey at Horton. His sister was Queen Elfrida, the murderess of her stepson, St Edward the Martyr. The older members of the Shire-mote we are describing must have known Ordulf. Lyfing was the immediate successor of Abbot Aylmer, chosen by the Earl to govern his new foundation, and Ordgar and his brothers, who were present at the meeting, were probably his relatives. Earl Ordulf's biographer relates that he always rose from his bed at midnight and remained long in prayer.

In the days of King Canute and Bishop Lyfing the monks prospered in Devon. Those of Exeter received a new royal charter. To Buckfast Canute granted the manor of Zeal Monachorum in the hundred of North Tawton, and probably other possessions. Under Abbot Ælfwine our community remained undisturbed by the troubles that followed on Canute's death, for Bishop Lyfing and Earl Godwin were the Abbot's friends. Indeed, we may safely say that the last half century of Anglo-Saxon monastic life at Buckfast was a period of profound peace and prosperity, a blessing that seems to have rested on our abbey throughout its long career.

One would almost be tempted to find an allusion to the peaceful times in the very name of Canute's donation of Zeal Monachorum to our abbey (for *zeal* is only a corrupt spelling of the Anglo-Saxon *sele* or *setl*), the station of resting-place of the monks.[1] The grant is recognised in the Hundred Rolls of Edward I.

The meeting of the Shire-mote recorded in this chapter, if not belonging to Canute's reign, was of earlier date than those to be selected in the next, at which also our abbot assisted.

If sometimes I seem to wander from my subject, as, for example, in giving the story of Earl Ordulf, I may plead in excuse that one cannot get a truer conception of the England of Saxon times and the thoughts of our forefathers than from listening to the tales they would tell their children in those old English homesteads.

[1] Davidson, *Anglo-Saxon Charters at Exeter*.

CHAPTER IV

A Journey from Buckfast to Exeter in the Reign of the Confessor. Bishop Leofric of Crediton installed by the King in his new Cathedral of Exeter. The Abbots of Buckfast and Tavistock in the Confessor's Reign at the Exeter Shire-mote. The Norman Conquest. St Mary's Abbey not disturbed. Domesday Book and the estates of Buckfast Abbey. Serfdom in Anglo-Saxon times.

TWICE every year, in May and October, Abbot Ælfwine was obliged to journey to Exeter in order to attend the Shire-mote, of which we spoke in our last chapter. It was only a ride of eighteen miles, and he might conveniently halt at his estate of Trusham, a little beyond Chudleigh, the half-way station between Ashburton and Exeter.

On leaving the Abbey, he would cross the Dart, unless it chanced to be too much swollen, by the usual ford at the north-west corner of the Abbey meadows, and pass through Ashburton, on the highway to Exeter. Of course, at these times of the year, he would find himself in the company of the neighbouring landed proprietors, journeying, like himself, to the Shire-mote, and of the priests having care of souls, who had to be present at the Episcopal synod, which was held before or after the council of the shire. The thanes travelled each with his escort, and they formed a numerous and goodly company, as they wended their way through that fairest part of Devon. For more than half their journey, the road skirted the great moor, separated by a broad valley, across which they could see the town of Bovey Tracey on the hillside. On arriving at Exeter, our Abbot Ælfwine would go to his own residence, which still exists, in the Cathedral close.

It is evident that the Abbot's absences from his community, by virtue of his secular offices, had to be more frequent than one could wish. The Abbots of St Mary's never incurred the censure of worldliness, from which some of their brethren were not immune, but of course there was always the danger that they might adopt the manners of ealdormen and thanes, though England was in Anglo-Saxon times more penetrated by the spirit of Faith than it has been at any subsequent period. Besides the fixed times of the Abbot's resort to Exeter, there were numerous extraordinary occasions from which he could not absent himself. Concerning two more of these meetings at which Abbot Ælfwine was present, I have a few words to say. Both these occasions occurred in the reign of St Edward the Confessor.

In the year 1050 the King obtained from Pope St Leo IX. permission to transfer the Episcopal see of the Bishop of Crediton to the larger, more central, and better fortified city of Exeter. The monks of the Abbey of St Mary and St Peter—they were only eight in number—were transferred to Westminster, and their monastery became the Episcopal residence. Bishop Leofric, one of the royal chaplains (to whom Edward had granted Holacumb, now East Teignmouth, but then part of Dawlish), had succeeded Lyfing as Bishop of Crediton.[1] The king resolved to honour the occasion by his presence and that of Queen Editha. In his charter he writes: " I, King Edward, with my own hand, lay this charter (*privilegium*) on the altar of St Peter, and leading Leofric the Bishop on my right hand, and my Queen Edith on my left, I place him on his Episcopal throne in the presence of my ealdormen and my kinsmen, my nobles and chaplains, the Archbishops Eadsin and Ælfric adding their confirmation and praise, with the others whose names appear at the end of this charter." Among these are Ælfwine and Sihtric, the Abbots of Buckfast and Tavistock. Among the Bishops present was Aldred of Worcester, who had been the successor of Lyfing as Abbot of Tavistock. Several of the thanes are those who figured on the occasion described in our last chapter; Ordgar with his brother, Odda, Godman the priest, and others, while Earl Godwin's name of course heads the laity.

In place of the monks, Bishop Leofric established at Exeter a large community of canons, living under the rule of St Chrodogang. If, as is said, he likewise transferred a small community of Benedictine nuns, whose monastery he needed for his clergy, it is some satisfaction that to-day the noble Abbey of St Scholastica stands on the estate which Bishop Leofric received from St Edward and gave to his church at Exeter, where now a flourishing community of Benedictine nuns renew daily the life of prayer and praise of their sisters at Exeter in days of old.

[1] Davidson, *Anglo-Saxon Charters at Exeter.*

The other instance in which Abbot Ælfwine is found in an assembly of the clergy and nobles has an interest of its own. Nine years after the event just narrated, St Edward was desirous of granting to Eadred, Bishop of Worcester, formerly Abbot of Tavistock, four parcels of land in Cornwall, which are now known as Treraboe in the parish of St Keverne, Trevallack in the same neighbourhood, Grugith,[1] and Trelan, all which Edward the Elder had given to Ethelward his thane. Among the signatories to this charter we find Bishop Leofric and Abbot Ælfwine.[2] A year later Bishop Aldred became Archbishop of York. The lands in question were at a later period among the possessions of St Michael's Mount, and in the reign of Henry VI. they were held by the Abbess of Syon.[3]

Abbot Ælfwine survived the Conquest. The fearful oppression of his race by the Normans must have deeply saddened his last days. But it is quite clear that St Mary's Abbey was revered by the conquerors and its lands untouched. Judhael de Totnes, the powerful Norman who built Totnes Castle and owned the land bordering on St Mary's territory of Buckfast, was a man of great piety, the founder of Totnes and Barnstaple Priories, and to the latter of these he retired towards the end of his life. That the Abbey existed, with its ancient possessions, in the reign of Henry I., who came to

---

[1] Davidson, *Anglo-Saxon Charters at Exeter*.

[2] There was another Abbot Ælfwine, the Abbot of Hyde or Newminster, but he died two years before the date of this charter.

[3] Oliver, *Monasticon Exoniense*, p. 414.

the throne only thirty-four years after the conquest, we know from a charter of Henry II. But when we next meet with an Abbot of Buckfast, in 1143, he is the head of a Norman community, and one would like to know at what date the Saxon community came to an end. My own opinion is that the Saxon monks remained unmolested till a colony of monks was brought over from Savigny, by the authority of Henry I., between 1105 and 1135. But the beginnings of St Mary's Abbey as a Norman foundation must be reserved to the next chapter.

It will be well in our next chapter to close the Saxon portion of our history with a brief account of its possessions under Edward the Confessor. They were all within the county of Devon and are minutely described in Domesday Book. It is not unusual for people now owning or dwelling on such lands, though not Catholics themselves, to tell you with a sort of pride that their homes once belonged to the monks. Some of them have had an interesting history in post-Reformation times.

The compilation of Domesday was only completed in 1086, twenty years after the Norman invasion. The English struggle for liberty had been overcome and the nation subdued. Yet we learn from Domesday that St Mary's of Buckfast was still under the rule of its Abbot, and that none of its manors had been usurped. As the men of Devon had risen against their oppressors, and Exeter had been twice besieged, it is clear that the Abbot had prudently kept aloof from a useless contest. In the times of tranquillity which followed, no change could have come over our community, till the religious revival under Henry I. introduced Norman monks, from Savigny,[1] and the reign of the Black Monks, which had lasted for three centuries and a half, was brought to an end, until they returned in 1882.

It would be superfluous to give here at length the detailed account of all our possessions as it is written in the record of the great survey, but I may be allowed to transcribe the few lines that concern the manor of Buckfaesten, in Mr Brooking Rowe's English translation.

"The Abbot has one manor which is called Bulfestra, and is the head of the abbacy, and that never paid geld. There the Abbot has one smith, and ten serfs, who have two ploughs, and there the Abbot has three pigs, and one mile in length in wood and a half in breadth."

Here we see that Buckfaesten was one of our smallest estates. No account of course is taken of the meadows immediately adjoining the abbey, nor of the kitchen-garden and fields which the monks cultivated by their own labour. Only eleven of the Abbey dependents, with their families, lived on this estate. For greater tranquillity, most of it was retained as a wood. The arable land only comprised two carucates or ploughlands, each of sixty-four acres, according to the Devonshire custom,[2] though a ploughland was much larger elsewhere. "The plough, writes Bishop Brownlow, "was driven by four oxen yoked abreast, and often four more in front of them. And thus the plough was called a *caruca*,

---

[1] J. Brooking Rowe, "Cistercian Houses in Devon," *Trans. Dev. Assoc.*

[2] Reichel, "The Hundreds of Devon," *Trans. Dev. Assoc.*

or four-horsed chariot; and hence the land ploughed by this team of eight was styled a *carucate*" or ploughland.[1]

That the monks purposely sought after greater seclusion round the sanctuary of St Mary appears from the account given of their neighbouring manor of Brent, with its ten teams, thirty acres of pasture, fifty-five sheep, with only five acres of wood, the manor being cultivated by ten villeins, eight bordars and five serfs—in all, twenty-three families.

Serfdom and slavery were being gradually but surely extirpated by the influence of the Church; but the time of its total extinction was yet distant, though the condition of the villein or serf had been greatly softened. The *villani* of Brent owned their homesteads and lands almost by hereditary descent, and their oxen and ploughs were their own property. The bordars, or cottagers, usually possessed no oxen. The serfs, few in number, were, as Bishop Brownlow puts it, "fast becoming merged in the cottier class above them." Voluntary manumissions were frequent; if the lord made one of his bondmen work on a Sunday, he became a free man, and so in many other cases. Thus, without any violent disruption of society, a class of free men grew up, and serfdom gradually disappeared. The history of our abbey will itself give us some insight into the state of the peasantry in Devon after the Conquest.

I must now for Devonshire readers give a brief survey of our abbey lands, and advise others to skip the next chapter, which they may find a dry one.

[1] *Slavery and Serfdom in Europe*, p. 96.

CHAPTER V

Lands of St Mary's Abbey in the reign of Edward the Confessor. The South Devon estates. Brent, Ash, Heathfield, Churchstow, Kingsbridge. Dodbrooke and the Lady Godeva. Trusham near Chudleigh. Zeal Monachorum. Down St Mary and Petrockstow in North Devon.

THE pedestrian who, starting from Buckfast, journeys on southward by the high road till he reaches the town of Kingsbridge at the head of an estuary on the South Devon coast, will be following the line along which lay the earliest colonizing settlements of our Benedictine monks in Devonshire. Not monasteries, of course, for they were only dependencies on the one monastery of St Mary of the deer-fastness. In the manner of speaking of the period, they were called "churches" or oratories at least, as the duty of establishing a centre for the celebration of mass and the administration of the Sacraments was the first obligation incumbent on the monastic colonizers. The estate was usually said to be given to St Mary, St Peter, St Petrock, and so forth, according to the dedication of the church. "Lands of Churches, which have been given to Saints in Alms," is the title of a section of the Devonshire Domesday.[1]

[1] Reichel, *Domesday Churches of Devon.*

But together with Christian worship, the monks trained the Saxons and Britons who remained on Saxon soil, to agriculture and pasturage, to the crafts of the blacksmith, the carpenter, and the mason, and their settlements grew into villages and towns, while the labourers were being prepared for the state of freemen to which the church laboured to raise them. Their condition was, as is universally admitted, in every way superior to that of the toilers on the surrounding lands, while the rule of the crozier was proverbially mild. The traces of the monastic agriculturists are distinctly visible at the present day. But to return to our colonies on the way from Buckfast to Kingsbridge.

Brent Hill dominates the landscape for the first six or seven miles of our traveller's journey, but its summit is no longer crowned by St Michael's Chapel. Below it is the village of South Brent, perhaps the earliest of the monastic settlements made from the mother-church of Buckfast. The Norman Tower of St Petrock's Church was clearly built not long after Abbot Ælfwine's day by one of his successors. Brent fair, held for three days at Michaelmas, began in olden times immediately after the people had satisfied their devotion by a visit to St Michael's, on Brent Hill. The annual fair was granted by Edward III. in 1340 at the petition of Abbot Philip. The two manors owned by the Abbey at Brent were part of the 36,000 acres of Abbey lands acquired at the Dissolution by Sir William Petre. That versatile knight showed his secret attachment to the faith by getting his acquisition ratified by the Holy See in Mary's reign. The unswerving constancy in religion of his descendants, the Lords Petre, kept the greatest part of the lands of Buckfast Abbey in Catholic hands down to the nineteenth century, and was undoubtedly a help to save Catholicity from extinction in Devon in difficult times. The Devonshire estates of the Petres passed into other hands during the last century.

Journeying southward, and before we reach the new Cistercian foundation of Wood Barton (an ancient home of the Fortescues), we find ourselves in Ermington Hundred. We are now entering the South Hams, a district from its fertility styled the garden of Devon. A small estate within the parish of Modbury, bearing the name of Ash, was occupied by the monks in Saxon times, but as it cannot now be identified with certainty, we pass to the neighbouring "church" and settlement of Heathfield, in the parish of Aveton Giffard, another of our settlements.

The richest and most populous of St Mary's possessions lay southward, and within a few miles of Heathfield; and it was at Heathfield, at least in Norman times, that the Abbot held his court of justice. Forty acres of rich pasturage lay within this monastic settlement, on which was a village of some twenty-five families, with of course its little church, and a residence for the steward of the Abbey. "There the Abbot," says the Domesday record of Heathfield, "has eleven oxen and five pigs and sixty sheep and sixteen goats."

This line of monastic settlements, which began with Buckfaesten, and ran southwards through Brent, Ash, and Heathfield, ended at what is now the town of Kingsbridge at the head, as we have just mentioned, of an estuary of the sea. The monks held here the two estates of Churchstow and Notone, Kingsbridge being only a part of Churchstow. The name of Churchstow, "the place of the church," tells us that the church here built to the honour of the Mother of God, was a statelier and more important one than existed on any of their other settlements, Buckfaesten, of course, excepted. Kingsbridge belonged to our Abbey down to the Dissolution, and thenceforward, till nearly the close of the eighteenth century, to the Petre family. Nowhere, except at Buckfast itself, are there so many traces of the work of the monks, especially in architecture and wood-carving.

Dodbrooke, however, which nowadays forms practically one town with Kingsbridge, was not part of the Abbey possessions. Among the few English landholders in Devon who were not wholly dispossessed of their estates by the Normans were the three noble ladies, Alveva, Alfhilla, and Godeva. The lady Godeva was the widow of Brictric the thane, and she was allowed to retain her land of Dodbrooke. The origin of the name is of course from one Dodda; we have met with "Dodda Child" already.

Kingsbridge has a special claim on us in this history, but its place is in a subsequent chapter. It was favoured by our Abbot, to whom it owes St Edmund's Church, and its position as the metropolis of the South Hams, and the marked character of the town, which it derives from its isolated situation,[1] gives it a peculiar interest.

[1] Robert Dymond, P.S.A., "Kingsbridge and Dodbrooke," *Transactions of the Devonshire Association.* July 1877.

The other holdings of St Mary's Abbey before the Conquest need only be briefly mentioned. Of Trusham, half-way between Buckfast and Exeter, and of its lovely surroundings, I have already spoken. Trusham had the good fortune to pass after the dissolution, or at least in Elizabeth's reign, to the Catholic family of Southcote, so that it is likely to have been in Catholic hands for some time. The two estates of Zeal Monachorum and Down St Mary in North Devon had not the same lot. The former, whose church is dedicated to St Peter, was held by the Seymours in Elizabeth's days, and subsequently by the Earls of Moray. Stow St Petrock, or Petrockstow, which was clearly at its origin a British church, is also in North Devon, five miles from Hatherleigh. Lord Clinton is lord of the manor.

No important addition was made to the Abbey estates from the Conquest to the Dissolution, with the exception of such lands in the immediate vicinity of Buckfast as were given by the neighbouring barons or purchased from them. The story of their acquisition is known, and forms a pleasant record. But with this brief and dry chapter I must end the story of St Mary's Abbey in Anglo-Saxon times. The year 1086, with its record of our possessions in Domesday, gives us the last glimpse of the old Saxon community at Buckfaesten. The Normans seem to have found the name a barbarous one, and softened it down to Bulfestra, though the peasantry kept to the old name, now abbreviated into Buckfast.

(The field is blazoned as *sable* by Leland; as *azure* in Sir George Carew's Scroll of Arms, here followed.)

SICUT CERVUS AD FONTES

ARMS OF BUCKFAST ABBEY IMPALED WITH ARMS OF CLIFFORD OF CHUDLEIGH.

[*To face page* 87.

CHAPTER VI

The earliest of our extant charters. A deed in the reign of Henry I., now in the possession of the Abbey. Judhel the son of Alured the Giant. Sir Roger de Nunant and his family. The "Mary Mass." The wood and meadow on the banks of the North Brook. "Priestaford." The knightly witnesses to the charter. The Earl of Totnes. The arms of Buckfast.

THERE is a manuscript on parchment lying before me as I write, which was almost certainly written in the dear old Abbey itself eight centuries ago, and has found its way back again. It bears no date and the seal has been cut off. But its authenticity is beyond a doubt. A thirteenth-century copy of it exists in the portion of our chartulary in the archives of Exeter Cathedral, which was discovered a few years ago, and published by Prebendary Hingeston-Randolph at the end of Bishop Grandisson's Register. It is the oldest known original charter belonging to St Mary's Abbey at Buckfast.

Our last historical landmark was the account of the "Lands of the Church of St Mary's at Buckfast" in Domesday Book. Domesday Book was completed in 1086, and the charter before me was written in the reign of Henry I., who came to the throne only fourteen years later, in 1100. It tells its own story, a delightful little episode, illustrative of the simple faith and piety of our ancestors, such as will be more than once repeated in these pages. But to make it understood, I must here insert a fragment from the history of Devon in the eleventh century.

Among the proud barons to whom the conqueror distributed the lands of the Saxon thanes of Devon, Judhel of Totnes, already mentioned, was one of the most powerful. One hundred and seven manors fell to his share, and the Abbot's territory at Buckfast lay in the neighbourhood in his estates. He seems to be the same as "Joel, son of Alured the Giant," mentioned by Orderic. Many a Breton legend is told of Alured the Giant, who ended his days as a monk at Cerisy, near Bayeux. His son Judhel incurred the anger of the Red King, who gave his Totnes manors to Sir Roger de Nunant, as the name is spelt in our charter.[1] The castle of Totnes was granted, or confirmed, to him by Henry I. Sir Roger's estates at Buckfast bordered on the land of St Mary's, and he himself, his wife Alice, his sons Guy and Henry, would of course often hear mass in the Abbey Church, and were our devoted friends and benefactors. It is possible that the charter was written in the reign of William II., and that the grant of land which it contains was made to the English community; but it may with perhaps more probability be assigned to the beginnings of the French colony from Savigny, of which I shall speak very shortly. And now to the charter.

[1] Often *Nonant* or *Novant* in later writers.

In the monastic communities of medieval England it was usual to have a daily mass of our Blessed Lady sung early in the morning, that the labourers might be able to hear it before going out to their day's toil. It was known as the "Mary Mass," and the "Mary bell" of the Abbey was the first announcement to them that the day had begun. Of course the whole population used to hear mass daily. This mass used in the larger monasteries to be always sung, and bequests for its maintenance[1] are frequent in wills during the Ages of Faith.

Sir Roger makes known to all present and future: "That I, Roger de Nunant, for the welfare of my soul and that of my wife Alice, and for the souls of my children, my ancestors, and my posterity, have given to the Church of Buckfast, and the monks who serve God there, with the consent of my sons Guy and Henry and my other children,"—Guy and Henry were present and consenting with a full heart, we are told in the next charter, when this one was read in our chapter-house—"as a perpetual alms, free and quit of all secular exaction and service, all my land of Sideham, with its wood, and with all my part of the water on both sides, that is to say, from the east side of the road that leads from the old ford of Northbrooke as far as New Ford on Dart, that they (the monks) may thence be able to find bread and wine to sing mass," *i.e.*, for the daily mass to be sung at the Abbey. He next affirms that he has affixed hereto his seal, and continues: "Whosoever shall presume to annul this deed shall not escape the malediction of the Mother of God, the Blessed Mary, and mine; and

[1] Bridgett, *Our Lady's Dowry*.

may all they who uphold and confirm it enjoy the protection of the same Holy Virgin. To myself and my men, however, I retain free right of way from the North Brook road to the New Ford, on our way to Ashburton market, with common right of pasture as far as the said land extends."

To one living at Buckfast the identifying of the little estate in question is easy enough. Sir Roger gave us the wood and meadow land which he owned along the beautiful stream known in his day as North Brook and the stream itself as far as it belonged to him. Now, as of old, it forms the boundary of the Abbey land, and if the New Ford across the Dart is not used now, yet the name " Priestaford," Priest's Ford, clung to the house above it till quite lately, and the path to the Ashburton market is quite distinctly traceable. Higher up the stream, in Sir Roger's part, among scenery of wonderful beauty, wood and meadow are just as they were, and there is still the " old ford " by which the track crosses North Brook.

His son Henry, the brother of Guy, confirms the gift almost in the same words, and by a subsequent donation adds to it the contiguous estate of Schirehill, with leave to the monks to draw a fosse round the wood if they chose. He speaks of his brother, who seems to have already departed this life, as " the Lord Guy, my brother." His younger brother, Roger the second, by another charter confirms all the donations made by his father and by " the venerable Lord, Henry de Nunant, my brother." Lastly, Sir Roger the third, the son of Sir Guy and of the Lady Mabel, gives the monks leave to come upon his land, as far as they need it, to strengthen their dam across the North Brook. This last Sir Roger, grandson of our first benefactor, closes this list of charters by a deed signed at the house of the Bishop of Exeter. It is undated, like the rest, and gives the names of some of the men attached to the Abbey lands. From the names of the witnesses, which include the Bishop of Exeter, the Archdeacon of Totnes, the Priors of Totnes, Modbury, and Plympton, this last charter was given before 1160. This is the same Sir Roger de Nunant, whose signature, with that of St Thomas of Canterbury and others, is appended to a charter of Henry II. in favour of Buckfast Abbey.

Sir Roger de Nunant the eldest, Lord of Totnes and its Castle, is the first of a long list of our knightly benefactors. It is pleasant to recall the scene of his visit to the Abbey and the ratification of his gift in the chapter-house, his two boys being allowed to be present, as Sir Henry is careful to remind us: "the Lord Guy, my brother, and myself being present." The Lady Alice, their mother, could of course not enter the precincts, but was perhaps waiting in the guest-house, just below the room in which these lines are being penned. Even the very North Gate through which the Nunants must have passed coming from their estate on that memorable occasion has not disappeared, for its early Norman arch still spans the ancient road. Sir Roger and his boys were not alone in the chapter-house with the Abbot (possibly Abbot Eustace) and the monks. There was a goodly company of witnesses present, and here are their names from the charter: Osborne the priest, surnamed Rufus; John de Hode, a Norman, perhaps an ancestor of the

Hodys of Brixham, as Brixham belonged to the Nunants; William de Waleys, or the Welshman; William de Baumeis; David, probably the royal huntsman, whose descendants held land not far from Buckfast, by the service of providing the king with arrows when he went to hunt on Dartmoor, name and office being seemingly hereditary; Roger *pe de levre* (pied de lièvre, or Harefoot); William le Denys, or the Dane; "and many others." No doubt the worthy knight and his friends prayed devoutly before our Blessed Lady's altar in the Abbey Church; equally certain that the Abbot made them good cheer in the guest-house, to which it is likely that our friend David was able to contribute something.

We would willingly linger on the family history of our earliest Norman benefactor. But it seems that the name of Nonant became extinct in the fourteenth century, the last heiress marrying into the Beauchamp family. One of the last of the race, Sir Guy de Nonant, together with the community of Plympton Priory, in 1279 presented William de Aldesworth to the Rectory of St Mawgan, styled in the Episcopal Register of Bishop Bronescombe *Ecclesia de la Herne*, the Church of *Lanherne* in Cornwall. But their power had declined; and in these later times they were seated at Broadclist, the Totnes barony having passed into other hands at the death of Henry, son of Sir Roger III. The family of Valletort succeeded to the Buckfast estates, and we shall often meet them in the course of our story. The noble Lady Adeleis (Alice) de Nonant appears in one of our charters of uncertain, but very early, date; she was possibly the widow of the first Sir Roger. The list of witnesses to this latter deed is remarkable; it contains among others the name of the well-known Roger de Cockington. As his father was Lord of Camoys, it is not surprising to find in his company Thomas de Herbert and William de Kidwelly, both from Wales.

The Lords of Totnes were our near neighbours, and I may not omit to record that St Thomas of Hereford (Cantilupe) was the son of an Earl of Totnes, and that George Carew, Earl of Totnes in Elizabeth's reign, had four sisters-in-law among the English Canonesses of St Monica's at Louvain, now at Newton Abbey in Devon.

The arms of Nonant, the red lion rampant on the silver shield, may be seen among those of our benefactors in the refectory at Buckfast.[1]

We have no means of ascertaining the name of Abbot Ælfwine's successor, referred to in Domesday, nor that of the Abbot to whom the good Sir Roger granted the manor of Sideham.

So far as is known, Sir Roger de Nonant, Lord of Totnes, was our earliest benefactor after the Conquest. Must we reckon as a contemporary benefactor, the Lord of Berry Castle, known then, as now, by the name of Berry Pomeroy? There is a story in Leland, unsupported and clearly erroneous,[2] of a supposed suppression of St Mary's Abbey at this period, and of one Ethelward de Pomeroy, by whom it is said to

---

[1] George Carew, Earl of Totnes, is an authority on heraldry. In his "Scroll of Arms" for our county, lately printed in *Devonshire Notes and Queries*, those of Buckfast Abbey differ from the ordinarily accepted version by the field being *azure*, not *sable*.

[2] J. Brooking Rowe, "Cistercian Houses of Devon," *Trans. of Dev. Assoc.*

have been refounded. For this story, the only possible foundation would be the exchange of Saxon for Norman monks about that period, or in the reign of Henry I., coupled with the known generosity of the Pomeroy family. But of the Pomeroys I shall have something to say when we come to the times of Seinclere Pomeroy, most probably Abbot of Buckfast, A.D. 1500, whose brother Henry was the great-grandfather of the leader of the Western insurrection for the defence of the Catholic Faith in 1549.

CHAPTER VII

The religious revival in England in the reign of Henry I. His charter granted to St Mary's Abbey. Extinction of the Saxon community. The Grey Monks at Buckfast. Robert de Mortaigne and Ralph de Fougères. Ipplepen. Blessed Vitalis and the Order of Savigny. The Synod of London in 1102. Norman monks introduced at Buckfast about 1105. Death of Blessed Vitalis of Savigny.

OF the great religious revival which marked the reign of Henry I. (1100-1135), we must needs speak with gratitude and reverence. But we may be allowed to regret one of its features, to wit, the universal displacement of English bishops and abbots, and the substitution of Norman prelates and Norman communities in their stead. The same fate overtook our monastery.

The revival was indeed needed to soften the calamities of that unhappy time, and its vigour showed how deeply the faith had been implanted in the English race. "Everywhere in town and country men banded themselves together for prayer; hermits flocked to the woods; noble and churl welcomed the austere Cistercians, a reformed out-shoot of the Benedictine Order, as they spread over the moors and forests of the

North. A new spirit of devotion woke the slumber of the religious houses, and penetrated alike to the home of the noble Walter de l'Espec at Rievaulx, or of the trader Gilbert Becket at Cheapside."[1] Religion also did much to effect the amalgamation of Norman and Saxon into one English nation.

Our remote corner of Devonshire must have escaped the horrors of baronial tyranny in Stephen's reign, and through the rest of this unhappy period. Judhel de Totnes, and the De Nonants and Valletorts who succeeded to his lordship in these parts, were men of piety and benevolent rulers. We cannot be sure that Saxon monks did not still hold St Mary's at the time of the gift of the first Sir Roger de Nunant, but the grants of his son and grandson, and probably his own, were made to a Norman community. To a Norman abbot and his monks was certainly granted the charter of Henry I., confirming "to the Monks of Buckfast the church and abbey, lands, tenements, churches, and other possessions" held by them. Its date and full tenor are not known, but its substance is briefly repeated in a charter of Henry II., who wills they should hold them "as in the days of King Henry my grandfather." For my own part, I think this charter of Henry I. was granted about the year 1105, for by that date, the ancient Abbey of St Mary of Buckfast must, I think, have passed to the monastic congregation of Savigny, founded by Blessed Vitalis of Mortain under the rule of St Benedict. His disciples were known as the Order of Savigny, and

[1] Green, *Short History of the English People.*

were popularly called the Grey Monks, from the colour of their habit, in reality white, but made of wool that had not been dyed. The story of Blessed Vitalis and his Grey Monks concerns too much the monastic history of Devonshire and of Buckfast to be altogether omitted in this place. On the west side of the ancient tower, restored in 1883, beneath a sculptured head of a monk, may be read the letters: B.V.O.P.N. (*Beate Vitalis ora pro nobis*) which were carved on that occasion at the desire of one of the monks, who wished to preserve the memory of the "flower of abbots," as he was styled in his epitaph written by Ralph of Caen, Canon of St Paul's in London. Moreover, for the space of nearly half a century, it is clear that the abbot and monks of St Mary's on the Dart lived under the sway of Blessed Vitalis and his holy successors, Abbots Geoffrey and Serlo of Savigny, to whom our monastic historians often give the same title of "Blessed." Abbot Eustace of Buckfast, who ruled our monastery in 1143, was of the same congregation. But we must, first, establish the historical fact of the aggregation to Savigny.

This aggregation admits of no serious doubt. Leland,[1] who first started the untenable conjecture of a suppression and a new beginning at the period of the Conquest, writes: "The Monastery of Buckfast formerly began with the Grey Monks, and next received the Cistercians." John Leland or Leyland, a priest, B.A. of Christ's College, visited our abbey

[1] *Collectanea*, vol. iii., p. 152, ed. 1770. See for this and what follows, J. Brooking Rowe's "Cistercian Houses of Devon," in *Transactions of Devonshire Association*.

in the course of his antiquarian tour (1534-1543) and catalogued our manuscripts. In the midst of the list he inserted the words I have just translated from his Latin. An absolutely conclusive confirmation of his statement is afforded by a charter of Henry II.,[1] granted between 1155 and 1161 (to which we shall come presently), in which occur the words: "Monks of Buckfast, who are of the Order of Savigny." It is true that the Savigny Congregation had ceased to have a *canonical* existence in 1148; but the monasteries in England declined for some time to accept the change. The charter of Henry II. only recites that of Henry I. Anyhow, it excludes all doubts as to the aggregation. In what circumstances it was effected may easily be concluded from the story I have now to tell.

In the partition of lands in Devonshire made by the Conqueror, a splendid spoil fell to the lot of his half-brother, Robert de Mortain or Mortaigne, whom Devonshire writers often call the Earl of Moreton. Five manors the Earl held in his own demesne; seventy-seven were held under him, among the chief holders being Reginald de Valletort, a name that will often figure in our pages, and the noble Norman Dru, or Drogo. Drogo seems to have obtained more possessions in our county than any one else, and his name ought not to be passed over, for his brother, Richard Fitz-Ponz, was the ancestor of the noble House of Clifford. The Earl's estates did not lie in our immediate neighbourhood, the nearest perhaps being those at Cornwood and Modbury.

[1] *Patent Rolls*, 1 Edw. IV., p. 2, m. 4 (J. Brooking Rowe).

All were forfeited to the king when his successor, William, Earl of Mortaign, "departed to Normandy, and there took arms against the king, on which the king (Henry I.), confiscated all his estates and possessions in this country."[1] How Earl Robert came to be indirectly mixed up with our history will shortly appear.

Ralph de Fougères, whose ancestral estates lay in Brittany, had probably in the person of his descendant Ralph II., still more to do with the settling of the Grey monks at Buckfast. The Fougères family were, till the reign of King John, Lords of Ipplepen, a few miles from Buckfast. Ralph II. made a gift of a manor at Ipplepen to the monastery of St Peter at Fougères. And now to the story of Blessed Vitalis,[2] and the Grey monks, who succeeded the Black Monks at Buckfast, only to give place half a century later, to the White Monks from Clairvaux.

Vitalis was born about 1050, at Tierceville not far from Bayeux. His parents, Reigfred and Roharde, spent their lives in works of piety and benevolence. The boy was educated in a monastery, probably at Bayeux, where his schoolfellows nicknamed him "the little abbot." From Bayeux he seems to have passed to the celebrated school of Liège for the study of theology and Canon Law. After his ordination, Robert, Earl of Mortaigne, made him his chaplain and canon of St Evroul, and he was one of the Earl's chief counsellors. Whether as his

---

[1] *Saxon Chronicle*, A.D. 1104.

[2] An authentic copy of the Acts of Blessed Vitalis was discovered at Fougères by M. Léopold Delisle. See Darras, *Histoire de l'Église*, tome vingt-quatrième.

chaplain he visited England at this period of his life, is uncertain; in 1093 he obtained leave to retire into the forest of Craon, though he had probably been practising at intervals the life of a hermit at an earlier date. In the year 1112, Ralph de Fougères, Lord of Ipplepen in South Devon, made him a grant of the forest of Savigny, on the confines of Normandy and Brittany: "That what I cannot obtain by my own merits, I may purchase from the poor in spirit, to wit, that Kingdom of Heaven, which is their heritage; that they may be my advocates in the heavenly city, whereof they are citizens alike and princes." His grant is made with the concurrence of the Lady Avis, his wife, and of his four sons. Henry, the youngest of these, who alone of the four had opposed the grant, became in the end a monk of Savigny.

Now it is clear, and is of moment for our history, that this grant of the devout Lord of Fougères and Ipplepen was only a confirmation of a previous one. For, as far back as 1105,[1] we have a letter of William, Count of Mortaigne, erecting a monastery of the Blessed Trinity for nuns, "with the help of Brother Vitalis, Abbot of Savigny," and I am confident he had held that dignity for several years previously. This brings me back to England and Devonshire. For we must not imagine that Blessed Vitalis had been all these years at Savigny; he had visited England, and probably Devon, and Buckfast, more than once before 1112 A.D.

Ten years before Ralph's concession to Blessed Vitalis, of Savigny, in 1102, occurred the memorable

[1] Mabillon, *Annales O.S.B.*, Lib. lxx., n. xciv.

discussion between Henry I., and St Anselm of Canterbury in Westminster Hall, on the question of investitures which were a fruitful source of simoniacal depravity. It was immediately followed by a council of the Bishops and Abbots of England, held, according to Matthew Paris, in St Paul's Church at London; the barons, by request of the Archbishop, being present. The ancient biographer of Blessed Vitalis, Stephen de Fougères, grandson of Ralph, and Bishop of Rennes, relates at length how Vitalis, who was present at the Synod of London on the invitation of St Anselm, denounced more than once in the Synod, with unparalleled energy, the faults of the clergy, despite the most determined efforts to silence him. This makes it extremely probable that he sat there as abbot.

But it is not unlikely that it was in this year, 1102, that St Mary's Abbey passed to the Grey Monks. The Saxon Chronicle has only these few words on the Synod: "At Michaelmas the King was at Westminster, with all the head men of this land, both clergy and laity; and Archbishop Anselm held a synod, at which many abbots, both French and English, lost their staffs and their abbacies, because they had obtained them unlawfully or had lived unrighteously therein." Even when there was no charge of unrighteous living, if an English abbot died or became incapable, a Norman at once received his abbacy, and the Chronicle admits that the rule of St Benedict was by these Normans well and strictly observed. But Matthew Paris tells us something more. He says that a number of abbots were deposed at this time who had obtained their dignities through money from laymen (which was too often done under compulsion), and he numbers among these those of Cerne in Dorset, and Tavistock in Devon, "and others, whose names we do not know."

The West-country monasteries had therefore been visited; Blessed Vitalis, of whom we read that he went "through all England," would certainly have visited the monastic possessions on the lands of his devoted patrons, William, Earl of Mortaigne, and Ralph de Fougères, in our county. His sanctity and eloquence drew many communities in France to adopt his discipline, and the year 1102 is the most likely of any for the introduction of the monks of Savigny at Buckfast. He was again in England in 1108 and 1118, always devoting his splendid gifts to the re-establishment of strict monastic rule, and his biographer relates that it was his custom to admit whole communities without requiring any renewal of their vows, if they had professed the Benedictine Rule. As Blessed Vitalis himself never used compulsion, the aggregation of Buckfast may have been altogether voluntary; it is also likely that under Norman oppression the Saxon monks had dwindled in number. Those that remained would have still been employed in the churches dependent on the Abbey, at Brent, Trusham, and elsewhere, as the newcomers were hampered by their ignorance of the language.

The observance of Savigny was almost identical with the Cistercian, but with the marked difference that Blessed Vitalis required his monks to employ themselves in preaching. Among the witnesses to an agreement between the Chapter of Exeter Cathedral and the Abbot of St Martin-in-the-fields, near Paris, appears the name of Abbot Eustace of Buckfast, in 1043. He was of course of the Savigny Congregation, and is the first of the present Abbot Anscar's predecessors after Ælfwine the Saxon whose name has come down to us.

It was in the month of September 1122 that Blessed Vitalis, whom we venerate among our Superiors, passed to his eternal reward. He had gone to visit the Priory of Dompierre. On Sunday, the 15th of the month, though he felt that his end was nigh, he celebrated mass and presided in choir at all the canonical hours. That night he rose before the rest to awaken the community for Matins, and with them sang the Nocturns of the day. These were followed by the Office of our Blessed Lady. The reader of the lessons, as usual, turned towards the Abbot's place to ask the blessing before reading the lesson. Vitalis uttered the words of the benediction: "Sanctæ Mariæ Virginis Intercessio nos Angelorum adjungat collegio" (May the intercession of the Blessed Virgin Mary unite us in the fellowship of the Angels). Even as the brethren were answering "Amen," the holy Abbot breathed his last.

He had always loved England. Three times at least he visited our country. Stephen de Fougères says that on one occasion his audience being composed exclusively of Englishmen and he speaking in Norman-French, to their wonder they understood his every word as if he were addressing them in their own tongue. His biographer relates also that on the day of his death, a certain abbot in a distant monastery, a man of exalted holiness and greatest renown, sitting among his brethren, was rapt in ecstacy for the space of an hour. When he returned to himself, his monks asked him what he had seen. He told them he had seen the soul of Abbot Vitalis, amid incomparable splendour, and surrounded by angels, ascend to Heaven. Needless to say that the Abbot was St Bernard of Clairvaux.

For ourselves it is a source of happiness that this great Saint of the Order of St Benedict should have known and loved Buckfast, and that his heart was gladdened by the sight of his children in our monastery, shut in by the dearly loved hills of Devon. To his mighty intercession is at least in part due the wondrous blessing vouchsafed to our Abbey, that it should be the first in all England whose long night of desolation should be ended.

At the time of his death, a hundred and forty monks formed the community at Savigny, and a monastery of nuns under his obedience was governed by his sister, usually called "Blessed" Adeline, as their Abbess. But now we must pass over forty-six years from the time we have assigned for the aggregation of St Mary's Abbey to Savigny, to reach one more landmark in our history.

Sir Roger de Nunant the First had held Totnes Castle for eighteen years at the approximate date I have ventured to assign to his deed of gift, viz., 1105. That gift would be most likely to follow soon after the royal charter establishing the Norman monks at Savigny. When he died I cannot say, but his son Guy had succeeded to his honours in 1123, and in

1140 his grandson, Sir Roger was among the barons in arms at the siege of Winchester. Blessed Vitalis was a favourite with Henry I., over whom he had great influence, so that the king would promptly confirm the transfer of Buckfast to his obedience. On the whole, my belief is that the transfer of our monastery to Savigny, was at once confirmed by royal charter, and on that occasion enriched by the donation of the Lord of Totnes, who was then in all likelihood near the end of his days. (See charters of Plympton, Barnstaple, and Totnes Priories in Oliver's Monasticon). In Marténe's *Thesaurus Anecdotorum*, t.I., p. 405, may be seen in a Bull of Eugene III., 1148 A.D., a list of English monasteries which in that year belonged to the Order of Savigny, and which the Pontiff incorporates with the Order of Citeaux. Only the English houses are named, and it is known that some of them demurred to the transfer, which accounts for the unusual vehemence of the final clauses. This hitherto unnoticed writing finally settles the question of the presence of the Grey Monks at Buckfast. The document is addressed to Abbot Serlo. I give the names of the thirteen monasteries in the order in which they are enumerated, with dates of foundation from Tanner: Furness, 1124; Buckfast; Bildewar, 1135; Neath, *temp*. Henry I.; Quarrer, 1132; Stratford Langthorne, 1134; Coggeshall or Coxhall, 1142; Basingwerk, 1131; Combermere, 1133; Byland, 1143; Swineshead, 1134; Calder, 1134; Rushen (Isle of Man), 1134. With the exception of Quarrer in the Isle of Wight, all are in places very remote from Buckfast, and with the possible exceptions of Neath, all were

founded after the death of Blessed
nearness to Ipplepen, the home
and patron, makes me incline to b
Mary's is the only house he persona
to his Order.

BUCKFAST ABBEY: DEVON:
PLAN OF ANCIENT FOUNDATIONS:

Cloister Garth.

[*To face page* 5*

CHAPTER VIII

Buckfast Abbey a Cistercian house. The General Chapter of Citeaux, 1148. Blessed Eugene III. The English monasteries of the Savigny Congregation hesitate to become Cistercians. Charter of Henry II. St Thomas of Canterbury. The Tracys of Devonshire. Foundation of Torre Abbey.

IN Cistercian annals the General Chapter held at Citeaux in the month of September 1148 offers a scene on which one cannot look back without emotion. More than three hundred abbots were there assembled under the presidency of Abbot Raynard of Citeaux. Thither had come St Bernard, whose career was nearing its close. Among the Fathers, even as one of themselves, was the illustrious Pontiff, Blessed Eugene III., formerly a monk of Clairvaux, who, after holding the Council of Rheims, had visited the monastery of his profession, and thence had accompanied St Bernard to the General Chapter.

"He wore by day and night his woollen robe and the monastic cowl. True, his bed was splendidly covered, and surrounded by its purple curtain, but if you uncovered it you found that he lay on a heap of straw; so over his monastic garb he wore his papal robes. When he spoke to the brethren, he wept, and his voice was broken by sighs; yet he consoled and encouraged us as a brother, and not as a Lord and ruler." So is he described by an eye-witness, a monk of Clairvaux.

More than one Abbot offered himself and his community on this occasion to the Order of Citeaux. Abbot Serlo of Savigny besought the fathers to receive his thirty monasteries under the obedience of Clairvaux. His prayer was granted, with the sanction of the Pontiff there present. It was ordered that the holy abbot should hold the sixth place among the Abbots of the Order. Five years later Blessed Serlo resigned his dignity, and as a simple monk retired to Clairvaux, where he lived yet another five years, dying there in the year 1158.

From September 1148 the congregation of Savigny ceased to have a canonical existence. But it is known that some years passed before all the English houses agreed to become Cistercians, so that we may say that the rule of the Grey Monks at Buckfast lasted for half a century. Cistercians held St Mary's Abbey for 390 years. If my dates be admitted, and we count the twenty-four years we have occupied down to the present date (1905) it has been tenanted by the Black Monks for about 366 years. We have no indication that the Savigny Monks rebuilt the monastery in their time. Cistercians were the greatest architects of their age, and it is the Cistercian fabric, on Cistercian foundations, that has been already in part restored, in the style that was in use when it passed under St

Bernard's rule. There is abundant evidence that his monks completely rebuilt our abbey, though they followed the ancient lines as far as they could, utilizing the existing foundations, as we have done theirs, but enlarging the monastery by carrying it further eastward towards the river.

The community of Buckfast had not much to change in their rule of monastic life. Of course they had to adopt the black scapular of Citeaux instead of their grey one over the white robe. The greatest alteration was the relinquishing of the apostolic ministry and of preaching, which formed part of the life of the Grey Monks. There can be little doubt that this was the cause of the demur made by some of the English houses when the passing to the Order of Citeaux was in question. Of course their labours in agriculture, in building, and in many arts and crafts, were very greatly increased. They remained patrons of the churches dependent on the abbey, and till the days of Henry VIII. we find them in the Episcopal registers of Exeter regularly presenting to the parishes of Buckfastleigh, Brent, Churchstow, and the rest mentioned above. Since the Conquest, the Cistercians, like other branches of the great Benedictine family, found a congenial home in the native land of St Stephen of Citeaux, himself born in the west country. "The Order took to itself all the quiet nooks and valleys and all the pleasant streams of old England, and gladdened the soul of the labourer by its constant bells."[1]

How well does not this description befit the

---

[1] St Stephen, Abbot, *Lives of English Saints*.

pleasant vale on the banks of the Dart, where these lines are being penned! Those days were the golden age of Cistercian fervour, a fervour that lasted till far into the thirteenth century. The fiery ardour of St Bernard, tempered by his ineffable sweetness of charity, was winning to God a mighty host, as well among the brave and chivalrous as among the poor and lowly. Vain were the efforts of the youthful nobles, who banded themselves together lest they should be carried away by his all-powerful word, vain the solicitude of mothers, hiding their children when the saint passed by.

No sooner were the Cistercians fairly seated at Buckfast than they felt the need, a very real one at the time of which we are writing, to have the lands and rights that had been held by their predecessors, secured to them by royal charter, for which, needless to say, they would have to pay. The Savigny Monks had been careful to obtain theirs from Henry I., but there could be no certainty that it would be respected, now that there had been a change of owners.

The duty of presenting their petition of course devolved on their powerful friend, Roger de Nonant, Lord of Totnes. But at this time (1150) this was out of the question. This Sir Roger, the grandson of our earliest benefactor after the Conquest, had sided with the clergy and barons who took up arms against Stephen. The rebellion first broke out in Devon, where Baldwin de Redvers held the Castle of Exeter against the King; and the Lord of Totnes, with the whole body of the barons of the West, were soon arrayed in behalf of Matilda's son Henry, afterwards Henry II.; De Nonant, with his vassals from our neighbourhood, was among those who fought under Matilda's banner at the siege of Winchester in 1140, with the sanction and by the exhortations of the papal legate. To the end of his reign Stephen was powerless to punish the nobles who had taken up arms against him, and Sir Roger kept possession of the honour of the barony of Totnes. But of course he could ask no favour from the king for his friends of St Mary's Abbey.

The good knight, however, did what he could for them. He confirmed the grants of his grandfather, of his father Sir Guy, and of his uncles Henry and Roger. By a deed of his own,[1] "for the welfare of my soul and that of my wife Alice, and for the souls of Roger my grandfather, Guy my father, and Mabel my mother," he finally and without reserve gives "to God and the Church of Blessed Mary of Buckfesten" (it is noteworthy that the name is here still given in Saxon) all that he owns of "the stream called North Brook, which flows between my land and the land of the aforesaid Abbey;" with the addition that they may come upon his land whenever they like, to strengthen their dam, and may draw off the water of the stream to wherever it suits them; adding, "moreover that they are to have [whatever they require] for singing Masses." Among the signatories we find the name of Ralph

[1] The Cartulary of Buckfast Abbey. Published by the Rev. F. C. Hingeston-Randolph at the end of Bishop Grandisson's Register.

Moine, one of the earliest instances of *Monk* used as a family name. To this Devonshire family belonged the celebrated General Monk.

About four years had the Cistercians been finally settled at Buckfast when messengers from Canterbury brought the request that they should sing mass for the repose of the soul of King Stephen, who had died "in the house of the monks"[1] at Canterbury, 25th of October 1154. He had deserved well of the monastic Orders, being the founder of Furness, Coggeshall, and Feversham Abbeys, in which last he was buried. On the 17th of December, Henry II. was crowned at Westminster. De Nonant was now in favour at court and the royal charter for Buckfast Abbey was solicited and obtained. It bears no date, and could not have been issued later than 1161, but is more likely to have been granted in 1155. From this time the Cistercian foundation began its legal existence at Buckfast, and its long peaceful career of nearly four centuries was inaugurated. The names at the foot of the charter have a more than ordinary interest for us monks of Buckfast. First comes Theobald, Archbishop of Canterbury, a monk of St Benedict, who had been Abbot of Bec. He was born at Tierceville, the birthplace of Blessed Vitalis. Thomas the Chancellor, afterwards St Thomas of Canterbury, signs in the next place, a still more pleasing memory. Then follow in order the names of Humphrey de Bohun, Roger de Nunant (here written Novant), Warren Fitzgerald, and William Fitzhamon, who had all four been companions in arms in the late civil war; Fitzgerald

---

[1] Stow.

being father-in-law to Baldwin de Redvers, Earl of Devon.

The charter is unusually brief, and simply confirms the Abbey and church in all the possessions it held in the reign of Henry I. But there exists a second and more ample copy, described by Mr Brooking Rowe, conferring on the Abbot the usual secular jurisdiction described in the phrases "soc and sac," etc., and exempting the monks from payment of taxes. In the former they are styled "of the Order of Savigny," in the second "of the Cistercian Order." It looks as if, the former being drawn up hurriedly, the latter had been intended to supply its defects. In the second the monks are declared exempt from "the customs of the moor," a reference of course to our Dartmoor privileges.

Sir Roger de Nonant (III.) died about the tenth year of Henry's reign. His successor lost half the barony in that of John, and not long after their estates in this part of Devon passed to the family of Valletort. The De Nunants had secured for us a tranquil time during the dreadful calamities of Stephen's reign. I had already noticed that Buckfast seems also to have escaped a visit from the Danish invaders, and indeed I may repeat it seems to have always enjoyed, within and without, the blessings of peace and content. From Edward the Confessor to Henry VIII. our Abbots never materially increased their possessions, nor is there any trace either of disagreement with their Bishop, or of internal dissensions, such as often afflicted their more ambitious neighbours of Tavistock.

From the opening of the thirteenth century, our

annals contain far more copious records, with here and there very pleasing and sometimes amusing pictures of medieval country life. But to the end of the twelfth century notices are very scanty. In the first days of January 1171 the Abbot had to announce to his monks the murder of St Thomas of Canterbury. One of the murderers, Sir William de Tracy, owned manors, Bovey Tracy among them, a few miles from the Abbey, but he fled for refuge to his estate of Wollacombe in North Devon. The subsequent misfortunes of the family gave rise to the Devonshire rhyming proverb:

> "All the Tracys
> Have the wind in their faces."

He is said to have built the Church of St Thomas at Bovey Tracy in atonement for his crime.

But I must bring this chapter and our history in the twelfth century to a close. There is a sentence in the close of the confirmatory charter granted to St Mary's in 1189 which I may not omit: "We grant them (the monks) pasture on the moor (Dartmoor) during the whole year for every kind of sheep and cattle." The significance of this will appear later on. The charter was granted by the hand of William Longchamps, Bishop of Ely, the Chancellor.

A glorious year in the ecclesiastical annals of Devon was 1196, when the splendid foundation of Torre Abbey for Premonstratensian Canons was made by William Lord Briwere. It was the noblest house of the Order in England, its choir being seventy-two feet long by thirty broad. The founda-

charter is witnessed first by the Bishop of
r, and thus by four abbots, among whom,
m, Abbot of Buckfast, the only one whose
 lay in Devon, takes the first place. He is
rst of our Cistercian line of abbots whose
 has come down to us.

CHAPTER IX

Sufferings of the Monks in the reign of King John. The Interdict of Innocent III. The holders of the Baronies of Totnes and Harberton. Peace restored. The Cistercian Abbeys of Buckland, Newenham, Dunkeswell, and Ford, in Devon.

THE thirteenth century, to which we owe our brightest Cistercian memories and the most wonderful creations of Cistercian Art, was ushered in by the fiercest storm that the Order ever had to weather in England, down to the days of Henry VIII. From the miseries brought on the country by the crimes of King John and the sufferings entailed on the monks by the Interdict of Pope Innocent III., not even the peaceful seclusion of Buckfast Abbey could save it, though it was not felt to nearly the same extent as in other parts of England. To add to the defenceless condition of our community, we were at this hour of direst need bereft of the protection of the De Nunants; for at the accession of John, the moiety of the barony of Totnes was given by the king to Reginald de Braose, and at the death of Henry de Nunant in 1206 the remaining portion was granted to Peter des Roches, Bishop of Winchester. As briefly as possible, I shall touch on the troubles of the Cistercians, more especially in Devon.

All went well with them during the earlier years of this reign. John professed himself a friend to the Order. Exeter was faithful to him; he enlarged its privileges and was a benefactor to the Priory of St Nicholas in that city. Hence it came to pass that the Devonshire Cistercians enjoyed so much of his favour that when his troubles with the barons began, the safe keeping of part of the royal treasures was entrusted to the Abbots of Buckfast and Ford, as we learn from a letter to our Abbot in 1215, asking for their return. He obliged John of Devon, Abbot of Ford, to come to court and assume the office—no very enviable one—of his chaplain and confessor. When in 1207 the king sent his officers to all the counties of England to enforce a tax of one-thirteenth from every church and monastery, he forbade them to exact anything from the Cistercians.

But on the 23rd of March 1208 the papal interdict for the whole kingdom of England was proclaimed, being Monday in Passion Week. "The churches were closed; no bell was tolled, no service was solemnly performed; the administration of the Sacraments, except to infants and the dying, was suspended; and the bodies of the dead were interred silently, in unconsecrated ground."[1]

The Cistercians, relying on their privileges, had at the first continued to say mass and chant the Divine Office as usual in their own part of their churches, which was separated from that frequented by the

[1] Lingard.

laity. This was done, writes Matthew Paris, "by the command of their principal Abbot (the Abbot of Citeaux); when it came to the knowledge of the Pope, they received a second order of interdict, to their greater confusion." In the following year, Cardinal Stephen Langton, Archbishop of Canterbury, obtained leave for the conventual churches to have Mass and the Divine Offices celebrated with closed doors once a week; but "the Cistercians, by reason of having presumed to do so before, were not allowed this indulgence."

The sufferings of the poor monks of Buckfast may be imagined. Their daily toil was no longer relieved by the chant of the Office they loved so dearly; no Mass or Sacraments to cheer them on their pilgrimage; as the solemn festivals of the Church came round, they could but pray in silence in their desolate church, or kneel before the great cross in the midst of the cloister-garth. In the year 1210 the king summoned to his presence "all the prelates of the kingdom; abbots, priors, abbesses, templars, hospitallers, custodians of the cells of the Cluniacs and of the other alien priories. The sums extorted are said to have reached a hundred thousand pounds sterling.[1] The Cistercians of England, willing or unwilling, without regard to their privileges, paid on this occasion forty thousand pounds of silver, and were forbidden for that year to go on their annual journey to the General Chapter.... The king extorted from all the religious houses, especially of the Cistercian Order, a writing by which they were

[1] Matthew Paris, *Hist. Angl.* The sum indicated would be equal to more than a million nowadays.

forced to declare that what he had wrung from them had been given freely as a benevolent subsidy for the welfare of the kingdom." The chronicler of Waverley Abbey in Surrey adds that the Cistercians resisted him at first: "Then by violence he wrung from them the sum of 33,333 marks, and they were scattered and dispersed among other houses of monks and canons. Waverley lost all its possessions; its monks and lay-brothers, dispersed all over England, bore the wrath of the king in patience. The Abbot, John III., dreading the royal anger, fled secretly by night."[1] How the monks fared at Buckfast, I cannot say, but of course they did not escape the exactions. William de Braose, Lord of Totnes, stoutly refused to do homage to the excommunicated monarch, urged thereto by his heroic wife Matilda. They were forfeited, Totnes, Cornworthy, and Loddiswell being granted to the Earl of Cornwall.

De Braose, with his wife and children, fled to Ireland; John crossed over in 1210, defeated Walter de Lacy, and among his prisoners were the wife of De Braose and her son William, whom he sent to England and starved to death, after most atrocious torments, in Windsor Castle.

"After the interdict had lasted six years, fourteen weeks and two days, Nicholas the legate, on the day of the Apostles Peter and Paul, by apostolic authority declared it at an end; and there was great rejoicing throughout the kingdom, and everywhere bells were rung, and they sang *Te Deum Laudamus*." This was in 1214. A year before it had been relaxed in favour of conventual churches. The monasteries had

[1] *Annales de Waverleia.*

been already restored. On the night following St Luke's Feast, 1216, King John died at Newark.

The storm was over, and a long period of tranquillity for St Mary's Abbey was to follow. The fruits of their useful labours surround us at the present day, but we must defer speaking of these to the next chapter. For the better understanding of the records in our chartulary, I must here add a word on the holders of the two baronies of Totnes and Harberton by which our own estate at Buckfast was surrounded, both of which baronies had been hitherto held by the De Nunants.

Harberton was now held by Reginald de Valletort, and the Valletorts were our neighbours till the death of Roger de Valletort in 1275. Reginald, brother of the murdered William de Braose, recovered his part of the Totnes barony; but before the end of the reign of Henry III., Totnes belonged to the family of Cantilupe. Reginald's granddaughter, Eva, married the brother of St Thomas of Hereford, William, third Baron Cantilupe, and brought with her as dower the castle and manor of Totnes.

Before closing the chapter it is necessary to advert to the other Cistercian monasteries of Devon, from whose history we may occasionally derive some light for our own history. They were four in all. Newenham was founded in 1245, Buckland in 1280; Dunkeswell, which has the most meagre history of the five, was founded by William, Lord Briwere, in 1201, and colonized from Ford. Ford was founded in 1141 by Adelicia, sister of the Viscount or hereditary Sheriff of Devon. Baldwin, the third Abbot of Ford, became Archbishop of

Canterbury. John of Devon made it celebrated for learning. He died in 1220.

Mr J. Brooking Rowe says that no Cistercian building in England remains in so perfect a state as Ford, but not a vestige of the monastic church is left. The twelfth century chapter-house, the north walk of the cloister, and the refectory, are perfect. Since 1841, Ford is no longer in the county of Devon.

CHAPTER X

Growing prosperity. Cistercian lay-brothers. The out-lying possessions of the monks on Dartmoor. Buckfast Moor. Agricultural labourers in the thirteenth century. Abbot Nicholas sells houses at Exeter. Abbot Michael. Architectural remains of the Abbey at the present day.

UNTIL the great plague of 1349, no such calamitous disorganisation disturbed the work of our monks as that which they underwent in the reign of John. Long before that time they had made their portion of the county of Devon "a good land, a land of wheat and barley, a land of flocks and herds."[1] In fact, judging from authentic records, I should say that in our immediate neighbourhood much more land was under cultivation in the thirteenth century than at the present day.

Now it is quite clear from the Abbey foundations, which have been unearthed since the return of the monks in 1882, that the original Cistercian monastery was built for a community of fifty choir monks, and no more. The dimensions of refectory, choir, and chapter-house, leave no doubt whatever on this point. Their duties in choir and the different

[1] J. Brooking Rowe, "Cistercian Houses of Devon," *Trans. Dev. Assoc.*

BUCKFAST ABBEY : The Cloister.

[*To face page* 72.

offices of the house left them small leisure, with the exception of the few, specially set apart for the work, to attend to agriculture. How, then, did they obtain the splendid results which it is admitted on all hands they did obtain?

By the system of aggregating great numbers of lay-brothers came to their Order. Fifty choir-monks at Buckfast meant one or two hundred lay-brothers, perhaps more. The houses now occupied by the Buckfast villagers, and separated from the Abbey by the width of the road, were built for that part of the lay-brothers, masons, carpenters, or blacksmiths, attached to the monastery, and were all built in medieval days, though now sadly disfigured. But a very large number lived out in granges, now farm-houses. I have seen near Buckfastleigh a stained-glass window picturing the Annunciation, in a farmer's kitchen, but it has since been removed. These more distant colonies became in course of time less amenable to discipline, and were for the most part suppressed by the Order in 1310, although a few trustworthy men were still left in them here and there. An example will not be out of place here.

On Dartmoor itself, and on the outskirts of that part which belongs to the Duchy of Cornwall, lie extensive portions of pasture-land, formerly the property of the Abbey, which were granted to the Commons of Devon by one of our Abbots. These are: Buckfast Moor, Holne Moor, and Brent Moor. The boundary stones, marked with a B, are still in their places, and the Abbey still possesses certain rights of seignory over them. Now, there is a document in our chartulary, of late pre-reformation date, which I may thus translate: "The Abbot and monks of Buckfast, *always, up to the time of the first Plague* (1348-49), kept on their moor of Buckfast a lay-brother, one succeeding another without interruption, living in a house on Buckfast Moor, having a shepherd under him to keep constant watch over the flocks and herds of the said monks on Buckfast Moor and Brent Moor, and to guide and shut in at night the said cattle within an enclosure of a hundred acres adjoining the said dwelling. The last of the lay-brothers who lived in the said dwelling was Brother Henry Walbrook, and the walls and ditches of the said house (and enclosure) are still to be seen."

Buckfast Moor alone is six miles by two, and on these vast pasture-lands our monks kept great flocks of sheep. The wool industry was a chief source of their income. A few years after the death of King John, in 1236, Abbot Michael and his monks were admitted into the guild of the Totnes merchants. The act of his admission is preserved in the roll now in the possession of the Corporation of Totnes.

Life on Buckfast Moor must have been as hard in winter as it was pleasant in summer. In earlier times there was, of course, a regular colony of lay-brothers there; after 1310 not more than one or two were left, with their secular dependents.

These dependents, who were being gradually trained to cultivate their own lands and pasture their herds, had by this time—thirteenth century— attained a very comfortable position, though many of them were still bound to the land, and their families went with it when it changed hands by purchase or otherwise. We shall find an example of this very shortly. Of course some were already absolutely free, but even such as were still in serfdom had their rights and privileges ascertained. In fact, Mr Thorold Rogers[1] affirms that the only difference in the condition of agricultural labourers in the thirteenth century and the opening of the nineteenth, was that the thirteenth century labourer was very much better off. He was paid for his labour. "All the necessities of life were abundant and cheap. Meat was plentiful; poultry found everywhere; eggs cheapest of all. The poorest and meanest man had no absolute and insurmountable impediment put in the way of his career." Mr Rogers finds in England now a population (more numerous than the whole population of England six centuries ago) "whose condition is more destitute, whose homes are more squalid, whose means are more uncertain, whose prospects are more hopeless, than those of the poorest serfs of the middle ages."

Still, these labourers were not free—an undesirable condition ; they could not leave their holdings unless they bought themselves out, or were fully emancipated by their lords. Their names are recited in deeds of transfer. A deed in our chartulary by Sir Roger de Nunant (about 1150) executed in the Episcopal house at Exeter in the presence of the Bishop, the Archdeacon, the Priors of Plympton, Totnes, and Modbury, and many others, declares that he renounces in favour of the Abbey all his rights to the services of "three men of their (the monks') land,

[1] *Six Centuries of Work and Wages.*

Ailwin Lepil, Osmer his son, and Roger of Nordtune." Serfs they certainly were. The final admission of every Englishman to complete freedom has been one of the greatest blessings of our race. But by the influence of the Church and of the monastic Order they received a preparation for the exercise of their freedom of which the fruit has not been lost. I now return to our history, starting from the beginning of the reign of Henry III. in 1216, when the good Abbot Nicholas was ruling at Buckfast, and doing his best to repair the ruin of the disastrous times of King John.

No period of our domestic history is more copiously illustrated than the reign of Henry III., thanks to numerous charters. For these charters I have a great fondness. They are never dry or formal. The simple faith of the age makes them often very beautiful. Then for Devonshire men they have the additional charm of those knightly family names, which with us are household words. Such is that of Hamlyn, to-day as well known in Buckfastleigh as it was in the days of Henry III.; of the Flemings and Fishacres, who gave their names to Stoke-Fleming and Combefishacre; of the Martins, lords of Dartington; the Furneaux, who are still, like the Hamlyns, our neighbours, to say nothing of Pomeroy and Ferrers and Peverel, with Audley and Monk, and others of still wider renown, who took a pride in their favourite Abbey, and would often be our honoured and welcome guests. There is a picturesqueness, too, in the little annual acknowledgments which the knightly donors would require to keep alive the memory of their gifts. A pound of wax, of course in the form of a candle, to be presented on Assumption Day, was a favourite one ; a red rose on the Feast of St John the Baptist was another. One, a lady, must needs have a pair of white gloves at Michaelmas. Abbot Nicholas—after consulting the cellarer and cook, I imagine—stipulates for an annual pound of pepper at Easter. This brings me back to my story ; the date of this agreement was about 1216, for Sampson and Roger Fitz-Henry were then provosts of the good town of Exeter, and Roger was elected Mayor for 1217. The deed is in the possession of the Dean and Chapter. Abbot Nicholas and his monks by this deed make over to John Lambrith, the land and all the houses, known as the houses of Aylmer Atlekyn, from the name of a former Saxon owner, who had probably given them to St Mary's. This transfer includes two shops[1] with the advantage of a door opening on the High Street. The worthy citizen perhaps dealt in pepper. His shop, "in King Street," is described as having the cemetery (then within the Cathedral Close) behind it. Abbot Nicholas just then must have been sadly in want of money, after his losses, so he sold these superfluous tenements for twenty-five marks of silver and the annual pound of pepper, besides obliging John Lambrith to a payment of ten shillings a year as an alms to St John's Hospital for the poor in Exeter, which numbered among its chief benefactors our neighbours, the Martins of Dartington.

In those days everybody sought to have his rights and possessions confirmed over and over

[1] *Sellas* was probably meant for *seldas; in regno vice*, I conjecture, stands for *in regio vico*.

again. The Abbot of Buckfast, presumably the same Abbot Nicholas, asked for and obtained from Sir Reginald de Valletort, who became Lord of Totnes in 1217, a confirmation of all the grants made by the De Nunants. This is signed first by Anthony, Prior of Plympton (1214-1225) and immediately after by "Robert l'Abbé." The family of L'Abbé, or Abbot, were lords of the manor of Washfield[1] at this period, a manor which afterwards passed to the Worths, to one of whose descendants I am indebted for valuable help in matters of antiquarian interest.

At some date between 1217 and 3rd May 1223, Abbot Nicholas had gone to his reward, and had been succeeded by Abbot Michael, nor can I find the name of any other Abbot—the charters simply using the phrase "Abbot of Buckfast"—till we reach Abbot Peter in 1242.

Buckfast shared in the tide of Cistercian prosperity that marked these years. The number of choir-monks increasing, the Church was prolonged eastward, as appears by its added thirteenth-century foundations. To allow of an enlargement of the refectory, it was built out at right angles to the cloister, and the walls of its southern extremity are still standing. (Our new colony has, however, in the restoration, elected to adhere to the twelfth-century plan.) For a supply of fuel, for charcoal-burning, and for their sheep, it became indispensable that they should acquire more woodland and pasture than they already held. This could only be obtained either in the vale of Dart towards Holne chase, or in the valley watered by North Brook, in the direction

[1] Worthy's *Devonshire Parishes*, vol. i., p. 133.

of Scorriton, the former stream flowing north, and the latter westward. Both these valleys are of wonderful beauty, the huge bulk of Hembury, crowned by the hill-fort to which it owes its Saxon name, being wedged in between them.

Towards the middle of the century, and after the death of Reginald de Valletort, who died in 1144, they received some gifts of land, to which several delightful little stories are attached, to be given in my next chapter; but during his lifetime they were only able to procure land by purchase. This powerful baron, the son of Roger de Valletort and Alice the Lady of Callington, had married Johanna, daughter and coheiress of Thomas Basset. He added his mother's and wife's estates to his baronies of Totnes and Harberton, though part of the latter was held by Henry de Pomeroy, Lord of Berry Castle. From him Abbot Peter bought part of his wood in South Holne, Sir Reginald adding: "If they chose to make charcoal from the aforesaid wood, they may dig a pit where they find it may best suit them, and with their horses and carts may freely go in and out through my land with their wood." He also lets them have a piece of moorland, as he says, "for the welfare of my soul and the souls of my ancestors and posterity"; but at the same time, requires payment down of forty-six marks sterling, which was duly paid. Sir Reginald died childless, his estates passing to his brother Ralph.

Agriculture and sheep-farming were only a portion of the labours of our Cistercians at this period. Their exquisite taste and matchless skill in architecture and in the adornment of their churches, argues a refined culture and an intellectual training that in this province has never been equalled in England. Had not the hand of the destroyer levelled the Church of Buckfast Abbey to the ground, we should perhaps have had a creation rivalling Tintern or Melrose.

All that could be recovered by excavation has been carefully collected, but the soft white stone used for the finer work had crumbled away under the soil. The slender columns of Purbeck marble, arranged in pairs, with some fragments of the arches that rested on them, belong to the days of Abbot Nicholas or Abbot Peter I., and tell us what the cloister windows must have been like. Of the same date is the piscina, one of the largest and finest in this part of South Devon. Some portions of window tracery, cut out of granite, proved too weighty to be carried off by those who for centuries used the Abbey ruins as a quarry. The fine tower at the south-western corner remains, but about 1480, all its windows were renewed in perpendicular style, and from existing fragments have been restored as they were when John Rede was Abbot, and Seinclere de Pomeroy, his successor, was among his monks. Coming back to the days of Abbots Nicholas and Peter, a great number of the famous Cistercian encaustic paving-tiles have been preserved. Some of these are large and plain, covered with a green or yellow glaze. But by far the greater number are small and square, some with geometrical designs, others with the fleur-de-lis, or representations of birds and fishes, the design being usually

SPECIMENS OF 13TH. CENTY FLOORING TILES.

[*To face page* 80.

white, on a red ground. As the mansion built in 1806 was constructed entirely out of the stones of the Abbey, the havoc wrought was complete. It is a wonder that we were able to find even such relics as a little copper door of a reliquary worked in Limoges enamel, dating from about 1220, and an Abbot's ring from which the stone had been removed. Another stone has been substituted, and Abbot Anscar now wears it. The restoration has been conducted with painstaking accuracy, so that the Abbot's place in the refectory is exactly where Abbot Eustace or Abbot William sat in the days of Stephen or Henry I. Even the doorway from the cloister into the kitchen is the same as of old, the lower portion of the chamfered stone door-jambs being Cistercian work; the same careful adherence to the old lines will be observed in completing the restoration.

But it is only by an effort of unaided imagination that we can recall the glory of St Mary's Church. Its plan is given in this little work, and shows that it was built on perfectly normal lines according to the fixed traditions of the monastic order, viz., the church on the north, the north-east corner of the cloister meeting the transept; the chapter-house being parallel with the church and entered from the east cloister, the refectory on the south, and the guests and cellarer's quarters occupying the west front of the monastery.

CHAPTER XI

Sir Robert de Helion's kindness to the monks of Buckfast. A distinguished company assembled in the chapter-house. Sir William Hamelin of Deandon. Sir Reginald de Valletort's land. A bad bargain. Trouble about the pigs. Sir Stephen de Bauceyn. Everything now as in days of yore. Abbots of Buckfast from 1242 to 1272.

THE village of Ashton, some four miles from Chudleigh, beyond Trusham, once a possession of St Mary's Abbey, is situated in one of the most charming parts of South Devon. The Lord of Ashton, about the year 1240—for I can only be sure that the story I am telling happened between 1238 and 1244—was a devout and kind-hearted knight, one Sir Robert de Helion. He was a great friend to the Buckfast monks, and no doubt would often ride over to visit the Abbot, when he halted at his manor-house of Trusham on his way to Exeter. The fine old manor-house of Ashton, once Sir Robert's dwelling, was for centuries the home of the Chudleighs, for the Helions were a short-lived race and their name had passed away before the close of the thirteenth century. The manor-house is now an ivy-clad and gabled farm-house.

Sir Robert was also the owner of an estate called in those days Hosefenne, but now Hawson, less than two miles from the Abbey, over which Sir Reginald de Valletort claimed manorial rights. Hawson Court is now the residence of E. F. Tanner, Esq., J.P., one of the most genial of landowners, a worthy successor to Sir Robert de Helion.

The austere life of our Cistercians moved the heart of the good knight to compassion, and he set himself to think how they might, at least a few times in the year, have their hearts cheered by some earthly solace, in addition to the spiritual joys of Church festivities. So he gathered together his friends and neighbours to witness—I presume in our chapter-house—a deed which he had prepared and fortified by very stringent conditions.

They were a goodly company. The Sheriff of Devon himself was there, Walter de Bathe, lord of Colebrooke; Sir Hugh Peverel of Ermington was next in dignity; Sir Guy de Briteville had come accompanied by Ralph de Challons of Challons Leigh, perhaps his son-in-law, who was to inherit the Briteville estates. Sir William Hamelin of Deandon, a friend of our house, who was often at Buckfast on similar occasions, had come from his Widdecombe home on the great Moor, and brought his neighbour Michael de Spitchwick, along with him. Sir William was the head of his family; he died without male issue, but from his brother Walter are descended the present Hamlyns of Buckfastleigh, to whose enterprise it is so largely indebted for its prosperity. The Vicar of Holne and many others were of the party.

Sir Robert's deed was read probably by the Vicar, to this distinguished assembly, and no doubt duly explained to them by the worthy knight. It set forth that, with the consent of his heir, he gave by this charter, "to God and to Blessed Mary of Buckfast, and to the monks who serve God in that place, all my land of Hosefenne, which is in the manor of the Lord Reginald de Valletort of South Holne . . . free from all exaction and service except the service of our lord the king, which is the fortieth part of a knight's fee," with the burden on the Abbot of an annual pound of wax on Assumption Day.

Now comes the pith of the matter. Out of the income to be derived from the Hosefenne estate, the Abbot must annually provide sixty-four gallons of wine. This is to be divided into four portions, of sixteen gallons each, to be drunk by the community on these four principal feasts: Christmas, Candlemas, Pentecost, and Assumption Day.

The allowance seems a liberal one. It is true we are now at the period when our Cistercians had to enlarge their monasteries to accommodate the influx of vocations, but more than seventy or eighty choir-monks there certainly could not have been at Buckfast at any period of its history. Of course the domestic lay brothers and those from the neighbouring granges who had come in for the festival would have their share.

But the good Sir Robert had his fears. What was to be done if a too strict Abbot or a stingy cellarer should try to curtail the allowance? This must be provided against. So he adds: "Should it ever happen that the Father Abbot (he of Citeaux), or the Visitor, or the Abbot of this place at any time, should have the presumption to take away or diminish this allowance of wine, after the truth of the matter has been enquired into and the seniors and the graver monks of the whole community have been heard, I or my heirs, shall have the power, without any contradiction, to resume the said land to their own uses. That this my gift may remain firm and inviolate for ever, I have confirmed this writing by adding my seal." Then follow the names of the distinguished witnesses.

The worthy knight must have had a light and grateful heart as he mounted his horse and rode away after partaking of the Abbot's hospitality, but I fear there was a smile on some faces, while he was explaining to the company the purport of his donation. Sir Reginald de Valletort only confirms it by a separate deed of his own, which concludes: "These are the witnesses: The Lord Hugh de Cardinan, William de Ferrers, John de Albemarle, Gilbert Fitz-Stephen, John de Shilston, knights; Warren de la More, William Finamore, and others." Fleet, now the residence of our popular representative, F. B. Mildmay, Esq., M.P., was then the home of Albemarle, otherwise Damarell; Sir John is styled by Risdon "of Milton Damarell." Not unknown to fame in the fierce "wars of the barons" are many of the names to be met with in the collection of the Abbey charters, but in their quiet Devon homes we only know them as devout and kindly children of the Holy Church.

Out of the many similar tales of domestic life told in our chartulary I can select but a few, else I should be tempted to say more about Hosefenne. It looks as if Sir Robert had made the purchase for the purpose of his donation. About twenty years previously Urglas de Holne had sold it to Nicholas de Laya, from whom Sir Robert de Helion bought it. I should weary readers who are not Devonians with stories of the personages who appear as witnesses in these transactions, such as David de Skeradon, who held his land, two miles away from the Abbey, by the service of presenting the king with three arrows whenever he came to hunt on Dartmoor— a decided sinecure ; or of Sir Martin Fishacre, whose father, Sir Peter, lies buried in the church of Moreleigh—near the newly built Trappist monastery— built by himself as a penance imposed by the Pope for having slain in a fit of rage the priest of Woodleigh; or of William of St Stephen, one of our nearest neighbours at Dean Prior; or of Henry de Pomeroy, the rebel Lord of Berry Castle; and so on.

So I shall content myself with one or two more stories, and at once give one as amusing as it is instructive, of which the date must be a little after Sir Robert de Helion's famous gift. Ralph de Valletort had succeeded to his brother Reginald, deceased in 1244. Abbot Peter, or perhaps William II., ruled at Buckfast Abbey. Sir Ralph made the Abbot what really seemed a splendid offer of an extensive wood, including Hembury Fort itself. The Abbot, no doubt rejoicing at his good fortune, paid down ninety marks of silver, and handed over to the knight a handsome palfrey, of the value of ten marks more, the deed of transfer being witnessed by our old friends, Walter de Bathe, Sir Robert de Helion, Sir William Hamelin, and so forth. There were one or two burdens attached to the sale, such as a fixed amount of wood, which Sir Stephen de Bauceyn was to receive every year from the forester of the Abbey; but the cellarer did not think them worth considering.

Very soon the Abbot found he had made anything but a cheap bargain. His neighbours, tenants of Sir Stephen de Bauceyn, turned out all their live stock, especially their pigs, to forage for themselves in the Abbot's wood. They claimed it as a right, and would pay nothing. They carried off as much timber as they chose, to build and repair their cottages; and every family claimed all they needed of timber for one draycart and two ploughs each, and for the repair of the same, to be furnished out of the said wood. Every three years each family required wood enough for a new waggon, at the Abbot's expense. At Christmas each family took away eight cartloads of firewood and one log, besides five cartloads and one log for each of their husbandmen.

No wonder the Abbot complained; but he was told it had always been so, and could get no redress. After a long period of disagreement, the matter was at last referred to arbitration, "by the advice of friends." Six freemen were appointed to settle the matter, and they decided against the Abbot on all points complained of, with three exceptions. First of all, goats were to be excluded from feeding in his wood. Secondly, the Abbot was to be paid for the pigs that fed there—the most important point—

at the rate of one penny a year for every pig over a year old, and a halfpenny for every pig under that age. Finally, the men of Sir Stephen de Bauceyn were not to cut the wood themselves, but it should be delivered to them by the Abbot's forester. Here, however, Sir Stephen's men managed to insert an important proviso, to wit, that whenever the forester refused it, and *whenever he could not be found*, they might help themselves. The advantages of this last condition are obvious.

The whole story is a good illustration of English life in the days of Henry III. But for the boys and novices of Buckfast Abbey in our day it has a charm of its own, for Ralph de Valletort's land—still wood and copse—is their favourite walk and place for recreation days, and is exactly as he describes it in his deed of sale, and they can recognise every detail of his description, for nothing is altered. There is still "the spring that gushes out under Stephen Mugge's house, and flows down to the meadow," and the ditch of Martin Keaula and the little streamlet trickling beyond Hembury down to Dart, and that rises below Hugh Kulla's house; even the old oak tree at the foot of the hill on the other side of Northbrook is still there. Only the little settlements of the husbandmen have disappeared, and there is no chance of meeting old Hugh Kulla at his cottage door. The wood surrounds Hembury and extends up the two valleys of Dart and Northbrook, and few more beautiful scenes can be found even in Devonshire. The final settlement of disputes was made on St Clement's day 1256, between the Abbot of Buckfast and Sir Stephen de Bauceyn. Sir

Stephen was a man of note in his day, and we shall meet with him again in our next chapter.[1]

[1] Owing to the loss of our Chronicle, and the want of Episcopal Registers of Exeter before Bishop Bronescombe (1257-1307), we can only compose the list of Abbots of Buckfast from deeds in which their names appear. Peter was certainly Abbot in 1242; William (II.) in 1246. In the next year, 1247, Abbot Howell of Buckfast signs a deed at Exeter. In 1257 William (III.) was Abbot, who had the dispute referred to in the above chapter, and was succeeded, according to Dr Oliver's list, by Durandus. In 1268 we find Abbot Henry. Simon was blessed by Bishop Bronescombe in 1272. Abbot Peter in 1243 bought eight furlongs of land at Engleburn, near Harbertonford, from Thomas de Reigny and his wife Johanna. On the Feast of St Lambert, 1246, William II. signs an agreement with Sir William de Saint-Stephen about land in Dean. (Add. MSS., Brit. Mus., 28649).

CHAPTER XII

Sir Stephen de Bauceyn slain in battle by Rees Vaughan. His land at Holne now called "Bozon's Farm." Sir Richard de Bauceyn. Faith and chivalry in the thirteenth century. The Chronicle of Newenham Abbey in Devon. The holy death of Sir Reginald de Mohun.

IF Sir Stephen de Bauceyn was present in person at Buckfast on St Clement's Day, 1256, he must have left immediately afterwards, in obedience to the royal summons. Things were going on badly in Wales for the forces under Prince Edward. Llewelyn, the Welsh prince, after conquering Glamorgan, had driven the royal army before him to the gates of Chester. It was the most heroic age in the annals of the Welsh people. On the arrival of the Devonshire knight, he was given the command of an army to repel the invader. It was in vain; the English were surrounded; two thousand were slain, and the gallant Sir Stephen perished by the sword of Rhys Vaughan, a noble Welshman, on whose land the battle was fought. This must have been early in 1257.

This "valiant and famous knight" was the younger son of Sir Guy de Bauceyn of Yardbiry, near Colyton. His brother Richard, who was also knighted, married Ellen, daughter of John de Shilston, and lived at Norton Bauceyn; Sir Stephen held manors at Holne, in our neighbourhood, and at Dodbrooke, adjoining the Abbot's manor of Kingsbridge.

On receiving the news of his brother's untimely death, Sir Richard de Bauceyn, his heir—Sir Stephen seems to have died unmarried—at once resolved, for the good of his soul, to present to the monks the manor at Holne, which had been the cause of dispute from the inroads made by its cultivators on the wood which the Abbot had bought from De Valletort. In his deed he gives—"for the souls of my father and mother, and of my brother Stephen Bauceyn, to the monks, who are the servants of God and Blessed Mary at Buckfast,"—all his land at Holne, wood and pasture, ways and paths, and the service of his freemen, whom he names. The gift was confirmed by Henry III. at Westminster on the 28th of October, Feast of SS. Simon and Jude, 1258. Though not the last of our royal charters, it is worthy of special notice. Its tenor is brief, only repeating and confirming the donation of "the aforesaid Stephen, who died in our service, for the welfare of his soul to the aforesaid Abbot and community and their successors." The witnesses are: Boniface, Archbishop of Canterbury (Blessed Boniface of Savoy, a Carthusian monk); Walter de Cantilupe, Bishop of Worcester (one of whose nephews was Earl of Totnes, and another St Thomas of Hereford); Richard de Clare, Earl of Ulster; Roger le Bigod, Earl of Norfolk; Hugh le Bigod, Justiciary of England; Humphrey de

Bohun, Earl of Hereford; James de Audley, and others.

The manor given to us by Sir Richard de Bauceyn (whose name is variously spelt) still bears the name of Bozon's Farm and is part of the estate of the Hon. Richard Dawson of Holne Park. Sir Ralph de Valletort died in 1257, leaving a son, Reginald, under age. As Lady of the Manor, Johanna, Sir Ralph's widow, made over by a grant to Abbot Henry her own dower-lands at Holne, and in the deed it is said that "to this writing, cut into two portions, the Abbot and the Lady Johanna affixed their seals." Among the signatures is one Alexander de Oxton. Oxton manor-house, on the road between Chudleigh and Exeter, was in the days of Protestant persecution a place of refuge for Ven. Philip Powell, O.S.B., martyr, and other hunted priests. This charter of the Lady Johanna was drawn up at her manor-house of Inceworth, in the parish of Maker in Cornwall, a possession of her husband's family. In a brief document, the same noble and pious lady commands "her men" at Holne to be henceforward obedient and dutiful to the Abbot as they hitherto had been obedient to her. The Bauceyn family continue for some time to figure in the county history; in 1261 Dame Agnes Bauceyn presents Robert de Hille to the rectory of Clist St Lawrence.

From what our chartulary and other documents tell us, it seems that from the days of Edward the Confessor till the dissolution almost the sole additions to the lands of the Abbey were in the two valleys of the Dart and of Northbrook, with some pasture-land on Dartmoor. I fear I have wearied my readers with the subject of these donations. Much might be added, but I forbear. Only I may be allowed to record the names of three sisters: Oresia, Turkasia, and Alicia, daughters of William Crocke of Crocketune, to whom we owed the wood of Birigge (Bridge) on the Dart, which may be the same wood that now forms part of the beautiful estate of Holne Park. It is Dame Turkesia who chooses a pair of white gloves for her annual present, as I mentioned before.

The year 1258, which we have now reached, was long remembered by our monks. On St Stephen's Day in 1257 Bishop Blondy of Exeter died. His successor's election was made on the 23rd of the February following. But of Bishop Bronescombe I must defer speaking to my next chapter. A month after Bishop Blondy's death, Sir Reginald de Mohun, Lord of Dunster and founder of the Cistercian Abbey of Newenham, died at Torre. Though the name of this holy servant of God is not in any of our charters—for his ancestral estates lay chiefly in Somersetshire—yet he was for certain well known to our community and Abbot. But it is for another reason that I wish here to insert from the chartulary of Newenham the singularly beautiful account of his holy death.

It is impossible in reading the annals of those days not to be struck by the simple piety of the Nunants, Helions, Bauceyns, and their knightly compeers. Faith and chivalry, intimately blended together, made the ideal knight, alike without fear and without reproach. There were many whose lives fell short of the ideal, but many realised it. Of these was Sir Reginald de Mohun. His death is thus told by the chronicler of Newenham. No doubt a like tale could be truly told of many others.

"On Sunday, the Feast of SS. Fabian and Sebastian, in the year of our Lord 1257 (1258), Sir Reginald de Mohun, Lord of Dunster and founder of Newenham, entered the way of all flesh at Torre in Devonshire; and this was the manner of his death: Sir Reginald, being stricken with a grievous sickness, sent for a Franciscan friar, Henry by name, a learned man who was then directing a divinity school at Oxford. He arrived at Torre on the Wednesday preceding the death of Sir Reginald, and heard his humble, devout, and entire confession. Early on the morning of Friday, as Friar Henry entered his room, Sir Reginald said: 'I have had a vision this night. I thought I was in the Abbey church of the white monks, and when I was on the point of quitting it, a venerable man, in the habit of a pilgrim, appeared and said to me: "Reginald, I leave you to choose whether you will come to me now in security and without peril, or wait till the week before Easter in your present danger." "My Lord," I said, "I will not wait, but will follow you now"; and I was going to do so, when he said: "You cannot follow me now, but in three days you shall be safe with me." And this was the dream that I saw.' The friar spoke many words of consolation to the sick man, and then went to his own chamber, and sat down at the foot of his bed, where he also fell asleep, and dreamed he was in the church of a Cistercian monastery and beheld a venerable man in white garments, leading by the hand a boy, more resplendent than the sun, whose garments were brighter than the clearest crystal, from the font to the altar, as is done with children after baptism. Asking who the child was, he was told: 'This is the soul of the venerable Reginald de Mohun.' The friar awoke, and understood that his dream confirmed that of Sir Reginald; for by the baptismal font is signified contrition of heart and true confession, because in penance sins are washed away even as in baptism. The going to the altar represented the entering of Sir Reginald's soul into heaven. The third day being come, Sir Reginald, who had been wont every day to assist at all the divine offices, asked Friar Henry to recite Prime and Tierce, as his time was fast drawing nigh. The friar began, and Sir Reginald said: 'For God's sake, recite quickly; my hour is at hand.' Henry then went to the church to celebrate mass, and on that day the Introit was *Circumdederunt*. When mass was over, the friar came to him in his sacred vestments, bearing the Body of our Lord. Sir Reginald strove to rise from his bed, but his weakness and the care of his attendants, of whom ten stood round him, withheld him. 'Alas!' he said, 'let me rise and meet my Saviour and Redeemer.' These were his last words, but he received the Communion, being in his senses, and was anointed. The friar, priests, and clerics there present recited the recommendation of the departing soul. As he was still living when it ended, they began it again, but at the words: *Omnes sancti orate pro eo*, without groan or any sign of pain, he slept in the Lord."

Seventy-six years afterwards, in 1333, his tomb was opened, and an eye-witness declares that his body, entire and incorrupt, exhaled a fragrant odour;

that it was exposed for three days to public view, and that he both saw and touched it. Though Reginald de Mohun died at Torre, yet both the brothers were buried in Newenham Church, before the High Altar. A few ruined walls are all that remain of the Abbey Church of Newenham.

We cannot but gain much by lingering over these records of the Ages of Faith and chivalry. Where Faith burns bright and clear the spirit of chivalry can never be extinguished.[1]

[1] For the extract just given from the Newenham Cartulary, I have availed myself, with some slight alterations, of Mr Davidson's translation in his *History of Newenham Abbey*.

ST MARY'S ABBEY, BUCKFAST, DEVON (North-west), showing the Mansion built in 1806 and the Ancient Tower.

[*To face page* 97.

CHAPTER XIII

Tranquillity of Devonshire during the War of the Barons in the reign of Henry III. Durand and Henry, Abbots of Buckfast (1253-1272). Walter Bronescombe, Bishop of Exeter. The Bishop holds his court in the chapter-house of the Abbey (1259). His zeal and activity. Social changes in Devon. Bondmen become wealthy landowners. Richard Tyulla. The hospital of the poor at Buckfast Abbey. Bishop Bronescombe a friend to the community. Priory of St Nicholas.

THE year 1258, which our story has now reached, stands forth in English history as one of its stormiest epochs. It was the year of the "Mad Parliament" at Oxford, and of a great success of the barons under Simon de Montfort in the struggle with King Henry III. and his foreign favourites. How little these fierce contests disturbed the tranquillity of our remote county, and how completely the peaceful work of the Catholic Church was left undisturbed by them, is forcibly brought home to us as we turn over the pages of the acts of Walter Bronescombe, Bishop of Exeter, now made accessible to all by the truly colossal labours of Prebendary Hingeston-Randolph. Richard, Earl of Cornwall, the king's brother, was Lord Paramount of Exeter and its

Castle, and would sometimes hold his court there, and we recognise some of our old friends in the names appended to his Exeter charters. But city and county flourished and prospered.

Under Abbots Durand (1258), Henry (1268), and Simon (1272), the Abbey enjoyed unbroken tranquillity. It is, indeed, remarkable that though the great Bishop's fiery zeal for ecclesiastical discipline and his Episcopal rights led him—I do not say always with reason and moderation—into disputes with the religious houses of Ford, Tavistock, Buckland, Plympton, Launceston, Bodmin, and others, and, perhaps even more frequently, with members of his diocesan clergy, there is no trace of any shadow of discord between the Bishop and the Abbot and monks of Buckfast. Nay, more, I have found no trace of any such disagreement in all the seven hundred years that our Abbey is known to have been the home of a monastic community. It is, indeed, a singular blessing, and may in part account for the still more signal blessing of its restoration. Even what I have already noted—that St Mary's patrimony seems neither to have suffered from Danish cruelty nor from Norman oppression—makes it look as if the blessings of peace had been granted as its inheritance from the beginning.

Bishop Bronescombe was enthroned at Exeter on the third Sunday after Easter, the 14th of April 1258. On the 19th of March 1259, we find him at our Abbey accompanied by two of his clergy, Master Bartholomew Larder (of Upton Pyne) and Master John Noble. The cause of his visit was, with the assistance of Abbot Durand and brother William of

Poundstock, monk of Buckfast, to hold a judicial investigation into some strange proceedings that had occurred at Exeter, while his predecessor, Bishop Blondy, was at the point of death. Whether it was that the two accused, Walter of Loddiswell and Richard of Totnes, were likely to be well known to the Abbot, or for some other reason, the Bishop elected to hold his court in our chapter-house.

The case was a very singular one. Already, on the 7th of February, the Bishop had addressed a letter to the Dean of Exeter to proceed to an examination of several charges of forgery of the late Bishop's signature. Those guilty, it seems, had confessed, and were now to repeat their confession and receive sentence in the chapter-house of Buckfast.

The register opens as follows: " On the Wednesday immediately preceding the Feast of St Benedict, being the fourteenth day before the Kalends of April (March 19), in the Chapter-house of Buckfast, before the Lord Bishop, appeared Walter de Loddiswell, chancellor and chamberlain of Richard, Bishop of Exeter, deceased, of happy memory, and Master Richard of Totnes, his notary, who, returning into themselves by repentance, voluntarily and on oath, in the presence of the Lord Abbot of Buckfast, of William of Poundstock, monk, etc."

In short, they confessed that during the Bishop's last illness, they had, in his bedroom, drawn up and put his seal to certain documents, especially for conferring benefices and the like, which his Lordship never saw, he being at the time unconscious; and they implicated some others as accomplices. They now submitted themselves to the Bishop's sentence, as they had incurred excommunication. As nothing had been carried away from the Bishop's Palace (and it does not appear that any harm had really ensued), they were absolved after canonical penance.

I take it for granted that Bishop Bronescombe stayed at Buckfast for St Benedict's Feast, the first time that feast came round after his taking possession of his Cathedral. I should have liked to know more of William of Poundstock, who seems to have been in the Bishop's confidence. The Bodrigans were then lords of the manor of Poundstock, and John de Bodrigan was in 1262 rector of the church. He had shown himself contumacious to the Bishop's orders in some matters not specified; and Bishop Bronescombe was no respecter of persons, as his acts abundantly prove. So he deprived the Rector for three years of the administration of his parish, at the same time absolving him from censures. On this occasion he held his court at Horseley in Surrey, and had with him one Brother Henry, a monk of our Abbey. This was on St Agnes's Day, 1262.

I may be here allowed a few words on this great and good Bishop, from whom three of our Abbots— Henry, Simon, and Robert—received their confirmation and benediction. He was the twelfth Bishop of Exeter, and, like his predecessor and his immediate successor, was born in that city, and at the time of his election was only in deacon's orders. Of a zeal and energy almost without parallel,[1] we find him

[1] See Prebendary Hingeston-Randolph's Preface to Bishop Bronescombe's Register.

visiting sixteen widely scattered parishes in little more than a month, from the Tamar to the wildest districts of Cornwall, where scarce a bridle-path existed; then after a week's rest crossing the great moor, and consecrating thirteen churches in one month. Nothing escaped his reforming zeal. The proud barons who dared to invade churches by acts of violence found themselves suddenly brought to their knees, and Sir William de la Pomeroye, the powerful Lord of Bury, and the scarcely less powerful Sir Henry de Tracey, had to petition the fearless Bishop to absolve them from excommunication; and even Edmund, Earl of Cornwall, found it useless to maintain a contest with Bishop Bronescombe. By his flock he was deeply loved, and his simple piety and beneficence won for him the title of "Walter the Good." The motto over the gateway of his manor-house of Clyst: *Janua patet; cor magis;* was the ruling principle of our Bishop, whose hospitable door was ever open wide to all, but his heart still wider. From affairs of State he held as much aloof as he could, but could not avoid being nominated the head of the commission appointed to settle the differences between the king and the barons after the battle of Evesham.

On the 21st of November 1259 Bishop Bronescombe consecrated our then newly finished Church of St Michael at Trusham, at which solemnity, of course, the Abbot and some of the monks of Buckfast were present. An aisle was added in 1430, but the church is to-day mainly the work of the monks, and on the 16th of August in the following year, William of Brideford was presented as Rector by the Abbot and community as Patrons. Brideford, or Bridford, on the Teign, lies a few miles to the north-west of Trusham, and was at that time a manor of the Valletorts.

A very pleasing little episode, bearing witness to the growing emancipation of our English peasantry who were rapidly passing from serfage to the condition of free yeomen, occurs at this period of our annals.

Some time before the death (1244) of Sir Reginald de Valletort he had made over to Henry de Valletort a portion of his estate at Holne, but with sundry burdens, Henry being, among other things, bound to pay for the feeding of Sir Reginald's hounds. As usual, Sir Reginald gives the names of the Saxon serfs, who were transferred with the estate, and rather odd names they are; Stephen Budd, or Bodda, Stephen Top, Asbert Wrench, and among them one Richard Tyulla. Twenty years have gone by, and on the 5th of June 1264, Richard Tyulla, in the presence of witnesses, grants his own charter to the Abbot and monks of Buckfast, making over to them, for himself and his heirs for ever, all his rights in the estate of Chalveleigh at South Holne, which was a gift to him from Sir Ralph de Valletort. The new landholder is careful to add: "To this writing I have appended my own seal," and to begin it in the usual form: "To all the faithful of Christ to whom this deed may come, Richard Tyulla wishes eternal welfare in the Lord." The list of witnesses embraces not only his Saxon neighbours Stephen Mugg and Wymund Cole, but the Norman knights Guarin de Bodetone and Nicholas de Kingdon. This is our earliest charter since the Conquest that is not a Norman grant. Saxon and Norman are now alike Englishmen, at least in Devon. Bodeton is now Button, a farmhouse, and the writer remembers asking the name of it, and getting for answer: " Button, sir; just as if you were to say, a button off your coat." It still retains a medieval arched passage of about the period on which we are now engaged.

But, indeed, about this time, the names of these Saxon owners of land became very frequent. We find Edward Husband—house-bondman is the original form of husbandman—Meliora, relict of Stephen Cole, Corbyn, and many another. The estate of Chalveleigh lay to the south of the stream called the Mardle, and was bounded by the property of Husband and Cole.

Abbot Henry had succeeded Durand before 1268, and was probably governing St Mary's Abbey at the time of Tyulla's charter. He lived till 1272, with which date I choose to close this chapter, as it gave us a new king and a new Abbot. As I shall not have many occasions of reverting to our charters of the reign of Henry III., I will only mention one more—a deed of Robert de Walworth, giving to the Abbey " along the course of the rivulet as far as the green path," a portion of his Walworth estate, " wood, meadow, pasture-land, moorland," and so forth. The donor adds that he had undertaken to defend and guarantee, for himself and his heirs, against all men, this portion of the Abbey lands, on payment of five marks of silver. This sum was duly paid to him by an official of the community, " Roger, who was over the hospital (*infirmitorium*) of the poor." The existence of this institution, with its special superintendent, is one more evidence of the beneficent character of our monastic foundations in the Middle Ages.

Abbot Henry's reign was not marked by any incident of note. Of course, he had often to journey to Citeaux for the General Chapter, and would be in attendance on Bishop Walter de Bronescombe when he visited the neighbourhood. In 1268 we find him signing an agreement with Richard Fitz-Alured, and presenting in 1264 Walwan as Vicar of Buckfastleigh, in 1269 Richard of Teignmouth as Vicar of Brent, and in 1270 Master Henry de Hamsterfort as Rector of Petrockstowe. A new order of things was, indeed, in preparation throughout the country, in which the Commons of England would make their power felt; but its influence had not yet been realised in Devon.

Bishop Bronescombe's esteem for our community appears from his taking Brother Henry with him on his journeys. In the Bishop's confirmation of Robert of Rye as Prior of St Nicholas at Exeter, granted at London on the 29th of June 1262, "Henry the Monk" again appears among the witnesses. It is likely that ecclesiastical studies, for which we find the community distinguished at a later period, were even at that time sedulously cultivated at St Mary's Abbey, and the Bishop needed learned men among his counsellors. Henry of Poundstock is perhaps identical with Abbot Henry, who died in 1272.

CHAPTER XIV

Abbot Simon, 1272. Amicia, Countess of Devon, founds Buckland Abbey. A dispute between the Bishop of Exeter and the Buckland monks. Abbot Robert, 1280. Defence of his rights against the Crown. Baronial rights of the Abbot in the reign of Edward I. A question concerning pasturage on Dartmoor. The perambulation of Dartmoor in 1240. A delightful summer ride. The Abbey moors no part of the Forest of Dartmoor.

CLOSE to the ancient parish church of Paignton in Devon, which still retains its Norman west entrance, may be seen some remains of the palace of the Bishops of Exeter.

On the Feast of St John the Baptist, 1272, Bishop Bronescombe, who had returned from visiting Chudleigh and Bishopsteignton, entertained a number of guests from Buckfast at this palace. He had that morning blessed a new Abbot for our monastery, who had been duly elected by the monks in place of Abbot Henry, lately deceased. Abbot Simon had taken the oath of fidelity to the Bishop as follows: "I, Brother Simon, Abbot of Buckfast, of the Order of Citeaux, do promise that I will for ever give submission, reverence, and obedience, as commanded by our Holy Fathers, according to the rule of St

Benedict, to thee, my Lord Bishop and Father, and to thy canonical successors, and to this Holy See of Exeter, saving our Order."

If we knew the day of Abbot Simon's death, we should perhaps find that he ruled for exactly eight years. At all events, his time could only have exceeded or fallen short of that term by a very few days, for his successor received his blessing at Chudleigh, 7th July 1280, from the hands of Bishop Bronescombe, only a fortnight before the Bishop's death.

On the 16th of November in this year, 1272, died King Henry III., his son Edward I. being absent in Palestine, whence he only returned in August 1274. Up to 1280, the year of Abbot Simon's death, I do not find any indication of the troubles by which the Church was harassed in the reign of this monarch in consequence of his need of money, and which Abbot Simon's successor had to meet immediately after his election. But the last months of his life must have been deeply saddened by the serious discord between the Bishop and the Abbot's Cistercian brethren at Buckland Abbey in Devon. This Abbey was founded by Amicia, Countess of Devon, in 1280, her foundation charter stating that: "We found this Abbey, which we desire shall be called St Benedict's of Buckland, which is in our manor of Buckland, for the perpetual maintenance of an Abbot and monks of St Benedict of the Cistercian Order." She then names those who are to be forever remembered in the prayers of the monks, including the King, Queen Eleanor, herself, her daughter Margaret (a nun of Lacock), and others. The monks forgot or neglected to ask the licence of the Bishop before saying mass in their new foundation, and were at once excommunicated and their church put under an interdict. Queen Eleanor interfered in their behalf, and the Bishop agreed to suspend his sentence for a time. On the 22nd of July, the dying prelate revoked all his censures pronounced against them. Before midnight he had given up his soul to God. Both the Abbots, of Buckfast and Buckland, who entered on office in this year, bore the name of Robert.

The only act of Abbot Simon's career on record is the presentation of Sir Peter of Dean, priest, to the parish of Zeal Monachorum, 6th December 1276.

Abbot Robert, his successor, found himself in difficulties with a royal commission at the very outset.

In the year 1280 Edward I. appointed special Commissioners to make enquiry throughout the kingdom by what right the landholders held their estates, franchises, or other privileges. Many estates came to be forfeited to the crown, and could only be redeemed by payment of an arbitrary fine. This was in virtue of the *Quo Warranto* Act. No doubt many abuses were remedied, but much hardship was also inflicted, on those, for example, whose title deeds had been lost.

Abbot Robert was called upon to show by what title he held through his official representative a court of justice at Buckfast, Heathfield, Churstow, and elsewhere on his demesnes. As holding lands of the crown by various charters, he was by his office a baron of the king. "The Church of Buckfastleigh" appears among the tenants-in-chief of the crown for twelve manors held in demesne, and to all such the title of baron, in its more extended sense of lord of a manor, was applicable. But at a very early period a distinction was made between the greater and lesser barons, and in the words of Sir Harris Nlcolas,[1] while the greater barons "held both a civil and criminal jurisdiction, each in his Court Baron, the lesser barons held only a civil jurisdiction over their vassals." Abbot Robert by his attorney rightly pleaded the charter of Richard I., granting him civil and criminal jurisdiction. The crown lawyers seem to have had no answer to his plea, and the case seems to have been allowed to drop.[2]

From this we can better estimate the secular position of our Abbots in the reign of Edward I. If it did not always conduce to the maintenance of monastic contemplation, and was a distraction from their religious occupations, it had been in earlier times of incalculable advantage to those who lived on their domains, and who were envied by the neighbours, although we do not find the Lords of Totnes disgraced by the atrocities recorded of many lay barons in England. Baronial jurisdiction, however, was in the time of Edward I. being gradually narrowed. Our Abbot's position was of course a higher one than most of the lords of the surrounding manors. But this was by legal right, not by encroachment.

A second question was brought forward, and I give it as stated in the "Hundred Rolls," as translated in the Dartmoor Preservation Association Publica-

---

[1] *Historic Peerage*, "Preface."

[2] Mr J. Brooking Rowe, "Cistercian Houses of Devon," *Trans. of Dev. Assoc.*

tions: "The Jurors of the Hundred of Stanborough say that the Abbot of Buckfast and his convent (community) have made purpresture (encroachment) of a certain great waste of the common moor in the south part of Dartmoor, to the injury of all the country, because, in the time of King Henry III., Howald, the Abbot, and the convent of Buckfastleigh, appropriated to themselves the aforesaid waste, and held it, and sell fuel, turf and pastures from year to year, and take rent therefor, by what warrant they know not, to the yearly damage of forty shillings." I may say at once that this charge, which was tried at Exeter in 1281, was not sustained; but the whole question, which was brought up at different times from the days of Henry III. even to our own, is so extremely interesting that I propose here briefly to give an account of the Dartmoor rights, and must begin with some information, necessary for non-Devonians.

"The great irregular tableland of Dartmoor," says the Rev. S. Baring-Gould,[1] "occupies two hundred and twenty-five square miles of territory. Of that, however, less than one-half is the 'Forest,' and belongs to the Duchy of Cornwall. Around the Forest are the commons belonging to the parishes contiguous to the moor." My readers, or most of them, may not need to be told that the word *Forest* does not necessarily mean a tract of land covered by trees, of which there are few on Dartmoor. "It was an extensive territory of uncultivated ground, kept in a virgin condition for the wild beasts of the forest, beasts of chase, and beasts and fowls of

[1] *A Book of the West*, Chapter X.

warren,"[1] with fixed boundaries, special officers, and laws.

Now, when the Black Prince obtained for himself and his successors a confirmation of the property of Dartmoor Forest, every Devonshire parish, except Totnes and Barnstaple, had immemorial rights of pasturage there, and could take off the moor "whatever might do them good, except green oak and venison," and the grant was made subject to these rights. Despite many deplorable encroachments, the exercise of these rights is in full use at the present day, and the flocks and herds of sheep, bullocks, and more especially of the wild Dartmoor ponies, add both to the value and picturesqueness of our great moor.

Now, was the Abbot of Buckfast the earliest of the encroachers on the Commons of Dartmoor? In other words, were the tracts of land known as Buckfast Moor, Brent Moor, and Holne Moor, parts of his manors of Buckfast, Brent, and Holne, as Abbot Robert maintained, or were they part of the *Forest?* Not only before the Dissolution, but since the Abbey lands have passed to other hands, has the question arisen. The decision, when any was given, has always been in favour of the Abbey. At the same time, it is clear that before the suppression, the Abbot, without relinquishing the seignory of the land, had allowed the free use of his pasture-land on the moor to the Commons of Devon. Their consequent rights, being of course irrevocable, are exercised at the present day, while in absence of any proof to the contrary, the lordship belongs presum-

[1] Rev. J. C. Cox, *How to write the History of a Parish.*

ably to the present owners of the Abbey. Some singularly interesting records bearing on the question are to be seen in the preserved portion of our cartulary, and I must give a brief notice of them.

Long before the days of the Black Prince, in the year 1240, Richard, Earl of Cornwall, the king's brother, had a dispute with four Devonshire knights, Sir William Hamlyn, our old friend Sir Robert de Helion, Sir Henry de Merton, and Sir William de Pruz, concerning the bounds of his (Richard's) Forest of Dartmoor, and those of the knights and free tenants—among whom was, of course, our Abbot Peter—whose manors were contiguous to the said forest, and who were represented by the four knights, who now asked to be allowed to make a perambulation of the forest bounds. The royal assent was granted, and an order issued from Westminster, on 13th June 1240, to the Sheriff of Devon, that he himself, accompanied by twelve knights of the shire bound by oath, should go with them, take careful note of the exact bounds, and forward the result to the king, "Wherever we may be, clearly and distinctly, and under thy seal, and the seals of the four knights aforesaid." This was done on the eve of St James, the 24th of the following month; and a more delightful summer ramble could not be conceived than that enjoyed by the distinguished company of sixteen knights, with Sir Walter de Bathe at their head. They must have been in the saddle from early morn till late at night, and I hope they got a dispensation from the Fast of St James's Vigil. All their names are given. There was the devout Sir William le Bruere, the founder of Torre Abbey, and Sir Roger Giffard, presumably of Awliscombe, whose line was to end with an Abbot of Buckfast, and our friends Sir Guy de Bryteville and Sir William de Widworthy, and Sir Hugh de Boley, a vassal of the Church, who held five knights' fee at Hilton of the Bishop of Exeter, and Durand, whom I cannot identify, but suspect was the father of our Abbot Durand. Needless to say, a crowd of moormen followed them, and, unless I am much mistaken, the Cistercian habit was to be seen among the riders, and if not my Lord Abbot himself, at least his cellarer was there, for in the cartulary the bounds of Buckfast moor and of Brent moor are appended to those of Dartmoor itself, and nothing was more easy than to take them at the same time.

It was a glorious ride. As the knights came from homes rather widely scattered round the moor, I presume they had slept the night before at Okehampton Castle, where Sir Hugh Courtenay would give his friends a hearty welcome. After hearing mass in the castle at an early hour, they rode to Costendonne, now Cawsand Beacon, their starting-point, a hill 1800 feet high, and then followed the track to Hound Tor, so-called from the stones of the summit, "weathered into forms resembling the heads of dogs peering over the natural battlements." Thence their route lay south, and as the perambulation says, "through a boggy place to the King's Oven," a name which remains to this day—changes are few on Dartmoor—and then, getting out of the fenny portion, they rode along the Walla Brook till it joined the East Dart, which they followed to Dartmeet. To follow them throughout their circuit would be out of place; suffice it to say that the "Abbot's Way" was a relief from the rough bridle tracks for a part of their journey, and that they reverently saluted Syward's Cross as they passed it. It is still in its place, the largest of the Dartmoor crosses.

The monks carefully copied into the cartulary the perambulation, and it is most unlikely that Abbot Howell, only seven years later, should have ventured on encroachments; and in fact, anxious as the Commissioners were to find such delinquencies, the charge fell through.

In 1531, Sir Thomas Denys, Sir Philip Champernowne, and others were again charged to investigate whether the moors occupied by the monks were part of their own manors or not. The verdict was that: "The three moors called South Holne Moor, Buckfast Moor, and Brent Moor, be parcel of the Abbot's manors called South Holne, Buckfastleigh and Brent;" and the document in our cartulary closes with these words: "And the said Abbot (John Rede) and his said convent daily hath done, and shall continue their daily prayer to God for your prosperous continuance long to endure."

Ten years later Abbot and monks had been cast adrift and the moors in question were in the hands of Sir Thomas Denys; and it is significant that we find the men of Buckfastleigh complaining that Sir Thomas refuses to allow them the pasturage on the foresaid moors "*which they used and had in the time of the late Abbot of the late monastery of Buckfast.*" In short, so far from encroaching, the Abbots, though they asserted the rights of their monastery, allowed the people to pasture their cattle on the Abbey land without payment. The council ordered that the people should be allowed to do " as in the Abbot of Buckfast's time."

But the Commissioners had not yet done with Abbot Robert. David of Skeriton, no doubt a descendant of that David who figures in our earliest charter, held his land by the services of finding three arrows for the king's use, when he chose to hunt on Dartmoor. From David it passed to Roger de Mirabel, who had forfeited it for felony; and it had been re-granted to Walter, the king's physician, and had subsequently been alienated to Buckfast. It was contended by the Commissioners that the alienation without the royal consent was not legal, but nothing more seems to have been heard of the matter.

CHAPTER XV

The new order of things in England. Cistercian decline. Parliament at Exeter in 1285. The Exeter Synod of 1287. Death of Abbot Robert. Extracts from the Buckfast cartulary. Edward I. visits the Abbey. Abbot Peter II. Distress of the monastic houses in the reign of Edward I. Abbot Robert II.

ON the Octave of St Martin, 1281, the case of the Crown against Abbot Robert of Buckfast was tried at Exeter, Walter de Fursden being his attorney. The Abbot appears to have made good his defence, as we have seen. Not only were no further proceedings taken, but he continued in the exercise of his ancient rights, in so far as they were not curtailed by subsequent Acts of Parliament.

Buckfast Abbey could not but be affected by the changes which began at this date, and which by the close of Edward I.'s reign had so transformed the kingdom that "with the reign of Edward we are face to face with modern England, the England in which we live."[1] The number of the greater barons was lessening day by day; that of the smaller landholders was rapidly increasing. Alienations of land to monasteries were checked by the Statute of Mortmain. "This restriction," writes the

[1] Green, *Short History of the English People.*

historian just quoted, "was probably no beneficial one to the country at large, for churchmen were the best landlords."

Moreover, as Cistercians gradually declined from their primitive austerity, their influence waned, and their numbers diminished. Mr J. Brooking Rowe rightly affirms that no scandal tarnished the fair fame of our monastery in its long career; "no greed of wealth, no undue accumulation of riches;" in what remains to be told of their story we find them still as of old, peaceful, studious, beneficent. But we know that the heroism of their early days of fervent austerity and penance had given place to a life, edifying indeed and useful, but not formed on the model of St Robert or St Bernard, in the strictness of silence, abstinence, and manual labour. The invariable consequences followed in the fewness of vocations and the decline of the reverence in which the Order had been held. The exuberant invigorating joyousness of their pristine austerity would have better supported them against outward attacks and oppression.

Edward I. and his Queen spent the Christmas of 1285 at Exeter. There they remained for fifteen days, and the king held a Parliament. From this it seems impossible that our Abbot should have been absent. The right of attendance of all the tenants-in-chief in Parliament was still unaltered, though the lesser barons did their best to shirk the duty on account of the expense. But at this time an effort was being made to secure their attendance, and so large a landholder as the Abbot of Buckfast could not be passed over. The king had been invited to Exeter by Bishop Quivil, but it is not clear whether the royal pair were lodged in the Bishop's palace or in the Dominican convent. The Abbot would, of course, during the Parliament, stay at his own town-house near the Cathedral.

A more welcome occasion occurred two years later, when Bishop Quivil held the celebrated Synod of Exeter. The acts of the Exeter Synod of 1257 are of great interest. Among other statutes it decreed that infants should be confirmed shortly after baptism; that no parishioner, save a patron or a noble, should have a fixed seat in the church; that no priest should say mass more than once in the same day, except on Christmas Day, Easter Sunday, or when a parish priest had an interment in his own church.

Specially dear to the Buckfast monks was another decree of the Synod of 1287. It was enacted that in every parish church of the vast diocese, besides the statue of the Patron Saint, there should also be a statue of our Blessed Lady. The statue of our Lady of Buckfast, however, now restored and venerated in our Abbey Church, seems to belong to the following century. It was also decreed that in addition to the four festivals of our Blessed Lady already observed in England, that of her Conception, the 8th of December, should be kept in the Exeter diocese as a holy day of obligation. Bishop Quivil built in Exeter Cathedral the Lady Chapel, in which he was buried. His decree making the Immaculate Conception a feast of obligation for his diocese was in 1328 extended to the whole Province of Canterbury.

I have not found the year of Abbot Robert's death, but his successor was in office in 1290. As the history of Buckfast is so largely identified with that of our county, and Abbot Robert's term of office marks the division between the old order of things and the new, I cannot help giving one lingering backward glance at some details of our domestic history between 1240, the year of the famous perambulation of Dartmoor and the date of the good Abbot's death. They all throw light on life in Old Devon, though they have not the dignity that surrounds events of national interest.

Mr Baring-Gould, in his *Book of the West*, describes Hound Tor Farmhouse as "nestling picturesquely enfolded in a sycamore grove." It was the first station made by Sir Walter de Bathe and his sixteen companions after leaving Cawsand Beacon. Should any of our monks ever visit it, they may recall to mind that it was once the manor-house of our friends, the knightly family to which belonged Sir Richard de Hound Tor, who signs one of our charters in company with Sir William Hamlyn and Sir William Brewer. The date of the charter is 1201, when Ralph de la More was Sheriff of Devon, and by Abbot Robert's time Hound Tor had passed to the Langdons.

In Abbot Robert's own time, on St Andrew's Day 1280, we find a case in which the Abbot has to exercise the power of wardship, granting leave to Michael Cole to marry Mariota, the daughter and heiress of Stephen Mugge, to any one of his sons whom he may choose, the said Michael being her guardian. Poor Mariota's own inclinations were not likely to be consulted in those days. If she wished to exercise her own choice, she could only do so on payment of a fine.

I do not know if the cellarer of the Abbey was sometimes slow in paying his debts. But in one deed I find inserted a special condition, that if the messenger sent for the money does not find it in readiness, he is to be allowed to live and board at the Abbey till he gets it; in another, that he is to get six pence—ten shillings it would be nowadays—for every day that payment is overdue. This last instance, also in Abbot Henry's time, was in the case of a lady entitled to a life annuity for some grants made to the monastery, and her quarterly payments were made "at the Abbey gate," that is to say, at the gate-house of which so much still remains and is transformed into two cottages. The lady's name was Eleanor de Ashleigh, in the parish of Lifton.

While entering on the new order of things, it is well to bear in mind that developments were slow in Devon, and that nowhere in England was the growth of change more gradual or more tranquil. Even in the formidable insurrections of the latter part of the fourteenth century, when the labourers rose all over the country, Devon remained quiet.[1] This was in part owing to the traditionally kind relations between landowners and labourers. But it was also due to the influence of the great Bishops of Exeter, in whose diocese Lollards and Wycliffites, with their preachings of revolution and sedition, were unable to gain the footing they found elsewhere.

[1] Bishop Brownlow, *Slavery and Serfdom*, p. 164, note.

Peter II. was our Abbot in 1290, if not for some years before, and governed his monastery for at least twenty-six years; Robert II. succeeding him in 1316.

The sixty years which preceded the Great Plague (1288-1348) were marked by many troubles and not a few scandals in the Exeter diocese, both among the laity and the clergy, secular and regular, though they were also distinguished by many saintly lives and by the virtues of our great and heroic bishops. The ecclesiastical history of the diocese is told with marvellous detail in the splendid Episcopal registers, and for the last forty years of that period its record is complete and minute.

Four Abbots ruled over St Mary's during these sixty years. As "not a single entry relating to acquisition of land or disputes leading to legal proceedings" can be discovered, there must have been profound peace in our valley, and the traces the Abbey has left in the Episcopal registers confirm this conclusion. The monks, however, had severe trials to encounter during the reign of Edward I., on account of that monarch's exactions—trials shared by every owner of land in England. How Abbot Peter managed to keep his community in existence is hard to imagine, and the small number of the monks was a necessary consequence of the king's rapacity. In 1294 Commissioners were sent to search the treasures of monasteries and churches, and under the derisive title of loans, they swept off both the money of the clergy and the sums deposited with them for safety. In another year half their income was exacted. The laity did not fare much better:

BUCKFAST ABBEY: Remains of North Gate, under which Edward I. passed on 1st April 1297.

[*To face page* 121.

first a heavy tax was imposed on every sack of wool, and then the wool was seized, to support the expense of the king's wars. Eventually all the clergy, secular and regular, of the Southern Province were !outlawed. But the spirit of the nation was roused; under the guidance of Archbishop Winchelsey, St Thomas of Hereford, and the Earls of Norfolk and Hereford, the crown was compelled to relinquish the right of levying taxes without the consent of the nation: the greatest victory over tyranny Englishmen had ever won.

During the struggle the monastic communities were reduced to beggary, but it is likely that at Buckfast, from its remote position, they suffered less than elsewhere. On the 8th of April 1297, Edward I. visited Buckfast Abbey on his way from Exeter to Plympton.

In 1307, the last year of King Edward's life, sixty-one Abbots attended the Parliament he had summoned to meet him at Carlisle, but neither Abbot Peter nor any Abbot from our county was present. The death of King Edward on the 7th of July in that year was followed by that of Bishop Bytton of Exeter on the 17th of September. The loss of this Bishop's register and the troubles of the time have left us no records of Abbot Peter's career beyond some agreements about the Abbey estates in Brent (1296) during the reign of Edward I. But we shall meet with him during the first nine years of Bishop Stapeldon's Episcopate.

CHAPTER XVI

Enthronement of Bishop de Stapeldon. Sir Hugh Courtenay as seneschal. Ordinations. Names of the monks. The language spoken by the community at the opening of the fourteenth century. Ashburton; its woollen trade and the monks of Buckfast. The chapel of St Lawrence. The service-books written by the monks. The Bishop's last visit. A manumission. Bishop Stapeldon murdered, 15th Oct. 1316.

WHEN Abbot Peter, on the 23rd of December 1308, returned home from Exeter, where, as in duty bound, he had assisted at the enthronement of the new Bishop, Walter de Stapeldon, he must have had much to tell them on the magnificence of the festival.

Perhaps he may have omitted to relate, as savouring too much of the world, how Sir Hugh de Courtenay, Baron of Okehampton and claimant to the earldom of Devon, had claimed and exercised his right of meeting the Bishop at the door of the church, as he dismounted, and walking on his right hand as far as the choir "to keep off the crush of people," and afterwards serving him at the first course at dinner in the Episcopal hall; in short, exercising the office of seneschal. Sir Hugh claimed in recompense for his services the right to carry away with him four silver dishes, one silver cup, two silver basins, besides the ewer and salt-cellars of the same precious metal. The said Sir Hugh did not forget in the deed solemnly drawn up on this occasion to claim hay and oats for the horses of his whole company.

It was hard on the Bishop, who was penniless, and had been obliged on that account to defer his enthronement till he had collected or borrowed money for the occasion. Though most frugal and hardworking, Bishop Walter loved magnificence, and it was a bitter humiliation for him to beg the Bishop-elect of Worcester, who was consecrated with him at Canterbury, to bear even his expenses for food and drink.

The Bishop had only arrived at Exeter the night before (21st December) from Crediton. In the morning he had held in Crediton Church his first ordination; and it is astounding to read that no less than one thousand and five candidates were present! Were not all the names given, it would not be believed; but every name is there, and the names of those by whom they were presented. There were one hundred and fifty-five sub-deacons, seventy-seven deacons, and forty-two priests; the rest received minor orders or the first tonsure.

Bishop Stapeldon's ordinations are given in full in his register, and if we had the surnames of our monks, it would assist our history. But the Cistercian usage of giving only their place of origin is still adhered to, with a few exceptions.

I give, as I find them, the names of those ordained

by Bishop Stapeldon; Brothers Walter of Totnes, Walter of Plympton, Adam of Lidford, Hugh of Brent, Adam of Bridestowe, John of Ashburton, Alan of Exeter, William Gifford, Walter Gifford, Michael de la Stone, Philip Cole; only eleven in eighteen years. The community must have dwindled in the hard times of Edward I.'s reign. Of course, I have no means of ascertaining how many were professed when already in orders, a numerous class at all times with Cistercians.

In addition to his monks the Abbot presented to Bishop Stapeldon some twenty secular clerics, whom he provided with a title, becoming responsible for their maintenance till they found a benefice, or placing them in his dependent churches. I am sorry to say that one of these, Peter of Pyne, was put back with this note opposite his name: "Not to be admitted till he has learned to sing." As the same misfortune befell several of his companions, I suspect one of the examiners was an enthusiast in Plain Chant. Poor Peter learned his chant, and was duly admitted on the next occasion. The Buckfast monks were usually ordained at Exeter Cathedral or in the Priory Church of Totnes. Our own church, though a large one, was unsuitable, as Cistercian churches were divided into three separate parts—for the people, the lay-brothers, and the monks respectively.

Not till the August following was the Bishop able to visit our Abbey, after closing a visitation of his diocese. On what day he arrived I cannot say, but he passed the 12th and 13th with our community and left on the 14th for Chudleigh, where he kept the Feast of the Assumption. As a matter of course, he gave a discourse to the monks in our chapter-house. And I can surmise with tolerable certainty, that the Abbot heard all about the work he was doing in the glorious choir of his Cathedral; the High Altar of silver, the wonderful stalls, the forty stained glass windows,[1] and the rest. The Bishop had appealed to Buckfast for help towards the expenses, and I hope Abbot Peter was able to assist him. At all events, our community granted a participation in all their spiritual works to all who should contribute.

It would be of wonderful interest if we could but listen to the converse held by the great statesman-bishop with the Abbot. They did not converse in English, but in Norman-French. English was, indeed, making its way, and the monks had to use it with the lay-brothers and the peasantry on their estates. Bishop Stapeldon disliked its use among ecclesiastics. In his statutes for the scholars of Stapeldon Hall (now Exeter College), his noble foundation at Oxford, he writes: "Whenever the scholars are met together, at dinner, supper, or otherwise, let them, as a rule, speak only French or Latin, so as to exercise themselves better in those languages, which will afterwards be to their greater advantage and reputation." A few years later, when it was laid to the charge of some ecclesiastics that they had been guilty of irreverence by making some remarks in choir, it was added as an aggravation that they had been uttered in English. That our

[1] See the Rev. Hingeston-Randolph's Preface to Bishop de Stapeldon's Register, an admirable biography.

monks now and then talked English among themselves is very likely, but in chapter or conference, Abbot Peter would certainly address them in French or Latin. That such was the usage in religious houses, we see from Bishop Stapeldon's letter to the Benedictine nuns of Polslo, written in Norman-French, with the admonition that if it should be absolutely necessary to say a word in places where silence is prescribed, the nuns are to whisper it in Latin: "I do not mean Latin according to the rules of grammar," writes the good Bishop, "but just a word, such as *candela, liber, missale, panis, cerevisia* (candle, book, missal, bread, beer), and so forth." Whispering in English he would not have tolerated; I am afraid the nun guilty of it would have been proclaimed at chapter next morning. His Lordship repeats the same for the Canonesses Regular of Canonsleigh, a house founded sixteen years before by the Countess of Gloucester for fifty Canonesses. Then, as now, there was one community of Benedictines, and one of Canonesses, in our diocese.

Bishop Stapeldon was not to enjoy in peace his walks with the Abbot by the Dart in the Long Meadow during his stay. The Burgesses of Ashburton, only two miles away, waited on him to ask him to get them from the king an annual fair to St Lawrence's Feast, which he promised at once. Then a messenger came with a letter from Sir Nicholas Lovetot, Rector of Stokenham, who wanted £18, supposed to be in his Lordship's hands, on behalf of Robert and Cecilia de Buthan, whose father had lately died, to whom the Bishop's secretary was directed to answer: "No effects." And so, on Assumption Eve, by the road which to the writer and his brethren is so familiar, he journeyed to Chudleigh, passing through Bishop Stapeldon's favourite borough of Ashburton, past Bickington, and through Chudleigh Knighton, till he reached the Episcopal manor-house, whereof the remains are still to be seen near Chudleigh Rock on Lord Clifford's estate, for Ugbrooke in those days belonged to the Bishop of Exeter.

The good people of Ashburton were then as familiar with the sight of the Cistercian habit as they are nowadays with the Benedictine. Being about half-an-hour's walk from the Abbey, it had been from old Sir Roger de Nunant's time the usual market for the Buckfast folk, and the cellarer and his men were as often to be seen there as at the present time. The weekly market was on Saturday.

In Abbot Peter's time Ashburton flourished exceedingly, and was really a large town, sending two members to the Parliament of 1297. During our Abbot's time, it was made one of the Stannary towns, and in the records of the coinage of tin at Ashburton in 1303 and 1305, may be read the old familiar names of our cartulary, Michael Cole, Stephen Mugge, and the rest, from among the Abbey tenants.

Nearly 22 tons of tin were coined at Ashburton in 1303.[1]

In the prosperity of the then thriving and active borough the neighbouring Abbey had a large share, whereof the fruits are enjoyed at the present day,

---

[1] R. N. Worth, "The Ancient Stannary of Ashburton," *Trans. of the Devon. Assoc.* 1876.

when the Ashburton woollen trade is all that remains of its industries. "The Cistercians," writes Mr J. Brooking Rowe, "were the great wool traders of the times in which they lived, and the owners of the large mills (at Buckfast) are but carrying out in the same locality the work of former years." But it seems certain that in the days of Abbot Peter the Ashburton woollen trade of our monks received its greatest development. "An exchange place for metal," says Mr Amery, "would soon become a mart also for raw produce, such as wool and skins. The farmer monks of Buckfast doubtless set an example of industry, and perhaps introduced the process of manufacturing cloth among the many useful occupations in which they employed their time."[1] He also notes that for the arms of the borough was adopted the seal of the Guild of St Lawrence at Ashburton, including the teasel, the badge of the fullers. The mention of this celebrated guild brings me back to Abbot Peter and Bishop Stapeldon.

In 1314—I am abridging from Mr Amery—the Bishop made over to St Lawrence's guild the chapel of St Lawrence, of which only the beautiful tower and one wall still remain, as their chantry. The priest, with a salary of £8. 13s. 4d. (perhaps over £100 of our money), was to "say mass in perpetuity for the Bishop, his predecessors and successors," and to keep a grammar school. The grammar school exists; though the chapel has been swept away, and mass has not been said at Ashburton for centuries.

The day after the Feast of the Assumption, 1314,

[1] Amery, "Ashburton and the Woollen Trade," *Trans. of the Devon. Assoc.* 1876.

was a proud day for Ashburton. The burgesses met in their new guildhall under their provost or portreeve, to read and put their seal to a deed by which they accepted the Bishop's noble gift, and bound themselves and their successors to provide the new chapel with missal, vestments, and all the needful for mass and the chaplain's maintenance. At the end, the names of the witnesses may be read, as follows (translated): "Robert, by the grace of God, Abbot of Tavistock; Matthias, Prior of Plympton; Peter, Abbot of Buckfast; Jocelyn, Prior of Totnes; Roger de Charleton, Archdeacon of Totnes; and others."[1] The Chapel of St Laurence was built in the form of a gridiron, as churches in honour of the martyr often were. Ashburton has always honoured the memory of Bishop Stapeldon as its chief benefactor.

A year later, he was again the guest of Abbot Peter at St Mary's Abbey. There we find him on 6th September 1315, and he probably remained some days with us. Here he perhaps received the king's letter on 1st September, asking for money to equip his army against Robert Bruce, King of Scotland. In the year before, the king had been defeated at Bannockburn, and the cares of state weighed heavily on the loyal Bishop of Exeter.

Abbot Peter died, probably in July 1316; for on Sunday, the 1st of August in that year, Abbot Robert II. received his blessing from Bishop Stapeldon at Crediton, and I find him soon after presenting to the parishes of Down St Mary and Petrockstowe.

One of the occupations of our monks at this period

[1] Oliver, *Lives of the Bishops of Exeter.*

was the writing and illuminating of missals and other books for the service of the neighbouring parishes, such as Ashburton and Staverton. It is instructive to read the Bishop's notes at the visitation of these churches. At Staverton he finds an Antiphonarium, Hymnarium, Collectarium, and Venitarium (chant for the Venite Exultemus) in one volume, "very good." A good Psalter in large letters. One Ordinal is described as "sufficient," another in a bad state. A Legenda (book of lessons for Matins) first-rate (optima), another worn out. One good Missal, new, with good notes for the chant, and so on; very creditable on the whole. But the pyx for the Blessed Sacrament (suspended, in form of a dove) had no lock. The processional cross was handsome, the frontal of the High Altar poor, the cruets tolerable. The priest exemplary; the parishioners say he instructs them well in spiritual things; no fault to be found in him, they say. As a rule, the parish priest, "the poor parson of a town," as Chaucer calls him, was beloved and esteemed. When otherwise, it was an exception.

At Ashburton, matters were not so satisfactory: the pyx quite unworthy, and made of wood; no nuptial veil, nor any frontal, except for the High Altar; books in a state of decay; windows made of wood; no cope. Unless all this is set right before Michaelmas, a fine of £20 to be paid for the benefit of the Cathedral.

Ten years had gone by since Abbot Robert's installation. A little after the middle of October 1326, messengers reached Buckfast Abbey with the appalling news of the murder of their Bishop by a

London mob. The contemporary accounts are given by Prebendary Hingeston-Randolph and Dr Oliver. With a brief summary of the same I shall close this chapter.

Edward II., as soon as he heard of the landing of his faithless queen, "the she-wolf of France," fled from London, on the 2nd of October, after entrusting the city to the custody of his faithful Bishop of Exeter. On the 15th, the Bishop, who was well aware of his danger, and wore an "acton" under his clothes as defensive armour, met the rabble as he was riding home from the country, between two and three in the afternoon. They had just come from the burning and plunder of his house. The fearless Bishop was assailed on all sides with shouts of "Traitor!" and turned his horse towards the north door of St Paul's. Before he could enter, he was seized, dragged from his horse, and hurried, wounded and bleeding, to Cheapside. There they proclaimed him a traitor, and struck off his head, two of his household meeting the same fate. The body was carried to St Paul's by the canons, after being stripped by the rebels, who set his head upon a stake. From St Paul's it was taken by the queen's partizans, and cast into a pit without any Christian rites. It was afterwards buried in St Clement Danes, and finally brought back to Exeter, where it rests under a canopied monument in the choir of the Cathedral. As a bishop, Stapeldon's life was irreproachable; as a statesman, his integrity and justice were without blemish. It was his misfortune to serve a weak and indolent king, and he died a victim to his unswerving loyalty.

CHAPTER XVII

Bishops of Exeter. James de Berkeley. John de Grandisson. Installation of Abbot Stephen, 1327. He reconciles Thurlestone Church. Bishop Grandisson at Buckfast Abbey. Abbot Stephen at the Council of London, 1329. The statue of our Lady of Buckfast. Abbot John of Churchstow, 1332. Abbot Gifford, 1333. The Devonshire Giffords. Abbot Stephen of Cornwall, 1348.

BISHOP STAPELDON'S successor in the See of Exeter, James de Berkeley, only survived his consecration for fourteen weeks. He died on the Feast of St John the Baptist, 1327. Not till the Octave of the Assumption, on the 22nd of August, in the following year, did his successor, John de Grandisson, "the most illustrious and most devoted of our Bishops," as Prebendary Hingeston-Randolph calls him, take possession of his Cathedral. His enthronement was celebrated without any pomp or display beyond the ecclesiastical rite.

The Bishop had entered his diocese on the 9th of June, and on Friday, the 24th of that month, in the chapel of his manor of Clyst, he confirmed the elections of Stephen, Abbot of Buckfast, and John of Chudleigh, Abbot of Ford, received their profession of obedience, and gave them the abbatial benediction.

A week later, on the 2nd of July, the Bishop issued his mandate, being then at his favourite manor of Chudleigh, to Abbot Stephen of Buckfast, to reconcile the parish church of Thurlestone, a village four miles from Kingsbridge, where the Avon from Dartmoor flows into the sea. In one of the sanguinary quarrels that abounded at this time, the parish church had been profaned by bloodshed, and in consequence had been placed under interdict. The Abbot reconciled the church according to the form assigned by the Bishop, sprinkling it "with water blessed by us," as Grandisson writes, on the 25th of the month, but it was not till the 20th of October that the Bishop removed the interdict, after the payment of the usual fine by the rector and parishioners. On the same day, he issued a commission for promoting to Holy Orders Robert Arch, a poor clerk of Crediton, for whose maintenance Abbot Stephen and his chapter assumed the responsibility.

The new Bishop found the finances of the diocese in the greatest confusion, owing to the state of chaos that followed Stapeldon's murder. He earnestly appealed to our Abbot, among others, for pecuniary assistance, and renewed his appeal by letters issued on the 15th of September. That Abbot Stephen responded, I believe, from the fact that on the 2nd of October, Bishop Grandisson was at our Abbey, the first religious house in the diocese to receive that honour. Five of his letters are dated from Buckfast on that day, and they are no bad indication of the Bishop's activity. The Vicar of Denbury, a parish not far from Buckfast, is granted leave of absence; the Abbot of Tavistock is informed that the Bishop intends to be with him on the 7th; the clergy of the diocese were commanded to afford free access to their churches to the collectors of money for repairing the bridge at Totnes, and to recommend them to the charity of the faithful at Solemn Mass on Sundays and holydays; and so on.

From the Episcopal Registers of this period we are made painfully conscious of a relaxation of ecclesiastical. discipline and a tendency to revolt against authority which it needed all the patient energy of Bishop Grandisson to control. The frequent enforced absences of Bishop de Stapeldon from his diocese were a misfortune; and, perhaps, the extraordinary number of ordinations during his episcopate included some who had no true vocation to the priesthood. The emancipation of the bondmen was now far advanced. Those that remained became naturally restless, and their lords used oppressive measures. Compared with other parts of the kingdom, the men of Devon remained tranquil on the whole, as may be judged from the total absence of disputes or lawsuits in the case of our monastery under four successive abbots; but even Devon did not escape altogether the contagion of lawlessness.

Abbot Stephen was among those summoned to attend personally, and not by proxy, at the Provincial Council convoked by Archbishop Simon Mepham for the 27th of January 1329, to be held in London, in St Paul's Cathedral. Among regulars, only the abbots were personally summoned, Buckfast taking the first rank among the five Cistercian houses. Before starting for London, those summoned held a meeting at Exeter, in which it was resolved to lay these three grievances before the Synod: that the lords of manors denied their bondmen the right of making wills; that lay-judges took upon themselves to judge and decide causes of a purely ecclesiastical nature; and that the jurisdiction of the Bishop of Exeter had been in some cases unduly hampered in his efforts for reform by appeals to the Archbishop.

The Bishop did not go to the Synod. He wrote to it that his house in London had been wrecked, that the murderers of his predecessor had been left unpunished, and that his own life would be in danger. He therefore appointed his proctor, who, with the abbots, archdeacons, and proctors of chapters and communities, should attend the Synod from the Exeter diocese.

In this Provincial Council the Feast of our Lady's Conception was made a holyday of obligation for the whole Province of Canterbury. The now restored statue of our Lady of Buckfast, which Abbot Boniface Nather solemnly blessed and placed over the Lady Altar of our present temporary church, belongs to this period.

The last act I find of Abbot Stephen's brief career is the presentation of Sir Thomas de Harewold as rector of Down St Mary, on the 11th of April 1332. He was dead before the Feast of All Saints, on which day John of Churchstow was blessed as Abbot of Buckfast in the Bishop's chapel at Chudleigh.

At the very date of his receiving the blessing he was obliged to inform the Bishop that, as it seems, during the brief interval since the death of Abbot Stephen, a serious robbery from his abbey had been committed. Large sums of money and other objects of value had disappeared, and no clue to detect the thieves could be found. It was clear that the guilty parties belonged to the neighbourhood. Bishop Grandisson three days later issued orders that in all the churches of the archdeaconry of Totnes sentence of excommunication against them should be published on Sundays and festivals "with ringing of bells, extinguishing of candles, and uplifted cross"; all suspected persons to be arrested and tried in the Episcopal Court. Whether the money was ever recovered is not recorded. No doubt, at Abbot Stephen's decease there was an unusual concourse of outsiders to the monastery, and lawlessness was ripe at that time. Abbot John ruled his monastery about eight months, dying towards the end of May in the following year.

On the 6th of June, Bishop Grandisson, in the chapel of his manor-house at Clyst, gave the abbatial blessing to our newly elected Abbot, William Gifford. He must have been comparatively young in the order of profession, having been ordained priest by Bishop Stapeldon in the Cathedral, on the 22nd of September 1319.[1]

---

[1] Unhappily the list of Bishop Grandisson's ordinations has been lost, but to the names of Buckfast monks who were priests in Bishop Stapeldon's time, as stated above, we must add

Abbot Gifford is the first on our list whose family name is given, a departure from the earlier Cistercian usage. But for us it is pleasing to read a name so illustrious in the annals of Catholic England. William Gifford was Bishop of Winchester in the days of the Conqueror; under Henry III. Walter Gifford was Archbishop of York, and Godfrey Gifford Bishop of Worcester. In the days of persecution, William Gifford, O.S.B., first President-General of the Anglo-Benedictines, was Archbishop of Rheims, and Bonaventure Gifford Vicar-Apostolic in England from 1688 to 1734, when he died at the age of 93. A great multitude of the scions of this noble house joined the ranks of the clergy and helped to fill our cloisters, as may be seen in books like the *Chronicle of St Monica's*, or *Foley's Records*, *S.J.* Among Bishop Grandisson's clergy I find at least five Giffords.

Aveton-Gifford, Wear-Gifford, Clovelly, Whitchurch, and Auliscombe were the principal seats of our Devonshire Giffords, who were subdivided into several branches. I am inclined to place our Abbot William among the descendants of Sir Roger Gifford, one of the Dartmoor perambulators mentioned in our Cartulary A.D. 1240. Sir Roger was a cadet of the Giffords of Wear and Aveton. Their lands bordered on our manor of Kingsbridge, and Sir Roger, like so many of his companions of the Perambulation, probably held also lands in our immediate neighbourhood.

For fifteen years almost to a day, Abbot Gifford

Peter, Robert, John of Churchstow, and the two Stephens who were afterwards abbots.

governed the community of Buckfast. He was among those summoned by name to the Provincial Council held in London in 1348. There he had the satisfaction of seeing justice done to his relative, Richard Gifford, priest of the Exeter diocese. Richard, with some other priests, had been cruelly ill-used by John de Sodbury and certain other royal commissioners. In such cases the fire and energy of Bishop Grandisson never failed him. He instantly excommunicated and ordered the arrest of the whole gang of petty tyrants. They submitted in sheer terror; without waiting for arrest, they sought his presence in abject fear as he was walking in his park at Clyst, or wherever they could find him. To a royal order to stop his proceedings, he replied by forcing John of Sodbury, whom he styles a notorious apostate and pestilent blasphemer, to crave pardon of the Synod.

The loss of our Chronicle conceals from us our domestic history. But as not a discord or trouble in a religious community escapes notice in these formidable Exeter Registers, we may fairly infer its history was peaceful. Abbot Gifford died in less than two months before the tremendous scourge known as the Black Death, or Great Plague, made its appearance in England. It unhinged the ecclesiastical order to an incredible extent, and we must devote our next chapter to some account of its ravages in Devon and their effect on our community.

On Whitsunday, the 8th of June 1348, Stephen of Cornwall was blessed as Abbot of Buckfast, in succession to Abbot Gifford, in the episcopal chapel at Chudleigh.

But before closing this chapter we may not omit to record the most splendid celebration ever seen within Exeter Cathedral from the days of the Confessor, which is also the last time we meet with our Abbot Gifford. On the 8th of July 1347, being Sunday, the day following the Translation of St Thomas of Canterbury, Richard Fitz-Ralph, Dean of Lichfield, was consecrated Archbishop of Armagh and Primate of Ireland by Bishop Grandisson in the Cathedral of Exeter. The Acts of his consecration record the presence of three Assistant Bishops— Salisbury, Bath and Wells, and St Asaph—as also of the Abbots of Buckfast, Torre, Hartland, and Newenham, and of the Prior of Plympton.

The consecration over, the new Archbishop " rode through Exeter on a palfrey covered with a white cloth, after the use of the Roman Curia."

Few prelates of his day are better known in history than Archbishop Fitz-Ralph. Renowned for his learning and his preaching, he is even more widely known for his opposition to the privileges of the Mendicant Orders.

CHAPTER XVIII

The Black Death; its ravages in Devonshire. Abbot Stephen of Cornwall, 1349. Abbot Philip Beaumont, 1349. Abbot Robert Simons. Bishop Ware's grave at Buckfast; his ring. The Beaumonts of Sherwell. Sherwell and Youlston. Chichesters of Raleigh. Chichesters of Calverleigh.

THE Black Death made its first appearance in England at Weymouth, in Dorset, on the 7th of July 1348. In Devonshire it had begun its ravages before the end of that month, and by abridging from Prebendary Hingeston-Randolph's admirable Preface to *Grandisson's Register*, I shall best be able to give an idea of the havoc it wrought in our county. As Cornwall suffered comparatively little, the greatest part of the fearful loss we are recording fell upon Devonshire.

The pestilence reached its height in Devon about April 1349. Abbot Stephen of Cornwall, at Buckfast, and Abbot John of Torre, died about the same time; their successors were blessed together at Clyst on 21st May 1359. At Newenham Abbey, three only were left alive out of twenty-six; at Bodmin, only two survived. The Abbot of Tavistock, the Priors of St James's and St Nicholas's at Exeter, were carried off, and the new Prior at the latter house only survived a few weeks. The Priors of Barnstaple, Pilton, Minster, Modbury, and St Michael's Mount, and the Abbot of Hartland, died within six months. At Ashburton there were four vicars in succession within three weeks. So fearful was the mortality among the secular clergy of our diocese, that in March 1349, the Bishop had to make sixty appointments to the places vacant by the deaths of the incumbents; in April, 53; in May, 48; in June, 46; in July, 37. These numbers represent, not the number of deaths, but only the number of priests the Bishop could find to supply the vacancies. He obtained a dispensation from Rome to ordain fifty illegitimates and a hundred others who had only reached their twenty-first year, as otherwise in many churches mass could not be said. There seems to have been no cowardly desertion of their posts by the diocesan clergy. The heroic Bishop Grandisson set the example, remaining at Chudleigh or Clyst in the thick of the pestilence during the whole time, and every day filling up by new institutions the ranks of the fallen. Through the months of November and December he ordered penitential processions at Exeter on Wednesdays and Fridays till Christmas.

From the disastrous effects of the Great Pestilence on ecclesiastical discipline England never recovered. Among the papers of Richard Dove, monk of Buckfast, is the regular form by which our novices were allowed to petition for an abridgment of their year of noviceship.[1] We read as follows: " I, Brother Richard, accepted novice in this Monastery of Blessed Mary of

[1] Brooking Rowe, from Sloane MS., No. 513.

Buckfast, of the Order of Citeaux, desiring by divine inspiration to make my solemn profession according to the Rule of St Benedict in this monastery, in virtue of the canonical permission granted to novices of religious orders, of my own free will and from no compulsion or fear, voluntarily, simply, and absolutely do by this writing renounce what remains of my year of probation, and earnestly petition to be now received to my profession as aforesaid." A note is here appended to the effect that this has been sanctioned by the General Chapter of Citeaux in 1373, because "in some parts of the world piety has grown cold, and monasteries suffer a lessening in divine worship from the fewness of monks." But, it is added, this concession is temporary and revocable at any moment; the novice must have reached at least his fifteenth year; he must have learned the whole Psalter by heart, as well as everything else appertaining to the monastic life; finally, he must himself make the prescribed renunciation and petition. Still, such renunciations are to be regretted, and they show a lack of vigorous life. How often they occurred at Buckfast, I cannot tell. Richard Dove lived in the earlier part of the fifteenth century.

To Abbot Gasquet's work, *The Great Pestilence*, I must refer my readers for a full account of the consequences of the Black Death throughout the country. Some of them, which concern Buckfast, will enter into our narrative.

Abbot Philip received his benediction together with Abbot John of Torre, on Ascension Thursday, 21st May 1349. He at once interested himself in behalf of the men of Buckfastleigh, for whom within his first year of government he obtained from the king a weekly market on Tuesday—the Ashburton market was on Saturday—as Buckfastleigh had now grown almost into a town, from a mere settlement of herdsmen which it had originally been. Brent was the richest of the Abbey manors, and the most populous, and Abbot Philip obtained for it by the same charter the annual fair for three days at Michaelmas, still represented by the September fair (which brings down to Brent the herds of Dartmoor ponies). On Brent Down in Abbot Philip's time, the sellers set up their booths; itinerant jugglers and musicians came to ply their vocation; and we learn with regret from Bishop Grandisson, that the ale sometimes flowed too freely, with the usual results, on such occasions. We may well hope, however, that at the Abbot's fair, in a place where his officers held judicial control, good order was kept. The fixing of the time for Michaelmas was in order to combine religious observance with gaiety, for on the summit of Brent Hill, overlooking the town, was the Chapel of St Michael—as also on Brent Tor, near Tavistock—and of course the good people of Brent and the neighbouring village would visit the sanctuary and hear mass there. No doubt Abbot Philip went there in person to open the fair for the first time. A feast to the people, in the shape of an ox or some sheep roasted at the fair, at the Abbot's expense, must be taken for granted, together with the barrels of ale to accompany it.

Here I am at an obscure point in our history. Nine years after Abbot Philip's election, I find Abbot Robert Simons in possession. But there is nothing to tell when he succeeded, and if he was the immediate successor of Philip. On the other hand, there is in Rymer's *Fœdera*[1] a royal proclamation, dated 1372, addressed to the Bishop of Exeter, the Earl of Devon, and seven other tenants-in-chief of the crown, who had estates near the coast, ordering them to array their men in all haste for the defence of the coast. One of the seven is John Beaumont, Abbot of Buckfast. Now, in 1372, Robert Simons, the date of whose institution I cannot discover, was Abbot of St Mary's. There is some mistake; but I conclude as certain that there had been an Abbot Beaumont between Abbot Stephen of Cornwall and Abbot Robert Simons. This was clearly our Abbot Philip— Philip being the favourite baptismal name with the Devonshire Beaumonts. This is confirmed by a curious incident in the time of Abbot Simons.

Bishop John Ware, a bishop in *partibus*, whose title is given in Latin as *Cumanagiensis* (Comagene?), acted for many years as Bishop-Auxiliary in the diocese of Exeter, and there are several commissions addressed to him in *Grandisson's Register*. After Bishop Grandisson's death he acted for some time in the same capacity in the diocese of Hereford. He must have been growing too old for work, for he returned to Devon, and retired to end his days at our Abbey, which of course he knew well as the most tranquil place in the diocese. At all events he died at Buckfast Abbey in, or a little before, the year 1393.

Before going further, I may as well mention that during our excavations on the foundations of the

[1] See Brooking Rowe, p. 79.

ancient church, we came upon a walled grave, in a most distinguished place, within what was the sanctuary, in front of the centre of the High Altar. It is the only one of its kind; the abbots are buried simply in the clay soil down the middle of the nave, each with his feet to the head of the next. I believe the walled grave, which is still open to view—as the church has not yet (1906) been rebuilt—to be that of Bishop Ware. It had been broken into and rifled. This was no doubt done at the same time as the rifling of the tombs of some of the Bishops of Exeter in Elizabeth's reign, as Prebendary Randolph records with just horror. The object was of course to steal any precious episcopal ornaments, and the vile thieves knew there was a bishop buried at the Abbey of Buckfast.

A ring which Abbot Anscar now possesses was found on the site of the ancient church. As it was of inferior metal, only a minute portion of the setting being of gold, the plunderers wrenched out the stone that adorned it and threw it away. So far is clear; I think it is not unlikely to have belonged to Bishop Ware, and to have been thrown away when the grave was broken into. Now to return to my story.

In 1393 William Beaumont (the name is often spelt Beaumond or Beamond with this Devonshire family) brought a legal action against Abbot Robert. He claimed from the Abbot a certain box containing his family muniments, with its contents. His father, the late John Beaumont, had, on the Feast of St Andrew, 1380, given this box, sealed, into the keeping of Bishop Ware at Exeter. The Bishop had taken or sent it to Buckfast Abbey, perhaps at the direction of John Beaumont, and his son now claimed it.

The Abbot's attorney, John Lacche, produced the box in court. He said that the only difficulty was that it had been claimed as his own by one John Brightricston, and he only asked that the said John should be allowed to plead for himself. He (the Abbot) had received it from Bishop Ware, with directions not to give it up to anyone but the rightful owner, but was not at all sure who was the owner. It was ordered that notice should be given to the other claimant, and time allowed him. He did not appear at the time fixed, and the box was handed over to William Beaumont. It is a curious case, and looks as if the papers in question could not be safely kept by John Beaumont. If, as I believe, his uncle had been Abbot of Buckfast, Beaumont must have known the Abbey well, had talked over family matters with the Abbot, and was aware that the sealed box could be safely concealed there.

William, the son of John Beaumont, plaintiff in this case, was the great-grandfather of Margaret, the daughter and heiress of Sir Hugh, the last of the Devonshire Beaumonts. Margaret married John Chichester of Youlston, from whom descend the Chichesters of Calverleigh, who have remained loyal to the ancient Faith, and represent the Beaumonts of Devon, who gave, as it appears from the proclamation I have quoted from Rymer, an abbot to our monastery, at some date between 1350 and 1358. A few words on the grand old family of Devonshire Beaumonts, long since extinct, will not be out of place here, more especially as our diocese owes a singular debt of gratitude to the Chichesters of Calverleigh, by whom they are now represented, though not by them alone.

Youlston, in the parish of Sherwell, four miles from Barnstaple, seems to have been the earliest home on English soil of the Devonshire Beaumonts.[1] Since the days of Elizabeth it has a title to a higher renown, for it was the birthplace of Blessed Cuthbert Mayne, the proto-martyr of the seminary priests. Blessed Cuthbert won his crown at Launceston, 29th November 1577. At Youlston, his ancestral home, it is likely that our Abbot Beaumont was born, and the precious relic of the glorious martyr, now at Buckfast, is one more link in a chain that is not one of memories alone.

Robert de Beaumont, under Baldwin the Sheriff, held the manor of Sherwell when the Domesday survey was taken. In the reign of Henry I., Roscelin (or Jocelyn) de Beaumont, Viscount Maine,[2] whose dwelling was at Youlston, married Constance, the king's daughter, and their daughter Armegard became Queen of Scotland by her marriage with William the Lion.[3] But our Beaumonts were never peers of Parliament; they remained simple Devonshire knights, and are unconnected with the noble English family of that name. The fifteenth in the

---

[1] Most of what follows on the Beaumont and Chichester families is taken from the excellent *History of the Family of Chichester*, by Sir Alexander Bruce Chichester, Bart.

[2] I do not know of any connection between this title of nobility and the family name of the Maynes, who lived at Youlston. It is perhaps only a coincidence, but such connection is not impossible.

[3] So Sir A. Chichester.

pedigree is that Sir John who gave the mysterious sealed box into Bishop Ware's keeping to be deposited at Buckfast. He was, I presume, a nephew of our Abbot, and I am not surprised at the story of the precious family papers, which William said in court were of immense value to him. The fact is that Sir John's mother, Joan Beaumont, an only surviving child, had married her cousin William, and made over the estates to him, and the papers had to do with these transactions.

Sir John was still living when he acquired some new and very desirable neighbours, though he little thought a day was to come when their descendants would be heirs to Sherwell and Youlston, and enjoy them down to this twentieth century in which we live. His friend Sir John, Lord of Raleigh, lived only four miles from Youlston, and had an only child, Thomasine, heiress to his ample estates. The road from Youlston to Barnstaple skirts Raleigh Park, just before you reach the town on the Yeo. Thomasine in 1384 married John, son of Sir Roger Chichester, both being aged nineteen. The Chichesters, an ancient Sussex family, not inferior to the Beaumonts in honours and achievements, thenceforward made Raleigh their principal seat, dropped their own arms, and assumed those of Raleigh.

In the tract of country bounded by Exmoor, the river Taw, and the sea, with its mighty herds of red deer roaming at large inland, and its wild and beautiful coast-line, the Chichesters were now the most powerful manorial family. As one looks on the beautiful recumbent statue of the Lady Thomasine under its sculptured canopy in Arlington Church, a student of Devonshire history must feel a kind of reverent affection for that medieval chivalry to which England owes so much.

A century later, the last Beaumont of Youlston, like the Lord of Raleigh in 1384, had an only daughter to inherit the vast possessions which fortunate marriages with the families of Scudamore, Willington, Punchardon, and others had brought to the house of Beaumont. Margaret Beaumont gave her hand to John Chichester of Raleigh in the reign of Henry VII., and Youlston became the home of the Chichesters. Anne Chichester, a daughter of this marriage, married John Rowe, of our neighbouring parish of Staverton. At Kingston, the home of the Rowes, mass was always said in days when it was pain of death to say it, as it was in the house of the Chichesters at Arlington, and afterwards at Calverleigh.

CHAPTER XIX

Wyclif and the Lollards. Troubles in Devonshire. Bishops Brantingham and Stafford. Abbot William Paderstow. Brothers William Stele and John Stourton. Abbot William Slade; his education at Exeter and Oxford; his reputation for learning.

A DANGEROUS period of English history is that of the thirty-seven years or more (1358-1395), during which Buckfast Abbey was governed by the energetic and intrepid Abbot Robert Simons. His birthplace I cannot find, but from this date forward the surname is frequently met with in Devonshire, especially among the clergy.

Abbot Robert lived through the national convulsion in which Wyclif and the Lollards played their part. The Great Plague practically emancipated the serfs that still remained in England. Food was very cheap and labour enormously dear; in fact, the labourer could set his own price on his work. In time this might have settled down to an improved condition for the population. But Wyclif's socialistic doctrines fired the peasantry with other thoughts. By the slaughter of the owners of land, the rich, and the clergy, they thought to inaugurate

St Mary's Abbey, Buckfast (View from North-east, with part of the old Foundations of Church and Cloister).

[*To face page* 150.

a new era of prosperity. In a dozen counties they rose in arms. Their march to London was marked by fire and bloodshed, and the murder of the Archbishop of Canterbury, whom they seized as he was making his thanksgiving after mass in the Tower, showed the ferocious spirit of their leaders. At the eighth stroke they cut off his head, and after nailing his episcopal hat to the skull, set it up on London Bridge. The citizens of London were roused from their apathy at the sight, and the insurrection was finally extinguished by the loyalty of the nation.

In Devonshire no armed rising occurred, for which we are largely indebted to the traditional firmness and zeal of the Bishops of Exeter. But the period was marked by sanguinary quarrels, and even the churches of the diocese were often polluted by bloodshed. The Abbot had to complain that his crops had been destroyed, his oak-trees cut down, and the fish taken from his weirs and fish-ponds. On one occasion, one, Richard of Trusham, who had lands in villeinage, declared himself not only a freeman, but the owner of all that he held of the Abbey, and by his own account it would represent a value at the present day of several thousand pounds. In this last instance, the Abbot recovered the cattle by force on his manor of Trusham, as he was legally entitled to do; in the other instances, he prosecuted the wrongdoers.

That he was known for a fearless and able man, appears from the fact that the Bishop of Exeter entrusted him with the charge of collecting the tenth that was required for the king from all church property in the county of Devon. Only a universally respected ecclesiastic could have undertaken a task of such difficulty in those days. From the report of the prosecution, we incidentally learn something of the value of the Dart fishery at that period. The salmon taken at Staverton alone are estimated at £40 a year. According to high authorities given by Prebendary Randolph, this would represent nowadays something like £800, though it seems incredible.

After all, half a dozen lawsuits in forty years was not much, if we take into account the lawlessness of the times. Our Abbot survived Bishop Grandisson for twenty-six years, living through the whole episcopate of Bishop Brantingham, who held him in high esteem, as appears from the appointment mentioned above; and he seems to have died about two months after Bishop Stafford took possession of his diocese, in August 1395. In the preceding chapter we have seen the transactions in Abbot Robert's time concerning the sealed box claimed by William Beaumont. I find him in 1373 summoned to attend the meeting of Convocation, and in 1374 the Bishop authorises him to say mass, or have it said, on feast days, in his private chapel at Brent. In the same year, Bishop Brantingham granted in favour of the Abbot an indulgence to all who should assist in repairing the bridge over the Dart, now known as Austen's Bridge, a little below the Abbey, and he grants another to such as should contribute to the ransom of some prisoners in the hands of the " French pirates," as he calls them. One of these, Deghere, seems to have been a Buckfast man.

Towards the end of his days the country had become calmer. He had lived through stormy times. In 1380 he had published in the Abbey church the episcopal excommunication of a royal sergeant-at-arms who had beheaded a Cornish priest and borne publicly the severed head on a pike to London. Even in Devonshire, the wanton murder of blameless priests was not unknown.

Abbot William Paderstow succeeded him in September 1395, and was at once appointed by Bishop Stafford to the office of collecting the tenth, held by his predecessor. I cannot find the date of his death, but he cannot have held office long. He had to exercise his manorial authority over Robert Knight, vicar of Brent. Knight was not charged with any laxity in his priestly duties, but had been already in trouble with Bishop Brantingham for certain high-handed proceedings, and for procuring illegal excommunications when he thought his rights had been infringed, even by the Bishop's officials. This is all I find concerning Abbot Paderstow (or Paderston). Before I come to his successor, the most distinguished among our abbots, I may as well put on record, for the sake of Devonshire genealogists, the few names I have been able to collect of our Devonshire monks, between 1370 and 1419.

The Abbots—Robert Simons, William Paderstow, William Beaghe, William Slade: Brothers Edward Stele, Henry Haredon, Robert Ash, Stephen Rowland, Richard Gorwet, John Stourton, Thomas Roger, John Barlynch, John Budde, William Budde, Walter Chester, Richard Dove, John Fytchet, William

Gyst, John Martyn, John Matthew, John Roddon, Edmund Coffin, John Northwhych, John Sturgeon, Robert Marchaunt, John Turgeyr.

The list is an instructive one. Almost all are Devonshire men, if not all, and several are from our immediate neighbourhood. The children of the recently emancipated bondmen find their home in the cloister with the sons of knightly houses, for the distinction between Norman and Saxon has by this time disappeared from the land, and noble and peasant are equal in the house of God. Exeter citizens are well represented. John Gyst was several times mayor of Exeter, while Brother John Gyst—his son, I presume—was a monk at St Mary's Abbey. The Buddes were Buckfast men, and a century earlier their ancestors had been serfs on the Abbey lands. The names of Fytchet, Martyn, Stourton, Matthew, and others, show that the descendants of the Norman knights still cherished their traditional love of the monastic cowl. On the whole, it affords a pleasing picture of the elements that formed the religious family of the Abbey at the opening of the fifteenth century.

Brothers Matthew, Fytchet, and Roger became abbots of Buckfast, of whom more hereafter. Edward Stele, monk at Buckfast in 1393, was probably the son of William Stele and Jane his wife, to whom in 1375 Bishop Brantingham granted a licence to have mass said in their private oratory Sir Thomas Fytchet and his wife Richardyne obtained a similar privilege in 1581, when our Abbot Fytchet and his brother, the future vicar of Brent, must have been little boys. The chief seat of the family was in Somersetshire. Somewhere on the site of our ancient church lies buried the good vicar of Brent, Edmund Fytchet, who left it in his will that he should be laid to rest with our monks.

If any of my readers should visit the village of Yarcombe, on the borders of Somersetshire, they may find there a farmhouse called Penshayne. It had once belonged to Otterton Priory, but about the time of which I am writing was a residence of the noble house of Stourton. In Bishop Stafford's time (1395-1419), Sir William Stourton was Justice of the Peace for Devon, and John Stourton was a monk of Buckfast. A generation earlier, I find Elizabeth Luttrell married to John Stourton (possibly the parents of the Buckfast monk), while her brother, Sir Hugh, is married to Catherine, a daughter of Sir John Beaumont,[1] and a relative, probably a niece, of our Abbot Beaumont; so that Buckfast Abbey and its abbot would be well known to the Stourtons of Penshayne at Yarcombe. The loyalty to the Catholic Faith of the Stourtons makes their connection with our community a matter of interest.

Such were the members of the community at the time when Abbot William Slade was elected to succeed Abbot Paderstow. There was a family of the name living at Salcombe Regis (where Slades are still numerous, and there is an estate called Slade) about this time, and I find, not long before, a William Slade, warden of Ottery, and another William Slade, or De la Slade, vicar of the neighbouring parish of Dean. In the Exeter Registers I do not find the date of Abbot Slade's installation. I

[1] Pole's *Devonshire Pedigrees*.

believe this to be owing to the long absence of Bishop Stafford from his diocese. He was away on affairs of State in 1401 and 1402, and I am inclined to refer our Abbot's election to this date.

William Slade's early education was at the school attached to Exeter Cathedral. In the glorious episcopate of Bishop Grandisson he could not but be deeply imbued with ecclesiastical traditions under the shadow of the noble Cathedral. No better guide for the education of youth ever lived than the great Bishop. Every year at Christmastide William Slade assisted at the beautiful ceremony of the Boy Bishop on the Feast of the Holy Innocents. Perhaps he may have been elected Boy Bishop himself. In due time he was sent to Oxford, where he lectured on Aristotle. "He was born in Devon, and brought up at the school in Exon, and from thence sent to Oxford, where he became very well learned, especially in Aristotle, whose works he did read openly in the schools, to his great commendation. When made Abbot of Buckfastleigh, he furnished the house with fair buildings, and adorned the commonwealth with his learning, leaving behind thirteen books of his own penning."[1]

Three of his works, the *Flores Moralium, Qæstiones de Anima*, and his Commentaries on the *Libri Sententiarum*, were seen by Leland when he visited our Abbey. A man of large and cultivated mind, eloquent and learned, a schoolman and architect, trained at Exeter and Oxford, must necessarily have done much to guide his monks, according to

[1] Hoker's MS. quoted in Oliver's *Monasticon Exoniense*.

monastic tradition, in their intellectual pursuits. His beneficent influence was not confined to his monastery. But I must defer to my next, an account of the work by which he is best remembered in Devonshire.

CHAPTER XX

Churchstow, "the place of the church." The town of Kingsbridge. St Edmund the Martyr's Church. The monks build a new church at Kingsbridge. Monastic remains. Leigh Barton. Cistercian wood-carving. Death of Abbot Slade. The blind Earl of Devon. A Tiverton legend. Boys educated for the Church at our Abbey.

AMONG the earliest possessions of Buckfast Abbey granted to it by the piety of the kings of Wessex was Churchstow, "the place of the church." The monks built a church there in honour of our Blessed Lady, on the summit of a lofty hill. As it was, and still is, the most striking and conspicuous object from the surrounding country, the village that grew up at its foot enjoyed for centuries before the Norman invasion the impressive name which it retains to this day.

Within the limits of Churchstow manor, and at the head of that inlet of the sea whereof Salcombe commands the entrance, a second village, now the town of Kingsbridge, came into existence at an early date, which soon outgrew Churchstow, and no wonder, for the fisheries afforded a ready means of subsistence. The villagers of this coast settlement were, as they describe themselves in 1414, " sailors or shipmasters, tradesmen and merchants, artificers and mechanics," and as late as 1877 they are described as unaltered in character. "Your agricultural labourer hereabouts can handle the oar as deftly as the plough, while his master holds shares in ships and in mercantile ventures on the sea. The local traditions are of great storms with their welcome harvest of wrecks, or of smuggling adventures. . . . Shakespeare would have found in the narrow drang-ways 'a very ancient and fish-like smell.'"[1]

Now, the sailors and fishers of Kingsbridge had for their parish church St Mary's, on the hill of Churchstow, two miles off. But they had also a little church of their own within their village. It was cruciform, and, being on the Abbey land, was certainly, as well as that of Churchstow, the work of our Buckfast monks, as builders and architects for the welfare of their Kingsbridge dependants. Though dependent on the mother-church of Churchstow, it had a quasi-parochial status of its own, but without the right of sepulture. That this little church, of which some traces still remains within the more recent building, existed as early as 1250, we have proof positive. But it is more likely to have been first erected at least two centuries earlier, and its dedication to the East Anglian king and martyr, St Edmund, put to death by the Danes in 870, suggests that our Saxon monks first established an oratory here in his honour after some signal delivery of Devon from the Danish hordes, before the time of Canute, and in the latter part of the tenth century.

[1] R. Dymond, " Kingsbridge and Dodbroke," in *Transactions of Devonshire Associations*, July 1877.

Otherwise the choice of this East Anglian saint by the monks of Buckfast would have been a little singular.

As Kingsbridge grew in size and importance, the Chapel of St Edmund not only became too small for the people, but they found it a serious grievance to have to carry their dead for burial to the top of Churchstow Hill. "Living by the labour of their hands," as they represent it in their petition to Bishop Stafford, "they could with difficulty even attend to the burial of their dead when so long and tedious a journey was necessary." But before addressing themselves to the Bishop, they had appealed to the Abbot of St Mary's, on whose manor they lived. He quite entered into their views. He had a residence in the town, and a fine barton at Leigh, two miles away, besides the "Abbot's Mill" in Kingsbridge itself. So it was decided that the monks should enlarge the existing Church of St Edmund, or rather incorporate it into a larger edifice, worthy of those erected at Trusham and elsewhere, and that the Bishop should then be asked to grant it full parochial rights.

The consent of the rector of Churchstow had to be obtained, as the right of his church would be affected.

In 1414 Bishop Stafford issued his *Ordinatio*, agreeing to consecrate the restored Church of St Edmund and its new cemetery. To indemnify the rector of Churchstow, it was ordained that on the Feast of the Assumption, the titular feast of St Mary at Churchstow (presumably also that of St Mary at Buckfast), every married householder of Kingsbridge should hear mass as of old in the mother-church, and offer one penny — equal to more than a shilling of our present money—for himself and family, the bachelors and maidens offering one halfpenny. As feasts of obligation, on which no servile work was allowed, all the Kingsbridge men were to keep holy St Edmund's day and the anniversaries of the dedications of both churches, with an offering of one halfpenny to the rector of Churchstow on each of the three days; while the flagon of ale hitherto paid as tithe by every Kingsbridge innkeeper was commuted for a payment of one penny. The *Ordinatio* was accepted and sealed in the chapter-house of Exeter Cathedral by the Dean and Chapter on the 20th of July; by Abbot Slade and the monks of Buckfast, in our chapter-house, on the 23rd ; by Roger Bachelor, rector of Churchstow, at Churchstow, on the 22nd ; by the petitioners representing the burgesses of Kingsbridge, on the 24th ; and by the burgesses, with seal of the town, on the 25th. On the 26th of August 1414, Bishop Stafford consecrated the church, and on the following day the cemetery of Kingsbridge.

During the two days that the Bishop and his assistant clergy were the guests of our Abbot and his monks, they had time to visit and admire the industrial and artistic labours of our monks in this their favourite manor. For here utility went hand-in-hand with the most exquisite and refined taste, as befitted the monastic order. Leigh Barton (wrongly called Leigh Priory nowadays), two miles out of the town, had of course to be visited ; now "an almost perfect monastic building situated in a peaceful, umbrageous dell away from the world, among green lawns and pleasant woods," writes the Rev. Mr Baring-Gould. It was full of life in those days, and it was harvest-season at the time. From a splendid description sent me by our architect, Mr Frederick Walters, with a ground plan, I learn that it is of late decorated or Early Perpendicular architecture, indicating (in Devonshire) a date probably between 1400 and 1414. It forms three sides of a quadrangle, two stories high, the upper being now reached by an outside staircase, the stonework of some of the windows still remaining.

But of course the Bishop and his company were entertained by the Abbot at his residence, towards the top of what is now the Fore Street. It has disappeared, and in a modern house in the same street we find portions of the carved ceiling of its stately hall. "It is panelled in squares, with moulded ribs, having at the intersections richly carved bosses, all of varied designs, some having human heads and faces (of hooded monks), others formed of leaves; each square of the ceiling divided by smaller diagonal ribs into four triangles, one or two of the bosses being of a sacred character." So far Mr Walters, who assigns it to the date of which we are writing. "Piquant and interesting must have been Kingsbridge of the Middle Ages, on which the Cistercians set their artistic and religious mark."[1] Nor did they ever rest from their artistic work. In the same house is a noble specimen of their old oak panelling, transferred thither when the earlier building was

[1] James Hine, *Trans. Dev. Assoc.*, July 1877.

destroyed, and assigned by Mr Walters to about 1480, and by him described as "about 6 ft. 6 in. in height, surmounted by a most beautiful and elaborate cresting, divided by upright pieces of oak, forming pedestals on which stand carved oak figures, apparently of the Apostles, though I have been only able to identify one or two of them." I need dwell no longer on these relics of old Buckfast; they are but one of a thousand evidences of the influences exerted on Englishmen by the monastic order; the influences of religious faith, industry, and a love for the beautiful in art.

Abbot Slade only lived long enough to see the anniversary of the dedication of St Edmund's Church, if, indeed, he had not gone to his reward before that day, for on the 8th of September 1415, Feast of our Lady's Nativity, his successor was blessed by Bishop Stafford. To trace the "fair buildings" he erected at Buckfast Abbey is not now possible; but I strongly incline to think, from inspection of the existing foundations, that he rebuilt in greater richness of architecture the north gallery of the cloister which adjoins the south wall of the church.

One little incident during his term of office I may not omit, as it connects St Mary's Abbey with the Courtenays, Earls of Devon. At some date between 1358 and 1377, Edward III., who must on that account take his place among our royal benefactors, had granted Abbot Robert Simon the manor of Kilbury, adjoining that of Buckfast, on which occasion it is likely that Abbot Robert undertook to rebuild the bridge over the Dart now known as Austin's Bridge, connecting Kilbury with his land across the river. Now the Courtenays had claimed some rights in this manor, and Abbot Slade sought a recognition of his title from the earl. Edward, known as "the Good Earl of Devon," resided in 1413 at his Castle of Tiverton. In his day he had been Admiral of the King's Fleet, and held the office of Earl Marshal, but he was now old and blind. His piety was conspicuous, and at his death he was, according to his will, buried at the Abbey of Ford, and he had ever been devoted to Cistercians. To obtain the favour he sought, we may take it for granted that Abbot Slade went in person to Tiverton and was graciously received by the good earl and his countess, the Lady Matilda, daughter of Thomas, Lord Camoys, and brought back with him the charter, which is the last in date of those in our Cartulary. It is brief, with no names of witnesses, and such as the earl would have asked his chaplain to make out as a personal favour to the Abbot, and runs thus:—

"Edward de Courtenay, Earl of Devon, to all the faithful of Christ into whose hands this writing may come, eternal welfare in our Lord. Seeing that the Lord Edward, sometime King of England, ancestor of our Lord the King that now is, gave and granted to Robert, late Abbot of Buckfast, and to the community there dwelling, the manor of Kilbury, with its appurtenances, to be had and held by the said Abbot and community and their successors: Be it known that we have remitted and made over to William, now Abbot of Buckfast, and the community dwelling there, whatever rights we have, or may have, in the said manor and its appurtenances. In witness whereof, we have affixed hereto our seal. Given at our Manor of Tiverton, the twelfth day of November, in the first year of King Henry, Fifth (of that name) since the Conquest" (A.D. 1413). Though Risdon seems to have been mistaken in ascribing to this earl the inscription which before his time had existed on a Courtenay tomb at Tiverton, yet its last lines are in singular agreement with the known piety and charity of "the Good Earl":

> " That we spent, we had ;
> That we left, we lost ;
> That we gave, we have."

Earl Edward died five years later, in 1419. His countess survived him forty-eight years, dying in 1467. Two of her grandchildren, Earl Thomas and his brother Henry, were attainted and executed during her lifetime, and with their brother John, who fell at Tewkesbury, sealed their loyalty with their blood. Thus ended the descendants of the " Good Earl of Devon." Henry Courtenay, Marquess of Exeter, beheaded on Tower Hill, on the 9th of December 1538, was a descendant of Earl Edward's brother, Sir Hugh Courtenay of Haccombe. Wriothesley, Windsor Herald, who was then living in London, and may even have seen the marquess executed with Lord Montague and Sir Edward Neville, says that they were "condemned for treason against the king by the counsel of Reginald Pole, Cardinal, which pretended to have enhanced the Bishop of Rome's usurped authority again."

I do not know if Matilda Camoys is the Countess

of Devon referred to in the amusing Tiverton legend given in Baring-Gould's *Book of the West*. I give it here slightly abridged from his pages :—

"One day the Countess of Devon was taking her walk abroad in the direction of Hensleigh, when she met a tailor descending the hill, laden with a large covered basket. As he passed, a cry came from the hamper. She stayed her steps and asked what he was carrying. 'Only seven puppies that I be going to drown in the Exe,' was his reply. 'I want a dog,' said the Countess; 'open the hamper.' The tailor tried to excuse himself, but the Countess insisted, and on the lid being raised, seven little babes were revealed. 'Alas! my Lady,' said the tailor, 'I am poor as a church mouse! My wife gave them to me all at once. What could I do but rid myself of them? See, they are all boys.' The Countess charged herself with their education, and when they were old enough sent them all to Buckfast Abbey, to be reared for the Church. Four became rectors of Tiverton (for Tiverton had four rectors), and the others their curates."

If Buckfast Abbey really educated boys for the priesthood, one can understand how this detail got into the legend in its Devonshire version, for nothing at the present day strikes the popular imagination more than the sight of our little *alumni* in their monastic habit. But to educate boys, even for their own Order, was foreign to Cistercian rule. However, after the fearful havoc in the ranks of the clergy caused by the Black Death, the rule had to give way to stern necessity. Cistercians in Devon gave their help in training boys for the Church, and we have a notable example in the history of Buckland, the nearest of the Devon monasteries to Buckfast. I give it from Mr Brooking Rowe's work and Dr Oliver.

In the muniment room at Powderham, the seat of the Courtenays, is an agreement made in 1522 between Abbot Whyte and one Robert Derkeham, who was clearly an outsider, and not a monk. Robert undertakes to help in the choir, evidently by playing the organ, and to teach four boys in the monastery, any one of whom he may choose to wait on him; to teach them also the music, and playing on the organ, and to teach this last to any of the monks who may wish to learn it. His remuneration was ample. He is to have a good table; an annuity of £2. 13s. 4d., equal to £25 nowadays; a gown every year of the value of 12s., the reversion of a tenement at Milton, and in the meantime the feeding of two cows, with a good garden, for which he is to pay half-rent. Robert's room was over the west door of the Abbey, the exact position of that in which these pages are being written, and he found it dreary and cold in winter. To make him comfortable, the Abbot further allowed thirty horse-loads annually of faggots for his fire, and every evening his servant brought him a wax candle, a quart of beer, and five ounces of bread. This was, of course, exclusive of whatever he chose to buy for himself.

The indenture distinguishes between the monks and the boys educated at the Abbey. With such Abbots as William Slade, and its larger revenue, our

Abbey would not be behind Buckland, if indeed it did set the example, in training boys for the priesthood, as indicated in the Tiverton legend. The doubtful assertion mentioned by Mr Brooking Rowe, that Bishop Bothe of Exeter (1465-1478) had been Abbot of Buckfast, and our lack of information on his early education, make me suspect that he was perhaps trained in a Cistercian school. He was the son of Sir Robert Bothe, of Dunham, in Cheshire, and nephew to Archbishop Booth, or Bothe, of York.

Up to this point in our history, the recovered portion of our Chronicle and the Exeter Registers published by Prebendary Hingeston-Randolph have facilitated the work. But these now fail me, and my notices of the Abbey from the time of Abbot Slade to the eve of the Dissolution must needs be scanty, though the list of abbots is fairly complete. Henry V. had succeeded to the throne of England, on the 21st of March 1412. Though Abbot Slade did not live long enough to witness the complete establishment of a new power in South Devon by the transfer of Budleigh, Otterton, Yarcombe, Sidmouth, and other possessions from St Michael's Mount to Syon monastery, yet he heard how the first stone of the new monastery had been laid by King Henry, on the 22nd of February 1415. A year later we find Margaret, the recluse of Bodmin, obtaining a licence from Bishop Stafford to migrate to "St Bridget-by-Schene." By reason of the nearness of the bulk of the estates of Syon, Buckfast had henceforward to regard that powerful community as its neighbour, a circumstance renewed in our own time, but in a different way. After many vicissitudes, the Bridgettine nuns of Syon, our only pre-Reformation community in existence, are settled at Chudleigh, on the borders of the manor of Trusham, once among the fairest possessions of Buckfast Abbey.

CHAPTER XXI

Abbot William Beaghe. Loyalty of the monks. A domestic incident. Abbots Rogger and Ffytchett. Abbot John Matthew, 1449. The Matthews of Glamorgan. Three of the Abbey settlements developed into flourishing market towns. Was Bishop Bothe of Exeter, Abbot of Buckfast? Abbot King and his restoration work. A Buckfast monk Prior of St Bernard's College, Oxford. Abbots Rede, Pomeroy, and Gyll.

In the days of Abbot Slade's immediate successor we meet with the single instance in the long history of our Abbey of anything like a domestic disturbance, although it is an amusing, not a scandalous story. Once more I must say, that if I had come across any indication of disorders, such as occasionally are noted in the Exeter Registers in regard to communities, otherwise of good renown, it would have been my duty to chronicle them, but I had none to chronicle.

Abbot Slade was succeeded, on 8th September 1415, by Abbot William Beaghe. Abbot Slade was among those who had lent money to the king for the French war on the security of the royal jewels; Buckfast, Tavistock, and Plympton, being the only religious houses in Devon that did so on

BUCKFAST ABBEY: Refectory rebuilt on old Foundations.

[*To face page* 170.

that occasion, when the moneys were conveyed to London by John Coplestone of Exeter. Abbot Beaghe, at his succession, at once gave a hundred marks for the same object, on behalf of his Abbey, so that, as Mr Brooking Rowe remarks, our Abbey had its share in the glories of Agincourt in the following month. The loyalty of our community is beyond question. With the exception of some insignificant legal proceedings, I find nothing to relate concerning Abbot Beaghe till the year 1421.

On the 26th of February in that year, the community were summoned to the chapter-house under their Prior, Thomas Rogger, where they found the Abbot, with Abbot William of Hailes in the diocese of Worcester; the Prior of Langbynington in the diocese of Lincoln; Abbot William's notary public, John Carnell, bachelor-of-laws; and Henry Fortescue, clerk, of the diocese of Exeter. No sooner were they all seated, than Abbot William handed the notary a paper to read, of which I can only give a summary.

Abbot Beaghe was old, infirm, and crippled, and clearly unable to govern his house, but had no mind to resign. His position obliged him to receive numerous guests, often of high rank, and to entertain them suitably to their condition. Not unfrequently he had to go to his town house at Exeter. He was generous and kindly in disposition, and the monks— no doubt the cellarer was the chief complainant— found that expenses were growing, and they were alarmed for the future.

The visitors seemed to think that the monks had been too hard on the poor Abbot, who was quite capable of representing the dignity of his office, although too infirm for its most onerous duties. They accordingly decreed that he should continue to receive his guests as heretofore. But he should only have at his disposal for this object a fixed sum, payable quarterly. If he wished to make a present to anyone who had come as a messenger from some great man, he was to make it out of this allowance; and if he required to ride abroad with fitting attendance, he must bear the expense out of the same sum. But all the government of the house was to be left to the Prior and his council, unless the Abbot's signature, for example, were needed, and then he must do as he was desired. The order is stringent, but always in the most respectful form, towards "the honourable and religious man, William, Lord Abbot," whose only fault seems to have been an excess of generosity, which his infirmities had made dangerous for the welfare of the monastery. He survived eleven years, Prior Rogger succeeding him as Abbot, 13th April 1432.

The name Beaghe is not to be met with, as far as my knowledge extends, in our Devonshire records of the period, but I suspect it is the same as Baghe, an Exeter family, whose monument Carew found "in St Thomas's by Exon."

Abbot Rogger only held office for eight years, but had already governed the house during the last eleven years of Abbot Beaghe's time. His record is a blank. The name was a very common one in Devon, and in some manor accounts of our Abbey lands, now in private hands, I find that in the reign of Henry VIII., Margaret Rogger held a tenement on our manor of Churchstow. Religious communities were largely recruited from such as were born on their estates.

Abbot Ffytchett, of whom I have written already, succeeded, 16th October 1442. About the time of his birth, Sir Thomas Ffytchett acquired Trill, near Axminster, under the shadow of the Cistercian Abbey of Newenham. Here the good knight, as in all his manor-houses in the diocese, had his private oratory by licence from the Bishop, and here it is most likely that Abbot Ffytchett and his brothers passed their boyhood, though they were not Sir Thomas's children. There were no other Ffytchetts in Devon outside this family; but besides the Abbot and his brother, the vicar of Dean, there was a third of the name among the diocesan clergy Their arms—Gules, a lion rampant or—are given by Risdon. Abbot Ffytchett was obliged to take legal proceedings for the protection of his fisheries on the Erme. " To him who can obtain permission to fish in the Erme," writes Mr Baring-Gould, " can be assured days to be never forgotten."

Seven years after Abbot Ffytchett's election, John Matthew succeeded him, 3rd October 1449. That he should have at once set to work to make Kingsbride a market town, was only natural, for the home of his family was at Dodbroke, now part of the united borough of Kingsbridge and Dodbroke. At the beginning of his time he obtained from Edward IV.—if indeed it was not a confirmation of a grant made to one of his predecessors—the privilege of a weekly market and an annual fair about the Feast of St Margaret, 20th July. Both are still maintained. He also obtained an annual fair for Buckfastleigh. This was the last stage in the development, under the fostering care of the monks, of Brent, Kingsbridge, and Buckfastleigh, from the days when they had been simple monastic colonies. In less than a century, abbot and monks were to disappear, and the monastic garb to be seen no more at Kingsbridge till an Abbot of Buckfast visited it again in 1905. But I have yet a word to say on the Matthews of Dodbroke, among whom Sir Bernard Burke rightly places John Matthew, Abbot of Buckfast, whose arms —the stork on the sable field—are to be seen on our refectory wall.

These Devonshire Matthews were descendants of those of Glamorgan represented by Viscount Llandaff at the present day. To the same race belonged the celebrated Sir Tobie Matthew, knight, priest, Jesuit, and courtier, who figured so largely in the reign of James I. It was in Abbot Matthew's time that the Devon branch of the family assumed the arms just described (which belonged to the Starkey family), when Jenkyn Matthew married Lucia, daughter of William Starkey. His grandson was that Edmund Matthew of Dodbroke who died in 1524. We have seen that our Buckfast abbots were nothing if not loyal, and with good reason. While John Matthew was a monk at Buckfast under the loyal Abbot Beaghe, his namesake and relative, Sir John Matthew, was serving Henry V. as master of the artillery at Agincourt.

A most tantalisingly obscure period breaks up this portion of our annals. From Abbot Matthew, elected in 1449, to Abbot John Rede the elder, in November

1498, a space of nearly fifty years, all is a blank, save a single indication that John King was Abbot in 1483, and one other exception to which I now come. It is all but certain that a name has been left out.

Speaking of this interval of time, Dr Oliver writes: "Scipio Squier, the herald, asserts that John Bothe was abbot here, before his promotion to the See of Exeter in 1465, but this wants confirmation." Mr Brooking Rowe adds: "On examining the events of his life before his consecration as bishop, it would seem that this could not have been." Nor do I venture to affirm it, but I do not reject it. Let us first see what the authority of Scipio Squier is worth, and then examine if the difficulties involved in his assertion are insurmountable.

On the 3rd of June 1595, Scipio Squier witnessed the will of Henry Tucker of King's Nympton, in Devon. At the end of the will is written: "Witnesses—Edmonde Squier, Pastor of King's Nympton, in Devon, and Scipio Squier, his son, the writers thereof."[1] Supposing Scipio to have been aged 21 at this date (his father died in 1620), he was born a little over a century after Bishop Bothe's death. His family had been settled in Devon, holding the manor of Little Fulford, before 1307, and had never left it. "Scipio Squier was a great local antiquary, and left some valuable heraldic manuscripts relative to the arms in Devonshire churches, which were among the collections of Dr

---

[1] For this and what follows concerning Scipio Squier, see Mr Charles Worthy's *Devonshire Wills*, pp. 105-106: Bemrose & Sons, 1896.

Jeremiah Milles, Dean of Exeter, and President of the Society of Antiquaries, 1765. He appears to have paid a visit to Exeter in 1607." At all events, his authority is not trifling in a matter connected with the bishops of Exeter, and a purely gratuitous assertion of such a nature is most unlikely. Even if a mistake, there would be some grounds for it. John Bothe, before being made Bishop of Exeter, was Canon of York, Archdeacon of Richmond, and Warden of the Collegiate Church of Manchester, a man of sterling virtue; "very courteous and affable to every man, and good to the poor," says Hoker. If he felt a vocation to the monastic life, he would of course not be allowed to relinquish his benefices during his noviceship, which in those days unfortunately too often lasted only six months; and even after his profession, many reasons might force him to delay for awhile sending in his formal resignation, though of course he could no longer exercise in person the duties attached to them. If the Abbot chanced to die soon after he had taken his vows, nothing was more likely than that a man of such eminence and experience should be chosen to succeed him; though, if my supposition is true, it would be probable that he governed our monastery for a very brief time, and perhaps succeeded to Exeter within a year or two after leaving the diocese of York. Besides, it would explain more easily how, at the translation of Bishop Neville from Exeter to York, the Archdeacon of Richmond was at once promoted by papal provision to Exeter, if he was already in the diocese and Abbot of Buckfast.

Of course I may be wrong, and I must leave to

those that come after me the task of throwing light on this dark period of our history; but even if Squier's positive assertion is incorrect, it can hardly have been without some cause, such as, for example, that a relative and namesake of the Bishop accompanied him to Devon and became Abbot of St Mary's.

It is pleasing to find evidence of the artistic activity of our monks about the time of Abbot King. To the year 1280 or thereabouts belong the restoration of the fine tower, so ably renewed from the designs of Mr Walters, at the expense of the Duke of Norfolk and the late Dr Mivart, so that now one sees it as it was in Abbot King's time; the later portion of the fine panelling of the Abbot's house at Kingsbridge, and the exquisite pulpit of Holne, which has on one of its panels the arms of our Abbey, belong to this period. Without a doubt, the Abbey church was restored at the same date, when a perfect wave of fervour for church restoration passed over our county under Bishops Bothe and Courtenay. Of Abbot King's career nothing is recorded in writing, and his name has only been saved from oblivion by a chance entry in the will of Ambrose Franke of Totnes, 25th February 1483. When he was elected, I know not.

The long history of old Buckfast is now drawing to a close. One very pleasing episode has to be told in this place—a story closely connected, if I mistake not, with the events of the day on which the monks of St Mary's Abbey were expelled from their home and cast adrift on the world.

Twice in the year 1484 were royal letters received by Abbot King in common with all the heads of

Cistercian houses in England. Richard III. was doing his best to win golden opinions as a religious and God-fearing monarch, and in May and December of that year he wrote to urge on the Cistercians the support of St Bernard's College, the Cistercian House of Studies at Oxford, now St John's. Long before Abbot King's time, Cistercians had frequented the schools at Oxford. But they had no house of their own. "Dispersed in divers inns and halls, they could not fulfil the customs and statutes of their Order as they ought to do; for which reason some devout scholars, finding themselves troubled in their consciences, refrained the University; and some, though they were elected accorded to the custom of their Order to go to Oxon to obtain philosophical learning, refused to do so, to the great detriment of science and renown belonging to that Order.

"This the Archbishop (Chicheley) considering, desired King Henry the Sixth that he might perform some acceptable thing to God in helping or contributing towards the necessities of these holy Cistercians, in building them a place where they might gain human and heavenly knowledge. Wherefore the said king, by his letters patent, dated at Lambeth, 20th March 1437, gave him leave to erect a college to the honour of the most glorious Virgin St Mary and St Bernard, in the street commonly called Northgate Street, in the parish of St Mary Magdalen, without Northgate, and on the ground of the said Archbishop, containing five acres or thereabouts. This he did, building it of freestone, in the place specified, on the east side of that street.

"Those that inhabited here were maintained by

the abbeys of their Order. They were governed by a Provisor, and he and they were subordinate to the Chancellor, who was their Visitor. When they had gotten a competency of University knowledge they were to be sent for home, and exercise the same in their own abbeys. They preached in the Church of St Peter in the East, Oxon, twice in Lent time. Adjoining to their lodging they had pleasant walks."[1]

This account speaks well for the religious fervour of our Cistercians. They had also a house of studies at Cambridge, but no monks from Devonshire do I find among its students, while St Bernard's at Oxford was largely, if not mainly, supported by the Devon monasteries. From John Staynbourne in 1461 to Philip Acton in 1535, St Bernard's had only seven Provisors (Priors) so far as is known, and of these the only one of whom any special notice is given by Wood, in his *Fasti Oxonienses*, was a monk, and afterwards Prior, of Buckfast. To complete what I have to tell of our monastery's Oxford connection, I may allow myself to anticipate some later events that enter into the tale of the last days of the dear old Abbey.

In the days of Abbot King, or perhaps of Abbot Rede, his immediate successor, two brothers, as it would seem, were among the children of a family that cultivated a part of the manor of Buckfast, named William and Arnold. Both no doubt were taught in our Abbey, but only one was professed here. William became a Benedictine monk at Tavistock. According to the then prevailing custom

[1] MSS. of Anthony à Wood, in *Monast. Anglic.*, vol. v., p. 744 (abridged).

of taking a surname from the place of their origin,[1] the two boys were known as William and Arnold Buckfast. William Buckfast figures on the list of the monks of Tavistock who received pensions at the Dissolution;[2] Brother Arnold owned also the surname of Gye, under which he appears in the list of eleven priests of the community on the day of the surrender.

Brother Arnold's progress in studies was such that his Abbot sent him to study at St Bernard's College, that he might be able by his teaching to help in maintaining the high standard to which Abbot Slade had raised the community. To Oxford he was sent, probably in Abbot de Pomeroy's time, for in 1518 I find in Wood, among the ten who supplicated for the degree of Bachelor of Divinity, as "Arnold Gye, alias Buckfast, a Cistercian Monk of St Bernard's College." His aptitude for government caused him to be retained or sent back to the College, for in 1528 he succeeded Father John Ford as Provisor or Prior of St Bernard's, till recalled to Buckfast as our Prior in 1532, in which office I find him on the fatal day of the surrender. What became of him after the expulsion, I know not. But there is a special reason for presuming that he returned for some years to St Bernard's at Oxford, which we know from Wood to have been at this time thronged with the poor expelled monks.

Prior Arnold was the only one of the Buckfast

---

[1] We have seen examples in a former chapter.

[2] At the dissolution of Ford Abbey, out of thirteen monks nine appear on the pension with the two surnames, the local one being given first.

monks to whom no pension was granted. It is possible that he may have died immediately after the Dissolution, but it is more probable that in defence of his conscience he resisted the intruded hireling thrust into office by the tyrant, and did what he could to confirm his brethren in the Faith. Since the death of the last legitimately elected Abbot, he alone was their lawful Superior by right of his office as Prior. To the strange coincidences that attended the Dissolution and restoration of the venerable Abbey, which have to be recorded in the sequel, this one, I think, will have to be added, that our last lawful Superior, though he bore not the title of Abbot, was born under the shadow of our monastery, and bore the name of Arnold Buckfast. It was a worthy thought of the first Abbot of the Restoration, Dom Boniface Natter, that the first novice (now professed) who was clothed after his entering on office, should bear the name of Brother Arnold.

Wood, who thought he was Abbot of Buckfast, relates that he left his arms "in one of the middle chamber windows of St Bernard's (now St John's College), wherein is a crozier thrust through a buck's face palewise." These are the arms of Buckfast Abbey, not of Prior Arnold.

I am not sure that he was the only Buckfast monk by whom the College was governed. John Ford, his immediate predecessor, is very likely indeed to have been one of the Fords of Ashburton or Bagtor, our neighbours, and a monk of St Mary's. John Ford of Ashburton, who obtained a grant of arms in 1527, married Mary Pomeroy of Ingsdon.

The next Abbot to John King seemed to have

been John Rede the elder, of whom Dr Oliver writes that he "occurs as Abbot," 24th November 1498, but without indication of the date of his election. Of the Redes there will be something to say when we reach his nephew (probably) and namesake, whom we must hold as the last true Abbot of Buckfast. But between 1498, when his name occurs, and the election of Alfred Gill as Abbot of Buckfast, we have a period of fourteen years. After reading the valuable essay on "Berry and its Ancient Lords," written by Mr Charles Worthy, I find reason to admit, as highly probable at the very least, that between Abbots Rede and Gill we should admit into the list the name of Abbot Seinclere (St Clere) Pomeroy, and I hope to be forgiven for giving a fragment of Devonshire history, interwoven as it is with the story of St Mary's Abbey, concerning these Pomeroys.

Raoul de la Pomeraie, "Ralph of the Orchard," was a Norman, whose castle, or what remains of it, now called Chateau Ganne,[1] may be seen in the Cinglais, not far from Falaise, got his title from the rich apple-orchards that surrounded his Norman home. He was proud of it, and the crest of the Pomeroys was a lion *seiant* with an apple in its paw. The Conqueror rewarded his military service by the manor known as Beri—the walled town—of which for that purpose he despoiled Aluric the Saxon. The stately and beautiful ruins of Berry Pomeroy Castle, two miles out of Totnes, are distant eight miles from Buckfast.

Ralph's descendants proved generous benefactors to the Church, as the White Monks of Ford and the

[1] Worthy, "The Lords of Berry," *Devonshire Assoc. Trans.*

Canons Regular of Torre, among others, could well testify. They loved their South Devon home, and of course intermarried with Valletorts, Moels, and other knightly houses in our vicinity. One of these alliances is of great importance to my history.

The last of the Pomeroys of Berry was the gallant Sir Thomas. In the reign of Henry VIII. he had served with distinction in France. In 1549 he headed the Catholic army in Devon, and fought for the defence of his Faith. He escaped sentence of death, but the noble castle and the fair manor passed away for ever from its ancient lords.

For some reason the Lords of Berry seem to have held aloof from Buckfast until the last century of their career. Our Cartulary never refers to them between 1100 and 1400, save on one occasion, when William de Pomeroy witnesses a deed of Reginald de Valletort. The Abbey lands that were surrendered by the intruded Gabriel Donne were those held in the reign of the Confessor, with a few additions of which the donors are known, but they were not Pomeroys.

Strangely enough, however, Leland, who in the reign of Henry VIII. visited Buckfast, says that it was re-founded after the Conquest, by one Ethelwerd de Pomeroy, which we have seen could not have been unless in the sense that the Lord of Berry had a hand in introducing the Norman monks in place of the dispossessed Saxons, which is likely enough. But what is to my purpose is the testimony of John Prince (1643-1723), who was vicar of Berry Pomeroy, and affirms "that one of this name and family was either the founder of, or a considerable benefactor to, this monastery, plainly appears from the Pomerai's arms, not long since to be seen in several places of the building." This last statement is beyond dispute. In the last century they were still faintly discernible in a farmhouse, originally part of the Abbey, and facing its entrance.

For this there must have been a reason, and I agree with Mr Worthy, that there are valid grounds for admitting that between 1498 and 1500, Abbot John Rede was succeeded in his office by Abbot Seinclere (St Clere) Pomeroy, by whom our community was governed till 1512. From his reign dates the legend, which Leland heard at his visit to Buckfast, not many years afterwards, of Ethelwerd de Pomeroy. In my opinion, there may, indeed, have been some benefaction to the monastery, of which the memory has perished, but I have no doubt it was in Abbot Seinclere's time that the Pomeroy arms were sculptured on our walls. A pleasing incident of Devonshire family history will introduce this Abbot to my readers.

Philip de Beaumont, the ancestor of our Abbot Philip de Beaumont, was the ancient Lord of Ilsington, on the outskirts of the great moor. He lived at Ankyston, now Ingsdon, a mile or so out of Ashburton, on the road to Chudleigh, and his manor-house, now the home of a community of nuns known as the White Sisters, occupied an elevated site, divided by a valley from the ancient village of Bickington, which in his time was a seat of the Giffards. Abbot Philip is not unlikely to have spent his boyhood at Ingsdon, and may have been born there.

Towards the year 1465, John Pomeroy, a younger brother of Sir Edward of Berry, had the good fortune to win the hand of a daughter of the house of Beaumont, who brought him as her dowry the manor of Ingsdon. He must have been of mature years, for his brother, Sir Edward, had died in 1446, leaving three children, of whom the second, our future Abbot, was named St Clere, a name also borne by a grandson of Sir Edward, the child of his youngest son John.

In the churchwardens' accounts for the parish of Ashburton, at the year 1500, is an entry of money, with the following note: "From a gift of the Lord Abbot of Buckfast St Clere Pomeroy — Geoffrey Harepath, and others." There is, of course, no division of punctuation to be looked for, and I think with Mr Worthy, that St Clere Pomeroy is here referred to as Abbot of Buckfast. This would at once account for the Pomeroy arms at the Abbey. The name of St Clere Pomeroy never occurs again in these accounts, though the names of the parishioners are constantly repeated. Besides, though a present to Ashburton from our Abbot would be natural enough, St Clere Pomeroy, when a layman, belonged to Ilsington parish, not to Ashburton, and his church offerings would go to Ilsington.

From the time that John de Pomeroy settled at Ingsdon, within a short ride of our Abbey, the Pomeroys are certain to have been visitors at St Mary's Church, and the young St Clere, after his father's death, would be often at his uncle's house, and perhaps under his guardianship. St Clere was the name of an ancient family of Budleigh, which more than once intermarried with the Fords and the Pomeroys of Ilsington, and I suspect that John Ford, Prior Arnold's immediate predecessor at St

Bernard's College, was a relation of Abbot St Clere Pomeroy, for the houses of Ford and Pomeroy were connected, and a monk of Buckfast Abbey. The old manor-house of Ingsdon (nothing of the ancient building is discernible now), at last given over to religion, seems thus to have been the home in boyhood of two abbots of Buckfast, Beaumont and Pomeroy. Nor should it be omitted that Sir William Pole, in the Pomeroy pedigree, gives the marriage and issue of Henry and John, brothers of St Clere, but not of the last named, who appears in the pedigree as unmarried. He must have been at least fifty-five years old at the time of his election.

In the same Ashburton accounts is a charge (1511-12) "for ringing the knell of the late Abbot of Buckfast." On Palm Sunday, 1512, Abbot Alfred Gyll was blessed as his successor.

Such is the absolute dearth of records at this period, that of Abbot Gyll's acts we know nothing. His family held land in the neighbourhood of Tavistock, and were till quite lately seated at Bickham, Buckland Monachorum. Abbot Richard Gyll, perhaps his brother, confirmed Abbot in 1530, was the last abbot of the Cistercians at Newenham. Robert Gyll was Prior of St Mary's, Totnes, during the whole time that Abbot Alfred governed Buckfast. Thomas Gyll, was the youngest of our Buckfast monks to whom pensions were granted at the Dissolution. For a century before they had figured among the Exeter diocesan clergy.

To what I have written above, I may here add that the present Viscount Harberton claims descent from the Ingsdon Pomeroys.

DOOR OF A 13TH CENTY ENAMELLED
AND GILDED BRASS LIMOGES WORK
CHASSE OR SHRINE.

[To face page 187.

CHAPTER XXII

The last Abbot before the Dissolution. Dearth of records. Isolation of the Abbot. The Convocation of 1531. The Act of Succession. The Oath of Supremacy; was it taken by the monks of Buckfast? Abbot Rede's integrity. Prior Arnold Gye.

JOHN REDE the younger, the last Abbot of Buckfast before the Dissolution, received the abbatial blessing from Bishop Veysey, 13th April 1525. Dr Oliver thinks he was a nephew of the former Abbot, John Rede. The 13th of April in that year fell on Maunday Thursday.

The Redes seem to have belonged to Dartmouth and its neighbourhood. Simon Rede, the last Abbot of Torre, who entered on office only two years before our Abbot, and survived till 1556, was buried in the Church of Stoke Flemyng, and his recumbent effigy is still to be seen in Townstall Church, Dartmouth. William Rede was a Cistercian of Ford Abbey at the time of its suppression.

The want of information for our history, in the latter part of the fifteenth century, does not affect our Abbey alone. The Exeter Registers during that period, and until 1521, were so neglected that all records from the Conquest till Henry III.'s reign were entirely lost, and little care was taken of what belonged to a later period. Perhaps the confusion caused by the Wars of the Roses, and the frequent absences of the bishops, contributed to this result. Bishop Catterick, the immediate successor of Bishop Stafford, died in Italy a month after his nomination, and was buried at Florence, in the Franciscan Church of Santa Croce. No complaint can be made against his immediate successor, Bishop Lacy, whose tomb is said to have been defaced in the reign of Henry VIII., to stop the concourse of pilgrims attracted to it by the fame of his miracles. But from that time forward our bishops were much drawn into affairs of State, and of twelve bishops in succession, beginning with Stafford, only two were born in the diocese. No doubt this also had to do with the neglect of records.

Abbot John Rede entered on office only a fortnight after Blessed Richard Whiting succeeded to the abbacy of Glastonbury, and had to meet the persecutions on the part of the Government that beset all the religious superiors of that time, so well told in Abbot Gasquet's *Last Abbot of Glastonbury*, and had his own trials to undergo. From his bishop he could not hope for support, for Bishop Veysey was a favourite at Court, and his courtly ambition "restrained him from being honest in bad times."[1] And the times were exceedingly bad. In February 1531, the Convocation of the Province of Canterbury had acknowledged the king as Supreme Head of the Church in England, *as far as the law of Christ permits*, and the systematic persecution of the clergy by

[1] Oliver.

pecuniary extortions began. A charge was brought against Rede shortly after that he had been in the habit of pasturing his cattle on the "King's moors" without payment, and on the 12th of July a commission was issued to Sir Thomas Denys and Sir Philip Champernowne, to enquire into the matter. Sir Thomas Denys was bent on mending the fallen fortunes of his house out of the Abbey lands—in which he was eminently successful;—but his trick was to ingratiate himself with the monks till the time for action arrived. So he decided in the Abbot's favour; and decided, "the beasts in the same pasturing to be and go in quiet manner, without any further vexation or trouble to the said Abbot, his title and interest of and in the same." He thoroughly deceived the monks, "pretending to be their friend, and obtaining offices of trust, and, of course, of emolument from them."[1] Eventually he became the owner of Buckfast Abbey.

The Abbot must have been sorely straitened for money in those days, but to resist demands was impossible. The vicar of Churchstow in 1533, put in a claim for a substantial addition to his annual income, which was of course fully granted. It may not have been excessive, but even if it had been, it was not the time to dispute it. But I do not find any indication of Abbot Rede having adopted the plan of giving out the Abbey lands on long leases, as was done by others in wholesale fashion at this time. Abbot Gyll of Newenham granted about twenty in 1533. Only one lease do I find granted by Abbot

[1] Brooking Rowe.

Rede in all his time of office, and that was a little before his death or expulsion in 1536.

A darker hour was now at hand. Already, in July 1531, the same month in which the royal commission held its enquiry concerning the Dartmoor pasturage, Abbot Rede had been made to feel painfully the complete isolation in which he stood. At the request of the English Cistercians the General Chapter of the Order had sent the Abbot of Chailly to make the visitation of the monasteries in England, but was hindered by a royal order, commanding him to return to France. Deserted by his bishop, forbidden under tremendous penalties to hold communication with Rome, deprived of the support of his Order, the Abbot of Buckfast was left to face the impending storm helpless and alone. In March 1333, the royal assent was given to the Act of Parliament forbidding appeals to the Pope. In the following month Anne Boleyn was proclaimed Queen, and evil tidings reached Devonshire from time and time, which caused superiors of religious houses to begin hurriedly granting long leases of their estates to those whom they deemed their friends, as I have said, an example not followed by our Abbot.

In March 1534, Parliament passed the Act by which it was made high treason to oppose the succession to the Crown of the issue of Henry and Anne Boleyn. The Oath of Succession, to be taken by the nobles, clergy, and others to whom it might be offered, was not contained in the Act itself. It was subsequently framed in such a form as to make it an Oath of Supremacy. As tendered to the religious communities, it included the formula: "Also that they would ever hold the king to be Head of the Church of England; that the Bishop of Rome, who in his bulls usurped the name of Pope and arrogated to himself the primacy of the most high Pontiff, had no more authority or jurisdiction than other Bishops in their dioceses."

Following close on this Act of Parliament came the news of the execution of the Holy Maid of Kent and her companions. Within the year our Devonshire monasteries were visited by the royal commissioners, who brought with them the form of the Oath to be signed by the monks of each community assembled in chapter.

It has been generally believed that, with the exception of the Carthusians and the Observant Franciscans, the Oath of Supremacy was universally signed by the monks. There are strong reasons for disbelieving this assertion. However, at Hartland Abbey in North Devon, it was signed by Abbot Priest and five others, 31st August 1534; as also by Prior Sturgeon and his community of Frithelstock, in the same year; by Prior Howe of Plympton, on 5th August; by Prior Ross of Pilton and two others, Richard Pilton and John Caw, in the month of September.[1] Here I may transcribe from Abbot Gasquet's great work a note appended to p. 248 of Vol. I. :—

"Canon Dixon says that the oath was taken in almost every chapter-house where it was tendered. This is generally stated as a fact, but as far as is known, there is no proof of it. The list of acknowledgments of the royal supremacy, printed in the

[1] Oliver, *Monasticon Exoniense.*

seventh Report of the Deputy Keeper, App. II., contains *all* the known documents as to the religious bodies. They number only 105, *a very small fraction of the whole.* Of these Mr F. Devon, the assistant keeper of public records, remarks:—'I believe it contains all the original acknowledgments of supremacy deposited in the branch public record office at the chapter-house. *The signatures are in my opinion not all autographs, but frequently in the same handwriting, and my impression is that the writer of the deed often added many of the names.*'" The same conclusion is confirmed by the history of Syon Monastery. On the whole, it is by far the more just and probable inference that a very great number of the religious were not involved in the guilt of this act of schism.

Buckfast does *not* figure in the fatal list, and there are a number of circumstances, as we shall see in our next chapter, to strengthen the presumption that the unhallowed oath was refused by the Abbot and Prior; that the royal commissioners found in the community a different spirit from that of Hartland or Plympton, and that their firmness was owing to Abbot Rede and Prior Arnold Gye. But in fairness to those by whom the Oath was taken, I must here summarise the just and wise remarks of Abbot Gasquet.[1]

At first sight we are startled at seeing the names of several of our martyrs among those who signed the Oath of Supremacy. But, difficult and strained as it may seem to us at the present day, there is at least sufficient evidence in what has come down to

[1] *The last Abbot of Glastonbury*, pp. 47 *sqq.*

us in contemporary writings, that among upright and learned men of that time, it was often thought that by signing the Oath of Supremacy they did not separate themselves from the communion of the Holy See. No doubt the overmastering dread of ruin to their monasteries to some extent warped their judgment. They felt sure that the king would return to Catholic unity some day or other, for in his early days he had been a loyal and devout Catholic. Many thought the headship of the Church of England might be allowed "in temporalibus," and that they could sign the document with this tacit reservation. Such reservations were by contemporaries really attributed to some leading ecclesiastics, and not without reason. Besides, since the Council of Constance and the Great Schism of the West, learned men might be found here and there in whom the divine origin of the papal authority was not so clear and undoubted as it had been during the first fourteen centuries of the Church, and as it continued to be in the faith and profession of Catholics. "I have, by the grace of God," said Blessed Thomas More, himself a martyr for the Primacy of the Holy See, "been always a Catholic never out of communion with the Roman Pontiff: but I have heard it said at times that the authority of the Roman Pontiff was certainly lawful and to be respected, but still an authority derived from human law, and not standing upon a divine prescription. Then, when I observed that human affairs were so ordered that the sources of the power of the Roman Pontiff would necessarily be examined, I gave myself up to a most diligent examination of that question for the space of seven years, and found that the authority of the Roman Pontiff, which you rashly—I will not use stronger language—have set aside, is not only lawful, to be respected, and necessary, but also grounded on the divine law and prescription. That is my opinion; that is the belief in which, by the grace of God, I shall die."

For that belief he died, and his death, and the deaths of his fellow-martyrs, have powerfully assisted in sweeping away the last vestiges of doubt or hesitation on this article of the Catholic Faith. What was possible under the reign of Henry had become impossible in the days of Elizabeth.

But while we may think that if the monks of Buckfast had really taken the Oath of Supremacy on this occasion, it would not be right to suppose their guilt to have been what it would be in our own times; it is but right to bear in mind that there is no evidence that they did so, but a valid presumption that they did not. But we must hasten to continue our story of the events of those days of infinite sadness.

Events were now following in quick succession that might have made the stoutest heart quail. The martyrdom of the Carthusians and their companions, of More, Fisher, and others, the suppression of the lesser monasteries, and the dismissal of all monks under twenty-four years of age, and of all who had professed under twenty, all combined to deepen the gloom that surrounded the community of Buckfast. We know not even the year in which the last Abbot of Buckfast died, nor whether he breathed his last in his beloved monastery. At the meeting of Convocation in June 1536, the intruded Gabriel

Donne assisted and signed as " Gabriel, *Abbas de Buckfestria.*"

As this royal nomination of a fallen monk who had forsaken the unity of the Catholic Faith, by a king in the same condition, was of course absolutely null and void, Gabriel Donne has no place in the list of the Abbots of Buckfast. During the two or three years from Abbot Rede's death or removal to the Dissolution, the lawful superior was of course the Prior. The last Superior of the Abbey of St Mary's at Buckfast was, therefore, Prior Arnold Gye, whom I believe to have been born on the patrimony of St Mary's, or, to give him what may be his true name, Arnold Buckfast.[1]

[1] The name of Gye occurs about this period as that of a family living at Sandford, a little north of Crediton. In Worthy's *Devonshire Wills*, I find that of James Mortymer of Sandford in 1558, whose trustee is "Robert Gye, gentleman"; in 1623 Jane Mortimer leaves the residue of her estate to "Cousin Robert Gye." A William Gye was a monk of Buckland at the Dissolution. In Sir William Pole's *Devonshire Pedigrees*, Robert Guy of Prouze, in Sandford, probably identical with James Mortimer's trustee, appears as the husband of Grace Dowrish. But the fact of Prior Arnold's assuming the name of Buckfast makes me think that he was only distantly connected with the Gyes of Sandford, and that he was born on the Abbey manor.

CHAPTER XXIII

Gabriel Donne. Abbot Rede's last act. The Cistercian house of Stratford Langthorne. Donne's earlier career. "The wolf rampant." Surrenders of Devonshire monasteries in 1539. Canonsleigh, Hartland, and Torre. The Eve of St Matthias, 1539. A strange coincidence. Sir William Petre.

THE meeting of Convocation that assembled on the 9th of June, and was dissolved on the 20th of July, in the year 1536, numbered in all 109 members. All had of course taken the Oath of Supremacy. But among them were some who afterwards shed their blood for the Primacy of the Holy See, and more who underwent for the same cause a life-long imprisonment, or went into voluntary exile, for their conscience.

Cromwell, as the King's Vicar-General, presided in person, and the terror of the royal vengeance awed the assembly into submission. The lesser monasteries had been already dissolved, and some of the greater ones had resigned themselves into the hands of the king. Anne Boleyn had been executed three weeks before the meeting of Parliament, and the king had married Jane Seymour the day after her execution. Efforts were indeed made by Convocation to stem the torrent of Lutheranism, especially by the Lower House, but in their protestation the members style Henry "the Supreme Head of the Church of England," and desire "that the Bishop of Rome, with his usurped authority, . . . be utterly and for ever renounced, forsaken, extinguished, and abolished." Such was the Convocation of 1536, which Archbishop Cranmer opened by singing the Mass of the Holy Ghost in St Paul's Cathedral.

The clergy of the Northern Province as yet stood firm. In their Convocation of this year they pronounced that "the King's Highness nor any temporal man may not be Supreme Head of the Church by the law of God; that lands given to God, the Church, or religious men, may not be taken away; that by the law of the Church, General Councils, and consent of Christian people, the Pope of Rome hath been taken for the Head of the Church and Vicar of Christ, and so ought to be taken." A formidable insurrection in Lincolnshire and the North strove to uphold this bold declaration. But the ecclesiastics of the Province of Canterbury had bent before the Terror, and eighteen bishops, with forty abbots and priors, signed the Acts of Convocation in the chapter-house of St Paul's.

Among the names of those who signed appears that of Gabriel, Abbot of Buckfast. A chain of circumstantial evidence leads us to the conclusions that Abbot John Rede was still living when Gabriel Donne was intruded into his place by Cromwell, either during the sitting of Convocation or shortly before; and that the Abbot, the Prior, and the community, had incurred the displeasure of the

Commissioners, probably from their resistance to the Oath of Supremacy.

Gabriel Donne's signature to the Acts of Convocation could not have been written later than the 20th of July 1536, when it was dissolved; and of Abbot Rede, Dr Oliver writes, "that we meet with his name in a lease, July 10, 1536," only ten days earlier. Mr Brooking Rowe says that "he was confirmed 13th April 1525, and lived about twelve years after," probably supposing him to have died just before Donne's appointment. At any rate, during the month of July he was removed from abbacy by death, or, as I believe, by a forced resignation.

Nor were the monks of St Mary's Abbey allowed to elect one of their own number to succeed John Rede. A stranger from a distant house, a royal favourite, and a tool of Cromwell "was foisted on the monks, and put in to carry out the designs of the king."[1]

The election, if choice had been allowed, would probably have fallen on Prior Arnold, an Oxford man, and for several years head of St Bernard's College at Oxford. But the Prior was so odious to the tyrannical government that he alone of the community was granted no pension whatever at the Dissolution. It is likely that under the influence of abbot and prior the community had proved so refractory that the Commissioners could recommend no one as likely to be a fit instrument for carrying out the royal will. It is a proceeding frequently met with in the history of the Dissolution.

[1] Brooking Rowe.

It is to be regretted that from this critical point we lose sight of Abbot Rede, whom we are obliged to regard as the last of our abbots until the election in our chapter of Dom Boniface Natter, on the 19th of November 1902. On his memory and the memory of his predecessors, as far as records survive, we can look back with reverence and gratitude. By their laborious and beneficent lives they set their stamp on the surrounding country, and governed their community in tranquil seclusion.

Though, of course, as already said, the only legitimate authority during the brief period that intervened till the surrender of the Abbey rested with Prior Arnold Gye, *alias* Buckfast, who on that account, though not holding the abbatial crozier, must be held to be our last Superior, Gabriel Donne entered at once at Buckfast on the work of temporal and spiritual destruction. The "wolf rampant" on his escutcheon was an apt symbol of his unhallowed mission, and his antecedent career a good preparation for it.

Gabriel Donne, a student of Trinity Hall, Cambridge, became a Cistercian in the Monastery of Stratford Langthorne of Essex, and in the Convocation of 1536 his signature immediately follows that of William Huddleston, the last Abbot of Stratford. His abilities were considerable, and we find him acting as proctor for his brethren in a lawsuit between the community and the vicar of West Ham, in 1517. Following Abbot Huddleston into the schism, he attracted the notice of Cranmer and Cromwell, and was employed in the arrest of Tyndale at Antwerp in 1535, returning to England in the month of June of that year. His services were rewarded with the abbacy of Buckfast, and, as we have seen, he sat as Abbot in the Convocation of June 1536. After the Dissolution he was gratified with a pension of £120, equal to £1200 in our own day; received various benefices, was made canon residentiary of St Paul's, and was appointed by Cranmer to exercise all manner of jurisdiction in his name in the diocese. Utterly unscrupulous, he became as Protestant as heart could wish under Edward VI., and in Mary's reign was again a Catholic. He died on the 5th of December 1558, within three weeks after the queen, and before there was time to be called upon for another change in his religion, and was buried in St Paul's, near the High Altar. He left much of his ill-gotten wealth for purposes of charity, and £120 to Trinity Hall, "which was applied to the foundation of a scholarship, and the establishment of an annual commemoration of the deceased, with a refection on the Feast of St Nicholas."[1] His arms are still to be seen among the shields in the roof of Trinity Hall Chapel.

During the two years and eight months of his uncanonical rule, "he alienated," writes Mr Brooking Rowe, "much of the monastic property," the prior and community being, of course, powerless to stay his hand. But he had a more important work to accomplish, namely, by oppression or cajolery to dispose the monks to a so-called "voluntary" surrender of the venerable abbey into the hands of

---

[1] Cooper's *Athenæ Cant.*; Brooking Rowe's *Cistercian Houses of Devon*.

the king. The royal agents in the work of suppression were enjoined to obtain such surrenders by every means in their power; if unsuccessful, they were to proceed by terror and compulsion.[1]

"With the king's hand on their throats," most of the communities made the surrender. Where the abbots proved obstinate they were deprived, "and others more pliant put in their room," writes Sir William Dugdale; as was, for example, the case at St Alban's and Evesham, and the dispossessed monks were turned adrift without a pension, to beg their bread. The intrusion of Gabriel Donne and his evil example and exhortations must have made the brief period that followed a time of inexpressible sadness for the monks, though no doubt his position as an acknowledged and favoured agent of Cromwell secured the monastery from wanton aggression by outsiders.

The government of our community by the unhappy apostate lasted for two years and a half after he had sat in Convocation as Abbot of Buckfast. In the latter part of February 1539,[2] the Royal Commissioners, William Petre, John Tregonwell, and John Smith, were hurrying on the dissolution of monastic houses in the county of Devon. On the 16th, Elizabeth Powell, Abbess of the Canonesses Regular of Canonsleigh, with her seventeen sisters, surrendered her monastery. The names of the nuns,

---

[1] *Gasquet*, vol. i., p. 278.
[2] Both the *Monasticon Anglicanum* and Oliver place the suppression of our monastery on the 25th of February 1538, but as in official documents it is dated in 30 Henry VIII., it seems that this must be an error for 1539.

Pomeroy, Chudleigh, Fortescue, Carew, Pollard, and the rest, belong almost without exception to our historical families. The monastery was razed. Thence the Commissioners, crossing the whole breadth of the county from east to west (Canonsleigh is on the Somerset border), four days later were at Hartland Abbey, of the same Order. Here, besides Abbot Pope, only four Canons Regular received pensions, "assigned and appoynted by John Tregonwell, William Petre, and John Smyth, esquyers, Commissioners." The surrender was made on the 21st; the assignment of pensions is dated on the 22nd. One of the canons is appointed to serve the Chapel of Bickington. As nearly as we can determine their route, we may now follow the cavalcade of the Royal Commissioners with their servants during the next five days.

From Hartland to Torre they could not easily have ridden in one day. But if they left Hartland on the 21st, they could well have rested at Okehampton Castle, which they would reach towards evening of the 22nd, having halted the night before at one of the numerous country seats on their way. The 23rd was the first Sunday in Lent, and after hearing mass in the castle, they would be early in the saddle and reach the great Premonstratensian Abbey of Torre in time to receive the surrender of the canons in their chapter-house the same night, for the surrender is dated on the 23rd, and was made by Abbot Simon Rede. The importance and wealth of this abbey make it probable that the Commissioners were detained there for the following day, or at least part of it, though no doubt the Abbot and the

Commissioners sat up till late at night. Of course all had been arranged beforehand, and Abbot Rede's pension, which would exceed £600 of our money, shows that he was high in favour with the despoilers.

The next day, Monday, was the Feast of St Matthias. It was the last day on which the monks of Buckfast could call their abbey their home, for on the morrow it was to pass away, as men thought, from the children of St Benedict for ever.[1] Gabriel Donne—I will not call him abbot, for to that title he had no right—was now busy in preparation for his guests and accomplices in the act of sacrilege he had undertaken to accomplish at the bidding of a lawless king. When offering up, with unworthy hands, the sacrifice of the mass on that day, he might well have pondered on the words he had to read in the Lesson from the Acts of the Apostles in the Missal, concerning the traitor: "Let their habitation become desolate, and let there be none to dwell therein; and his bishopric let another take." A year of years had indeed to pass away, but on the first day of the 365th year, on this same Feast of St Matthias, which had brought to an end eight centuries of monastic life in the Abbey of St Mary of Buckfaesten, the bishop of the diocese was to bless and enthrone, with all the splendour of the ancient rite, another abbot to begin anew the venerable line of monastic rulers, and take the place usurped by the fallen Judas. None of those concerned in appointing the day for the blessing of Abbot Boniface Natter on 24th March 1903 were

---

[1] Cistercians are of course a branch of the Benedictine Order, and their profession is made "according to the Rule of St Benedict."

aware of this coincidence, if, indeed, coincidence it should be called.

Whether it was on the day of St Matthias, or on the following, that the Commissioners rode from Torre to Buckfast, I cannot say, but the Feast of the Apostle was the last of which the monks were to see the close as possessors of the Abbey, for on the 25th it was surrendered. On his journey from Torre through the loveliest part of South Devon, William Petre was revisiting the scenes of his boyhood. Torbyran, where he first saw the light, is about five miles from Buckfast Abbey. The circumstance may well have awakened his better thoughts, for in his character evil and good were strangely mixed.

It will help us to a deeper insight into the scene enacted in our chapter-house on that memorable 25th of February, if I give some account here of this personage, whose descendants held for two centuries and a half the bulk of the lands that had belonged to our Abbey from the days of St Edward the Confessor. He was the eldest of the eight children of John Petre, Esq., and was born about the year 1505, at the family seat of Tor Newton, in the parish of Torbyran aforesaid. His father was a gentleman of small estate. William was sent to Oxford, where he entered first at Exeter College, was elected Fellow of All Souls in 1523, and in 1533 took his degree of D.C.L. It must have been some years before the last date that the Earl of Wiltshire, father to Queen Anne Boleyn, chose him as tutor to his son, the unhappy George Boleyn. At Court he attracted the notice of Henry VIII., and continued in favour under four sovereigns of England. Dignified, graceful, courteous, a keen observer of men, he was the most accomplished courtier ever known. "Wriothesley was rough and stubborn, Paget easy, Cecil close, Mason plain, Smith noble; Petre smooth, reserved, resolved, and yet obliging"; such is Prince's judgment of Petre and his contemporary statesman. At the time of the suppression of our Abbey he was not yet knighted. Out of the Abbey lands he obtained, in Devonshire alone, 36,000 acres, and in these estates was comprised the greatest part of our property, though not the Abbey itself.

Withal he retained a yearning for the old religion. In Queen Mary's reign he obtained from Paul IV. a special sanction for retaining the Abbey lands for himself and his heirs for ever, without scruple of conscience, and with absolution from all censures. After Elizabeth's accession he gradually withdrew himself from Court, and spent the last years of his life in retirement and works of charity at Ingatestone, in Essex. He is generally believed to have died a Catholic, and is the founder of the noble house that has ever remained, under many trials, unswervingly loyal to the Faith.

Unlike most of his fellow-Commissioners, he was no calumniator of the monks, and the Devon monasteries were at least fortunate in being spared the foul ribaldry and brutal insults of men like Layton and his compeers.

CHAPTER XXIV

Haste of the Royal Commissioners. Hostile attitude of the people. Arrival of Petre and his company at Buckfast. The last scene in the chapter-house. Names of the monks. Dismantling of the Abbey after the expulsion of the community.

THE Royal Commissioners were accompanied on their visitation of the monasteries by a large and well-armed retinue, a precaution of absolute necessity, without which their lives would have been in danger. True, the ferocious revenge taken on the defenders of the monasteries by the king, and the wholesale executions of eighteen months earlier, had quelled for the time the spirit of resistance that was to break out a few years later, only to be extinguished by the butchery of four thousand of the Devonshire peasantry. Besides, Devonshire men are slow to move, but they bitterly detested the foul work that was going on, and looked on with scowling faces as the band of licentious ruffians went about their work. Here and there some partial disturbance had arisen, as at the suppression of the Priory of St Nicholas at Exeter, but no serious rising took place at this time.

BUCKFAST ABBEY: First founded in Eighth Century; suppressed 1538; restored 1882.

The hostile attitude of the people accounts in part for the haste with which Petre and his company rode from monastery to monastery through the length and breadth of Devon, and the brief stay he made at each house. As all had been arranged in time beforehand, it is but natural to suppose that the monks were assembled in the chapter-house immediately on the arrival of the Commissioners, to append their signatures to the act of surrender, and that during the next twenty-four hours the Commissioners employed their time in taking over from the Abbot the charters, seals, and above all the inventory of the goods of the house, as all objects of gold, silver, or jewels had at once to be packed up and forwarded to London, and a special search was made for jewelled mitres, rings, vestments of cloth of gold or silver, and all such-like articles. The rest was put up for sale, especially the lead from the roof and the church bells, the buildings demolished, and their materials sold piecemeal. Once the inventory had been obtained, the rest of the work was left by the Commissioners to inferior officials. The monks of Buckfast knew the fate that awaited them, and there were sad hearts in the dear old Abbey, and great "grief in the convent and all the servants of the house, departing one from another, especially such as with their conscience could not break their profession. It would have made a flint melt and weep to have seen the breaking up of the house, and the sorrowful departing." So wrote an eye-witness of the suppression of the Cistercian Abbey of Roche, seven months before that of Buckfast.[1]

[1] *Gasquet*, vol. ii., p. 318.

Taking the cross-roads in an almost straight line from Torre to Buckfast, Sir William Petre would have passed close by Torbryan, his native place, and through Woodland, where his mother, Alice Colin, was born. But it is more likely that the large cavalcade kept the king's highway to Abbot's Kerswell—I am writing for Devonshire men—and thence to the ancient borough of Ashburton. Thence after a twenty minutes' ride their horses' hoofs clattered on the stone pavement under the arched south gate of the Abbey, and passing the grey old tower that still stands in its massive strength, they drew rein in front of the principal entrance. (In a room over that entrance, now restored, these pages have been written.) While the servants of the Abbey were busy with their horses they entered in and found themselves in the guest-house, where of course they met with all due courtesy, for Gabriel Donne and William Petre, old friends, were alike the Lord Cromwell's agents, and a goodly refection awaited the travellers. A brief talk round the fire, while the monks, who had said vespers in their choir for the last time, were assembling in chapter, and the Commissioners with their notary were led through the south gallery of the cloister, past the door of the refectory, and then turning to the left, found themselves at the door of the chapter-house, in front of which three inscribed tombstones of departed abbots diversified the bright green and yellow tiles of the pavement.[1]

[1] The description is no fanciful one; much has disappeared in the course of restoration, as it could not be preserved, but the writer is accurately describing what he himself unearthed, though it was in a crumbling state.

Round the chapter-house ran a low bench of red sandstone, on which the few remaining monks were seated. None could have been received to profession for years past; the younger monks had been compulsorily dismissed; death had of course come as a relief to some of the aged, and only ten choir-monks remained—of course not counting the pseudo-Abbot—including the Prior, Arnold Gye. The walls of the chapter-house have not yet been raised on the old foundations, but one can stand on the very spot occupied by Sir William Petre, with Gabriel Donne on his right, and recall the last scene in our history that ushered in the long night of desolation. The act of surrender was then read, I suppose by the notary.

By the document, which was in Latin, the Abbot and monks were made to say that "from just and reasonable motives we by these presents do give, grant, surrender, and confirm to our most illustrious Prince Henry, by the grace of God, King of England, Lord of Ireland, Supreme Head of the Church of England, all our said monastery or abbacy of Buckfast. . . . Before me, William Petre," etc. The deed of surrender was then laid on a table in the middle of the chapter-house, and each monk, beginning with Gabriel Donne, signed it in succession.

Throughout England there were not found many, even among those who had refused the Oath of Supremacy, to refuse the signatures. That all the signatures to be seen on these deeds are genuine we could not affirm, for there are instances, like that of Darent Convent, where they are all in the same handwriting, and clearly forged. As the penalty for refusing to sign was the refusal of a pension, it is possible that the signature of the Prior of Buckfast was inserted by someone else. It was a principal object with the king's agents that the monks should appear to have made a voluntary and unanimous surrender, and a more unscrupulous body of men it would be hard to find at any epoch of our country's history.

So ended the memorable 25th of February 1539. Perhaps the hardships of the dispersed monks were less severe than in some other instances, for an inspection of the list of names shows that they were all, or nearly all, Devonshire men, belonging to the class of landholders, and in all probability they left at once for the homes of their families. The names are the following: Arnold Gye, *Prior;* John Cowle, John Watts, Richard Taylor, William Shapcott, Matthew Pryston (Preston), Richard Splatt, Thomas Gylle, William Avery, John Doyge. All but the Prior were pensioned. It is impossible to decide on what principle the amount was fixed. Six of the number received £5. 6s. 8d. each; but John Cowle was allowed £6, and John Doyge £6. 13s. 4d., while Thomas Gill had but £5. As superiors usually were paid at a higher rate, the exclusion of the Prior becomes more conspicuous.

The old Devonshire families of Doidge, Amery, and Shapcote have numerous descendants, bearing these typical Devon names, in the county; Splatts and Prestons still linger among us. The other names are common to all parts of the country.

Once the surrender had been signed, the monks were not allowed to linger in their monastery. More than half of them would have been able to reach the homes of their families in one day. The dismantling of the building began at once. The lead was stripped from the roofs. The church bells, five in number, were bought from Sir Thomas Arundel for £33. 15s., by the men of Buckfastleigh for the parish church. But the buildings were not razed.

That the Abbey, or a portion of it, was used as a residence during the whole of the nineteenth century, is certain, and I think it may have been so at intervals at an earlier period. There was a curious legend among the country-people, that owing to a curse laid upon it by the monks at the time of their expulsion, none of its owners should ever die within its precincts, until, I presume, it returned to its rightful proprietors. During the last century the prophecy would seem to have been a true one; but the spell is broken now, for since it came into monastic hands in 1882, one death has occurred, that of an old Crimean veteran, a monk and priest of the Abbey, Dom Herluin Capelle, deceased on the anniversary of his profession, 11th July 1885, Feast of the Translation of St Benedict.

Of course a ghost story in such an ancient building is the correct thing, but the story of the Abbey ghost has received an unexpected elucidation, if I may so call it, which I shall relate in a subsequent chapter.

CHAPTER XXV

Buckfast Abbey after the Dissolution; its lay impropriators. Sir Thomas Denys; providential consequences of his purchase of the Abbey. The Catholic insurrection of 1549. Descendants of Sir Thomas Denys. The Rolle family. The building levelled in 1806.

THE history of our Abbey from the Dissolution to the return of the monks could only be told by relating the history of its lay proprietors during that interval. This I could not attempt to do, but a few notes on its vicissitudes will add to the completeness of our story.

For a long time it remained the property of the descendants of Sir Thomas Denys of Holcombe Burnell. The ancient Devonshire family of Denys bore with pride the three Danish battle-axes on its shield. An ancestor of St Thomas was the William le Deneis whose name appears in the list of witnesses to our earliest Norman charter, in the reign of Henry I. But by the time of Henry VIII. the family had become impoverished, and Sir Thomas set himself to repair its fortunes. This he was enabled to do out of the spoils of the monastic houses, and he availed himself of the chance to the utmost.

"He lived under eight kings and queens of the realm, and was greatly preferred by several of them." Of course, he changed his religion as often as a new religion came in. From some words in his will—he died in Elizabeth's reign—I suspect he was always a Catholic at heart.

As for a century or more the Abbey manor bore the name of Buckfast-Dennis, it would be pleasing if we could meet with any signs that the house of Denys had not abjured the ancient Faith. Although this cannot be shown, yet there is reason to believe that for a long time there were descendants of Sir Thomas who secretly adhered to the religion of their fathers. The subject is to us of such interest that I cannot forbear it altogether.

A devout and charitable priest was Sir Richard Denys, the youngest brother of Sir Thomas, and rector of Powderham. His will was proved at Exeter, on the 24th of June 1533, and in it he leaves all his belongings to be divided between the poor and the priests and friars, who are to say mass for his soul. If his brother was no follower of the good priest's holy example, yet it bore fruit in his nephew George, of whom it can hardly be doubted that he was a younger son of Sir Thomas. I here translate from Davenport's *History of the English Franciscans*, published at Douay in 1665, according to Dr Oliver.

"Brother George Denys, born of a noble Catholic family in the county of Devon, who had been the royal standard-bearer at the siege of Boulogne under Henry the Eighth, before the final suppression of the Order of St Francis received our habit at Greenwich in Queen Mary's time (as was told me some forty years ago by his brother, a man of rank, and an eye-witness of the events, who was then full of days and good works). Being only a novice, he betook himself to foreign parts (a proof of singular fervour), wearing his habit; and going from Brabant to Liege, was professed in our Order, and lived long after, being buried in the cloister, and there I saw his epitaph, which has since been removed."[1]

Father Christopher Davenport, writing after forty years, is clearly in error when he calls his informant a brother of George Denys, but that is a mere slip of memory. The man of rank, who from the praise bestowed on him by the Franciscan was probably a Catholic, must have been a nephew of George Denys. Davenport lived in Cornwall during the reign of Charles I.

Returning to our history, we find the monastery and church, the cemetery, grange, and farm buildings granted by the king to Sir Thomas Denys immediately after the Dissolution; the furniture, church plate, and other valuables, including the church bells, being conveyed away or sold for the benefit of the crown. With the buildings he obtained a portion of the adjacent land, including the manor pound. Six fodders of lead (a fodder weighed upwards of two thousand pounds) were carried off from the Abbey.

The purchase of the entire buildings by Sir Thomas Denys had providential consequences. It saved the Abbey itself from being built into and around, as has been done at Tavistock. It preserved the foundations intact for the future restorers, and

[1] Oliver, *Collections*, p. 22, note.

kept the Abbey isolated from the village, with its charming meadow-land surroundings, shut in by the Dart. To this day, the space between the North and South Gates is exactly as it was, with two small exceptions, with respect to buildings, in the year 1620. What was still more, the little estate of Buckfast-Dennis, by the possession of the manor-pound, remained in possession of manorial rights.[1] It is, therefore, not without reason that we look on the action of Sir Thomas Denys as a material help towards the future restoration of the venerable monastery.

The knight's eagerness for spoil was so well known that he was charged, rightly or wrongly, with having made away with a portion of the lead from the roofs. In great alarm he wrote the following letter, which I have modernised as to spelling :—

" Right Worshipful,

"After my hearty commendations: [I] do perceive by Mr Totyll ye be my very good master according to truth for six fodder of lead, supposed by Grove, Master Arundell's servant, that I should have the custody of. Wherefore [in] truth I never saw no such lead nor parcel thereof; and if I had, I am sure the matter is not so light but he would have had for his discharge a bill of my hand of the receipt, or some other sufficient witness to testify the same. I never was at Buckfast but one time since I did purchase it; therefore if it may please your

[1] For these and other particulars I am largely indebted to the late Mr Searle Benthall, a former proprietor of Buckfast Abbey.

mastership and the rest of my masters in commission with you to enquire for the truth hereof, if then [it] shall appear that I or any one of my servants to my knowledge or consent ever had any part of the said lead, I will promise you by this my writing to give you for every fodder of lead a hundred pounds, and in this way I trust you shall come to the knowledge of the truth, and know him (Grove) to be as he is and I a true man. Good Mr Barnes, for your gentleness in this behalf shewed, I shall think no less, but myself always bounden to gratify you or any friend of yours during my life with such pleasures as shall lie in my whole power, as knoweth the Holy Trinity, to whom I commit you.

"Yours assured,

"THOMAS DENYS.

"To the Right Worshipful William Barnes, Esquire, give this."[1]

He had good reason for his anxiety. Had he been guilty, it might have cost him his life. The Commissioners referred to in the letter were Matthew Colthurst, Robert Grove, who acted as receiver, William Barnes, Thomas Mildmay, and John Wiseman.

Whether it was at the time of the suppression, that the statue of our Blessed Lady in the Abbey church — now restored — was broken to pieces, I cannot say. It is more likely that the sacrilege was committed shortly after the accession of Edward VI.

---

[1] Copied by Mr Brooking Rowe from Land Revenue Records (bund. 1392, pile 31, No. 1).

The destruction of the sacred images and the suppression of the abbeys were among the principal causes of the formidable insurrection of the men of Devon and Cornwall in 1549, when the "abbey men," as they were called, were among the most determined of the insurgents, to whom the abbey lands of Buckfast must have sent many a stalwart recruit. The seventh article of this declaration ran as follows: "We will have the holy bread and holy water every Sunday, palms and ashes at the times accustomed, *images to be set up again in every church, etc.*"

The fourteenth article required two abbeys to be re-established in every county. Above all, they insisted on the mass being said in Latin as before, and "the Sacrament hung over the high altar, and there to be worshipped as it was wont to be. . . . We will not receive the new service, because it is but like a Christmas game; but we will have our old service of Latin mass, and procession, in Latin as it was before." Drs Moreman and Crispin were their spiritual guides from among the clergy of the Exeter diocese. On Whitsunday, the 9th of June, they compelled the parish priest of Sampford Courtenay to sing mass as usual. In a few days an army of 10,000 men marched from Crediton to Exeter and laid siege to the city. Sir Thomas Pomeroy and Sir Humphrey Arundal, knights; Berry, Coffin, and Winslade, esquires; Underhill and Segar, labouring men, were their leaders. Mr Raleigh, the father of Sir Walter, for attempting to expostulate with a countrywoman on her way to church, narrowly escaped with his life.

Lord Russell, who was in command of the royal

forces, with Sir Peter and Sir Gawen Carew, had his headquarters at Honiton. The first engagement was at Feniton Bridge, but Russell, finding his numbers too small, returned to Honiton. Reinforced by a body of German horse, and 300 Italian arquebusiers, he gave battle to the insurgents at Clist St Mary, on the 4th of August. The insurgents, whose standard was raised on a cart, whereon were a crucifix and relics of saints, were at first successful, and captured the enemy's artillery, which they turned against them. On the following day a second battle was fought on Clist Heath, and the superior discipline of the royal army prevailed. Four thousand peasants were butchered in cold blood, the vicar of St Thomas at Exeter was hanged from the steeple of his church in his sacred vestments, and the country was ravaged by fire and sword for miles round. Sir Thomas Denys was active in repressing the revolt. He showed himself more remiss in quelling the Protestant insurrection in Queen Mary's reign. Whether mass was again said in the desecrated church in Mary's reign, I cannot say for certain, but as the church had not been destroyed, though left to decay, it is by no means unlikely.

From Sir Thomas Denys the ownership of our Abbey passed to his son, Sir Robert, who died in 1592. As his brother was a Franciscan and his sister had married into the very Catholic and recusant family of Kirkham, he is likely to have been one of the large class of sympathisers with the Faith, who in those days, as Father Gerard tells us, went among Catholics by the name of schismatics. This is also probable as regards his son, Sir Thomas, who took to wife Anne, the daughter of William Pawlet, Marquess of Winchester, the most powerful Catholic family in England.

This Sir Thomas left no male issue, but his eldest daughter Anne, married to Sir Henry Rolle of Stevenson, carried the manor of Buckfast into that distinguished family. It is worth noting that Sir Henry's grandfather was that John Ford of Ashburton, of whom I have spoken elsewhere. Buckfast Abbey passed to his son, Denys Rolle, called by Prince "the darling of his country." Dr Oliver, in his *Ecclesiastical Antiquities of Devon*, gives an engraving of his beautiful monument in Bicton Church. He married Margaret, daughter of Lord Paulet of Hinton St George, in Somersetshire. Sir John Rolle, who died in 1706, held the manor of Buckfast at the time of his death.

It is said that Sir Richard Baker, the historian, was at one time the owner of Buckfast, but his tenure could only have been of a temporary nature. During the eighteenth century it belonged in succession to the families of D'Oyley and Bradford. Robert Bradford owned it in 1769. The next owners seem to have been the Berrys. They were succeeded by the late Mr Searle Benthall, who sold it to Dr James Gale, from whom it was purchased by the monks. An account of the restoration will be given in the next chapter.

Until the year 1806 it had been left to decay under the slow hand of time. In the *Gentleman's Magazine* for 1796, a description is given by Mr Laskey of the ruins as they then were, in which we are told that "on the north side [of the still existing Abbot's Tower] appear the walls and foundations of this once splendid seat of superstition, the Abbey church, and remains of its tower all lying in such massy fragments, that it is scarcely to be conceived by what power so vast a fabric could be disjointed. The walls appear of the thickness of 9 or 10 feet, and entirely composed of small stones in layers and a compost of lime and sand, which we supposed to have been thrown on these layers hot, after the manner anciently used in such large buildings, which, incorporating together, formed a mass as solid as the native rock. The ruins of this church appear to be about 250 feet in length, and the ruins of the tower towards the south seem like huge and vast rocks piled on one another."

The ruins were left in this condition till the year 1806, when Mr Berry levelled the still standing walls, out of which he built a modern house.

CHAPTER XXVI

St Mary's Fountain in the forest. Père Muard. Arrival of the monks at Buckfast in 1882. The first mass. The temporary church. The Feast of St Robert, 1886. Excavations. Autonomy granted to the community.

THE long night of solitude and desolation that in 1539 settled down on the Abbey of Our Lady at Buckfast seemed destined to be everlasting, but it was not so ordained in the counsels of God's providence. Three hundred and forty-five years were to pass away, and then once more the Adorable Sacrifice was to be offered up within these hallowed precincts by monks of St Benedict, and the first mass said there was to be that of the Patronage of Our Blessed Lady. How this was fulfilled I shall now briefly relate, but shall be obliged first to revert to certain events of somewhat earlier date.

In the second week of May 1849, a venerable French priest might have been seen wandering about, under the guidance of a countryman, through a tangled forest in the desert tract known as the Morvan, not far from Avallon. Sitting down by a clear spring of water, he asked his guide what was the name of the spring, and was told that it had been called St Mary's Fountain from time immemorial, though people knew not why. The servant of God knew then that he had arrived where he was to find the term of a desire that had long consumed him. Father John Baptist Muard—for such was his name—had long been known for his piety and zeal. The Society of Priests of St Edmund of Pontigny had been his first foundation. He had known by supernatural illustration that a greater work awaited him before he should die. He was to found a body of Benedictine monks, whose austerity should approach that of the stricter Cistercian observance of La Trappe, but who should have the active work of the ministry in view. Beside the fountain where he sat down now rises the Abbey of Ste Marie-de-la-Pierre-qui-vire. He died on 19th June 1854, and was buried in presence of a vast concourse of the clergy and people of the diocese. The Archbishop of Sens lost no time in petitioning the Holy See for his canonisation. His work grew and spread, and the French monasteries founded from that of La Pierre-qui-vire have since then, under the guidance of the Holy See, been erected into the French Province of the Cassinese Congregation of the Primitive Observance. Expelled from France in 1880, it was not till two years later that the children of St Benedict, welcomed with fatherly kindness by the venerable Bishop of Plymouth, the late Right Reverend William Vaughan, found a resting-place on English soil. On 28th October 1882, the first Vespers of the Feast of our Lady's Patronage were chanted by Benedictine monks at Buckfast. The Mass of our Blessed Lady was said next morning for the first time since the Reformation, by the two priests who formed part of the little company—six choir-monks, whose lot it was to be the first to enter on their ancient inheritance. Eight months later, on the anniversary of Père Muard's death, the deed was dated which conveyed Buckfast Abbey once more to the monks of St Benedict. But as yet it had not a corporate existence of its own. Its monks formed part of the community of St Mary's of La Pierre-qui-vire, and for several years the late Abbot Stephen Denis, who governed that monastery—a prelate whose memory will forever be in blessing—was the Superior of the monks at Buckfast. At the date of the first coming of the monks he was represented by Dom Thomas Dupérou, who died Abbot of Sacred Heart Abbey in Oklahoma.

The object of the monks on the acquisition of Buckfast Abbey was to erect at least a temporary church till such time as the former one could be rebuilt on its ancient site. The existing neat little church, towards which the venerable Bishop Vaughan, Lieutenant-Colonel Graham, father of Bishop Graham, Dr Macnamara of Torquay, and other friends generously contributed, was opened on Lady-day, 1884, by his Lordship the Right Reverend J. L. Patterson, Bishop of Emmaus. Dr St George Mivart, having visited the monastery, devoted his energies to pushing the work of its restoration, and the tower that still remained was admirably restored under the direction of Mr F. Walters, architect, to which work the Duke of Norfolk and Dr Mivart mainly contributed. A committee was next formed, through the untiring zeal of Dr Mivart, with Lord Clifford as its chairman, and numbering among its members Cardinals Manning and Newman, the Duke of Norfolk, the Earl of Denbigh, Archbishop Ullathorne, Bishop Hedley, Lord Herries, Lord Braye, Sir Paul Molesworth, Messrs Hussey Walsh, E. Gresham Wells, W. H. Lyall, H. Matthews, Q.C., G. S. Lane-Fox, with Dr Mivart and Mr Lilly as secretaries. Mr F. Walters was appointed architect.

Many other generous benefactors assisted in the work of restoration. But it is to the noble munificence of Lord Clifford that the Abbey mainly owes its restoration, and he holds with regard to the community even more than the place held by Roger de Nunant towards their predecessors of the twelfth century, in recognition whereof the arms of the Clifford family are sculptured over the door of the cloister. Under Mr Walters' direction as architect, the work began by taking accurate plans and measurements, down to the smallest detail, of the ancient monastic buildings. The London Society of Antiquaries gave £20 towards the work. The work of rebuilding then began with the south portion. Not a foot of new foundations was laid, the old ones being everywhere built on, and the old walls and all the offices thus came to be raised on their ancient site, cloister and cellarium, staircase, refectory and kitchen, being restored to their places. Even the jambs of the arched doorway leading from cloister into kitchen are, up to a certain height, the ancient ones, and the fireplace stands over the old hearthstone, which had been found under the turf, still blackened by the fire. The style chosen for the restored Abbey was that of the twelfth century, when the Abbey was restored by a colony from Clairvaux, in the reign of King Stephen. The Norman architecture, known in France by another name, had always been deemed by Père Muard the most suitable for the monastic spirit of his children. The designs of the restored Abbey are simple and severe, yet pleasing and graceful, and in the refectory the carved stone capitals, bosses, doorways, and windows are reproduced details from Fountains, Rievaulx, Furness, Chertsey, etc.

On 29th April 1886, Feast of St Robert of Citeaux, the restored portion of the Abbey was opened to the public. The Bishop of Clifton sang the High Mass, the Bishop of Plymouth assisting pontifically, attended by the Right Rev. Provost Brindle, Canons Woollett, Lapôtre, Graham (now Bishop of Plymouth), and Brownlow. Lord Clifford, the Earl of Devon, the Comte de Bari, the Rev. Lord Charles Thynne, Sir Paul Molesworth, a large body of clergy, secular and regular, the members of the Restoration Committee, and a numerous and distinguished company of guests, were present at the Pontifical Mass, and dined in the refectory. The sermon was preached by the Prior of Fort Augustus, Father Jerome Vaughan.

Since the opening of the south portion of the Abbey, excavations and researches have gone on, with a continual addition to fragments and relics of antiquity collected in the museum formed in the basement of the tower. It was found that the Cistercian abbots lay buried down the nave of the ancient church. A rather singular discovery was made in the last week of June 1892. The eastern part of the foundations of the ancient walls of the church was being covered with concrete to preserve and prepare them to support the future erections, the expense being defrayed by a bequest left by the late Dowager Lady Clifford. Here, as throughout the whole of the church, the nave was formerly separated from the aisles by a massive wall 5 feet in width, of which only the foundations remained. It was discovered that the lowest part of these foundations was formed by flat stones, laid edgeways, in two tiers, the upper at right angles to the lower. On the outer edge of the wall—that is to say, looking into the north aisle—by removing the stones from the upper tier, a cavity 6 feet long by 2 feet wide had left room for a tomb, in which a skeleton was found by the workmen. Its position was just eastward of the transept, and the stones on which it rested about 3 feet below the level of the sanctuary, so that the tomb would have been visible to anyone walking in the north aisle. There had always been among the country people before the arrival of the monks a superstitious legend of a yearly apparition on the night of 3rd July on the foundations of the ancient church, and the Rev. Mr Worthy, a former Vicar of Ashburton, in a MS. I have seen, connects it with a certain knight, Sir Wm. Kingdon, who was supposed to have been buried in the north aisle, and who for an undetected murder ought not to have been laid in a hallowed place. I incline to think that the remains are those of a member of the Audley family. They were great benefactors to the Abbey. James and Thomas Audley were buried in the Abbey church about the close of the fourteenth century, and their armorial bearings were displayed in a window only a few feet from the place where the skeleton was found.

For sixteen years the two monasteries of Pierre-qui-vire and Buckfast had been under the government of one abbot, Dom Etienne Denis.

The time had come for the erection of St Mary's into a separate community. At the canonical visitation held in December 1898, by the Right Rev. Abbot-General Dom Dominic Serafini, now Archbishop of Spoleto, the erection was decided upon. A few lines extracted from a letter of his Grace, dated 18th February 1899, are worth inserting here :—

"*To the Monks of the Community of Buckfast Abbey.*

"Dear children and brethren in our Lord,

"In compliance with the wish expressed in the Provincial Chapter, and with the consent of the community of the monastery of La Pierre-qui-vire, we have decided to grant to your community its autonomy, with the right of being governed by its resident Superior.

"While the autonomy carries with it certain privileges, it imposes on you yet more strictly certain obligations of your monastic life. For if fraternal charity has hitherto been one of the brightest adornments of Buckfast Abbey, as we had the happiness of witnessing at our visitation last December, now that your monastic family is constituted in a still more intimate unity, it becomes your duty to draw the bonds of that union more and more closely together, both one with another, and with the Superior who will be given to you with the blessing of Divine Providence.

"It is pleasing to us to trust, dear brethren, that, notwithstanding the different and far-distant lands that have given you birth, you will persevere in the traditions of mutual charity that have distinguished Buckfast Abbey from the beginning, and that you will ever keep before your eyes the sentence which our holy Lawgiver borrowed from St Paul, and established as a foundation-stone to his monastic institute—a sentence which enabled our Fathers in the days of old, with so much advantage to the Church and the Christian State, to train the mighty race of Cenobitical Monks: 'Whether slave or freeman, without distinction of Jew or Gentile, we are all one in Christ, under one Lord we serve as soldiers in one army; since God is no respecter of persons or of nations.'"

By a formal decree, dated Ash Wednesday, 1899, the canonical separation and erection were effected. This decree, however, did not restore to the monastery its ancient dignity of a Benedictine abbey. For a time, it was under deliberation whether this should not be done by a Papal Brief declaratory of the nullity of the suppression under Henry VIII., but it was finally decided to proceed in the usual way, the venerable abbey being again erected by a decree of the Abbot-General.

CHAPTER XXVII

The election of Abbot Boniface Natter, 19th November 1902; his blessing and enthronement, 24th March 1903. The ancient statue of our Lady of Buckfast. The west front of the Abbey completed. Abbot Boniface and Dom Anscar embark on the *Sirio*.

ON the morning of the 19th of November 1902, after the High Mass of the Holy Ghost had been sung, the monks assembled in Chapter to elect the first Abbot of the restored Abbey. Three hundred and seventy-seven years had passed since, in 1525, an Abbot of Buckfast had been canonically elected. The Right Reverend Dom Leander Lemoine, Abbot-Visitor of the Province, presided. The choice fell on Dom Boniface Natter, then absent at Subiaco, as one of the Abbot-General's Consultors. The election was confirmed on the 17th of the following month, and he was installed in choir at Buckfast on the Feast of St Maurus, 14th January 1903.

Dom Boniface Natter was born at Moosbeuren, in Wurtemberg, on the 24th of April 1866, and was christened Anthony. The Natters were of Austrian descent. More than one of the family had emigrated to England in the eighteenth century from Wurtemberg, and seem to have been naturalised here. Lorenz Natter was the most distinguished among these. He was a gem-engraver and medallist of great skill and taste, a high authority on antique gems, and was for a time employed at the Mint. He died at St Petersburg in 1763.

John Claude Natter, another of the family, who died in 1822, enjoyed considerable celebrity for his coloured typographical drawings, and executed numerous works in Great Britain and Ireland. Abbot Boniface showed the present writer some papers in German concerning another relative, one Captain Natter, who had the reputation in the family of having been "an English pirate." From the papers, he seemed to have been employed by Trinity House in some capacity. But it is not unlikely that he may have engaged in privateering on behalf of the British Government. The tendencies and abilities of his ancestors, at least in some particulars, were inherited by Abbot Boniface, whose tastes and sympathies were genuinely English.

He was born on the same day of the year as Père Muard, the holy founder of Pierre-qui-vire, and a train of circumstances in which the guidance of God's providence is recognisable, led him to leave his native Suabian village for France when only twelve years old, and enter among the *alumni* of that monastery. One who knew him in those days, and was a priest when he arrived there, but has now gone to his reward, often spoke to me of his fervour and piety at that age, and the charm of his boyish ways. His devout parents had instilled into his mind the simple and manly faith that moulded his whole being, and in his riper years taught him to repel with abhorrence whatever savoured of worldliness. Thus prepared, his monastic surroundings penetrated his very soul, and to the day of his death his ideal of true nobility, of strength and dignity, was for him realised in his profession as a Benedictine monk. I knew him very intimately, and am stating the simple truth.

He had to quit the monastery for a time at the expulsion in 1880. On the 13th of November 1882, he was clothed as a novice at Buckfast, made his simple vows on the 30th of November 1883, and his solemn vows on the 3rd of May 1887. On the 23rd of November 1890 he was ordained priest by the late Bishop Vaughan of Plymouth.

During the greater part of his career, Dom Boniface was Master of the Alumnate. In training the boys for the monastic life—one of them is now his successor in the abbacy—he was most successful. His standard of religious life was simple and uncompromising, and such as had a genuine vocation soon learned to love and revere it. There was no mistaking it. It was an ideal of the antique cast, manly, cheerful, orderly, austere, and large-minded. And their principles had to be of the highest order. What he taught, he showed by his example.

But though he scouted the idea of a divided allegiance between the usages handed down by our Fathers and the ways of the nineteenth or twentieth century, he was keenly interested in the national life of England. He was more English in heart than many born in England, and obtained from his Superior permission to be naturalised. Perhaps family traditions had something to do with this. He was a Conservative in politics, and intensely loyal. For three years before his election he lived in Italy as one of the Abbot-General's Consultors, and felt keenly any disparaging remark on his adopted country; so much so, that one of his Italian brethren —it was at the time of the Boer war—used to call him in joke, "Chamberlain." He rather enjoyed it.

Always kind, courteous, and hospitable, he won respect by his simplicity and kindliness. His intellectual gifts were considerable, and he was a good theologian. But he was more a man of action than a student; and though an excellent linguist, he never gave himself much to literary studies. His artistic taste was, however, very good.

From childhood he had been most devout to our Blessed Lady, and his first work as Abbot was to place in the Abbey church, for public veneration, the restored pre-Reformation statue of our Lady of Buckfast. It was while praying at the sanctuary of Genazzano that he seemed to hear a distinct intimation of the work that awaited him in England. His piety was deep but unobtrusive, though he was not always able to restrain his tears when before the altar. I feel strongly the danger of rashly canonising our departed friends, and I know well that he had his failings, but what I have written is based on constant intercourse during many years that we lived together.

The election having been confirmed by the Abbot-General, there remained only the solemn blessing and enthronement of the new Abbot. In pre-Reformation times, as our Abbots were not mitred, they were usually blessed by the Bishop of Exeter in the episcopal chapel at Clyst, Chudleigh, or Paignton. (This had been done for the last time when Bishop Veysey blessed Abbot Rede on the 13th of April 1525.)

Bishop Vaughan had died on the 25th of October 1902; his successor in the diocese of Plymouth, the Right Reverend Charles Graham, was to perform the sacred rite for both the first and second Abbots of the restored line.

At this point one of those strange coincidences occurred which seem to bring past and present together. It so happened that while our Abbot was desirous to have the ceremony on the Feast of the Purification, the Bishop's engagements obliged him to fix it at a later date, and it was eventually decided that it should be on the Feast of St Matthias. To no one at the time of making the arrangement did it occur that in so doing, the crowning act in the restoration of St Mary's Abbey would fall on the anniversary of the day in 1539 whose sunset was the last that saw the monks in possession of the venerable Abbey. None remembered that the year that was to open with the reign of the new Abbot was the three hundred and sixty-fifth, the last of a year of years, from that time when men fondly thought the light of our sanctuary had been extinguished for ever; nor did anyone reflect on the inspired words read at the mass of the feast concerning the election of him who was to fill the traitor's place. Here I need only subjoin the account of that memorable day's festivities as it was written by an eye-witness, slightly abridged and altered.

"Two memorable feasts of St Matthias has the old tower of Buckfast Abbey witnessed. One was in the thirtieth year of Henry VIII., a day of sorrow and humiliation, the last on which the poor harassed Cistercians could call their beloved cloister their home. The second was in this third year of King Edward VII., and the dear old Cistercian habit was again to be seen under the shadow of the venerable tower, although now the White Monks were there as honoured guests of the Benedictines, the original founders of St Mary's Abbey on the banks of the Dart. Instead of the ribald crew of Henry's Commissioners, the Lord Bishop of Plymouth, surrounded by a large body of his clergy, with dignitaries of the Catholic Church in their robes, abbots, monks, and religious in the habits of their different Orders, among which the white cassock and rochet of the Canons Regular were conspicuous, had come to enthrone, after a lapse of 365 years, the newly elected Abbot of Buckfast. The white cornettes of the Sisters of Charity, who, on their way from their little dwelling to the church, passed under the very arch of the northern gate that had echoed to the tramp of armed retainers on 24th February 1539, added picturesqueness to last Tuesday's day of rejoicing. To thoughtful minds it gave food for reflection, that the strange coincidence of dates had been undesigned by man. The gay flags and festoons of verdure on all sides were in keeping with the all-pervading feeling of glad thanksgiving.

"So great was the concourse that the stalls of the choir were given up by the monks to their ecclesiastical visitors, the community betaking themselves to the organ gallery. One layman, Lord Clifford of Chudleigh, the quasi-founder of the restored Abbey, is allowed a stall in the choir, by privilege of the Abbot-General. Viewed from the body of the church, and more especially from the tribune erected for the day, the black, white, and purple robes of the occupiers of the choir, and the pontifical vestments of the mitred prelates, formed a scene that was a fitting adjunct to the sacred rites. To some of those present it must have suggested that if a vision of this day could have been unrolled to the eyes of some monk in the hour that he was driven forth by the spoiler, he would willingly have said his *Nunc Dimittis*.

"At eleven, Terce was sung in choir, and Bishop Graham commenced the Pontifical Mass. To the great regret of the community, Abbots Gasquet and Ford, who had most kindly promised to be the two assistant Abbots for the occasion, were both hindered by indisposition; their places were taken by the Abbots of Erdington and Dourgne (France). By them the newly elected was presented to the Bishop, and after the reading of the Apostolic mandate, the ancient oath of fidelity to the Holy See, in its medieval wording, with the promise to observe the Rule of St Benedict, and to administer the goods of the monastery unto the well-being of Holy Church, of his brethren, of the poor and pilgrims, was heard again in Devon after a lapse of well-nigh four centuries. Most touching of all was the closing ceremony, when, after the newly mitred Abbot had given his blessing to the kneeling crowds of the Faithful during the singing of the *Te Deum*, his monks one by one did homage to their prelate and received from him the kiss of peace.

" The sermon was preached after the Gospel by the Right Rev. Mgr. Croke Robinson. Looking on the great event of the day as a landmark in the history of Catholic England and a signal evidence of the indestructibility of the Catholic Church, the preacher passed in brief review the succession of her triumphs following on periods of persecution, as at the conversion of Constantine, and the epochs of St Gregory the Great, Charlemagne, and the close of the Western Schism. So in England, Tudor tyranny, Stuart bigotry, Orange malice, had brought the Faith almost to destruction under Hanoverian oppression, and no ray of hope was visible when in 1773 Alban Butler lay on his death-bed. Then came the revival; through Milner, O'Connell, Catholic Emancipation, Newman and the Oxford Movement, Wiseman and Manning, down to the almost Second Summer of to-day. The highest advance is marked by this day's festival. Glastonbury, Fountains, Furness, and Rievaulx, still lie in desolation, but Buckfast was dead and had risen again; was lost, and is found. To-day is the anniversary of that day of sadness when the old monastic community, 365 years ago, came to an end, by the instrumentality of a traitor abbot; and the subdeacon at the altar had just chanted the words of St Peter, announcing to the infant Church that they were assembled to appoint one to take the traitor's place. Nor had this coincidence of dates been knowingly designed by anyone; it was only discovered after all arrangements had been made, and was a sign of God's hidden counsels.

The three historic revivals of monastic life at Buckfast had originated in France—the eldest daughter of the Church, yet the cradle of the revolutionary spirit. After alluding to the part of the noble house of Clifford in the restoration of the Abbey, Mgr. Croke Robinson wished to all non-Catholics present the greeting of peace implied in the Benedictine motto, 'Pax,' and closed his most eloquent discourse by wishing many years of life to the Abbot, and eternal prosperity to the community.

"Dinner was served at 2.30 in the fine schoolroom, as the beautiful refectory, a gem of architecture, could not have contained the guests, about 130 in number, who had accepted the Abbot's invitation. As the event of the day was an historic one in the annals of Buckfast, a fine tableau was exhibited, giving names and dates of the Abbots of Buckfast from the reign of St Edward the Confessor, with the Abbey arms, impaled with those of the house of Clifford, in the centre; while, to recall the connection of Buckfast with Devonshire history, the family arms of Abbots Gifford, Slade, Matthew, Gill and Rede, impaled with those of the Abbey, were displayed across the north end of the room, facing the Bishop. The portrait and arms of Leo XIII. held the place of honour, and by the side of the Holy Father was a portrait of King Edward VII. in his coronation robes. This last was by special desire of Abbot Natter, who, though not born in England, and of Austrian descent, is legally a British subject, and yields to none in loyalty to his Sovereign. In honour of the guests were ranged round the walls the escutcheons of the Bishop of Plymouth and the late Bishop Vaughan, Lord Clifford, Sir William Butler, the Cassinese and English Benedictine congregations, Abbots Gasquet, Ford, and Natter; and of the Abbeys of Downside, Erdington, and St Augustine's, Ramsgate; being the work of a monk of the Buckfast community, and much admired. Letters to the Abbot, expressive of warmest sympathy and congratulation, and regretting their inability to be present, were received from the Duke of Norfolk; the Earls of Ashburnham, Devon, Denbigh, Gainsborough, Morley, and Mount Edgecumbe, Earl Fortescue, Viscount Halifax; the Lords Herries, Clinton and Seaton, Lord Edmund Talbot, Count Torre Diaz; lJames Hope, Esq., M.P.; F. B. Mildmay, Esq., M.P.; and many others.

"Among the guests present with the Lord Bishop of Plymouth were: Lord Clifford; the Right Revv. Abbots of Erdington, Ramsgate, and Dourgne; the Right Rev. Mgr. Provost Lapôtre; the Right Rev. Mgr. Croke Robinson; and the Very Revv. Canons Hobson and Poole. Benedictines of other communities were represented by the Rev. Sir David O. Hunter-Blair, O.S.B., Bart., head of Hunter Blair's Hall, Oxford; the Revv. L. Lonergan, Adalbert Amandolini, P. Nugent, O.S.B.; the Canons Regular by the Very Rev. Father Allaria and the Prior of Bodmin; the Cistercians by the Prior of Wood Barton. The Superior of the Marists of Paignton and the Rev. Father Durand, of the Basilian Fathers, represented the congregations of later days. The diocesan clergy, worthy successors of those heroic secular priests of the Exeter diocese, of whom nine are said by Strype to have been executed for religion in 1549, when they joined the stalwart Catholic laity who rose for the restoration of the Faith and the monastic houses, formed the largest body of ecclesiastics present.

"If the Catholic element among the great crowd of lay guests counted the historic names of Clifford, Chichester, Berington, Strickland, and Knowles, it was pleasing to see many others, in whom difference of creed was no obstacle to a warm-hearted sympathy with a revival of ancient memories of Devon on this day of gladness. Such were Dr Gibson, Mayor of Totnes, with others of the county magistrates, and William Hamlyn, Esq., the lineal descendant of those Hamlyns of Widdecombe whose family name so often appears in the ancient charters of St Mary's Abbey. Ireland was well represented by Lady Butler and not a few other guests, among whom Dr Macnamara of Torquay gave a noble example of Celtic generosity by an offering of £1000 towards continuing the work of restoration.

"Just before dinner, the following telegram was received from Rome: 'The Pope sends special blessing to Abbot Natter, Lord Clifford, and all present at religious ceremony to-day, and all benefactors, past, present, and future. Ad multos annos.' Several other telegrams of congratulation, notably one from the proto-monastery of Subiaco, arrived during the day. After reading the telegram from Rome, the Abbot expressed the pleasure he had found in the congratulations even of those who were not Catholics, and added that Catholic obedience to the Pope in things spiritual in nowise lessens but confirms the loyalty of Englishmen to the King. He therefore proposed the health of the Holy Father and King Edward. He was himself proud of being an Englishman by the allegiance he had sworn and would ever maintain.

"The Bishop, in proposing the health of the Abbot, wished him many years of happy and prosperous rule, and expressed himself delighted with all that had been done on that day. His lordship described in brief the Abbot's career from the time he had known him. He related also the early days of the community, and how on one occasion a monk who had to be ordained was acting as cook, and in his stead a novice, who had scarcely ever seen a fish before, was put to take his place in the kitchen, with the result that the fish was burnt on one side and raw on the other. In subsequent visits, his lordship was always careful to inquire 'if it was the cook who was to be ordained.' The long line of monks he had seen to-day showed how the community had grown, and their teaching and example would bear abundant fruit in those around them.

"The Abbot returned thanks to those present for the way in which they had received the toast. Though 365 years had elapsed since Abbot Rede, the continuity was complete, and he was his lawful successor. He wished all prosperity to his lordship, who could always rely on the services of the community.

"Mr Tozer proposed the health of the clergy, to whom Catholics must ever look for help, guidance, and consolation. Too often those who had been educated in the faith took these things as a matter of course; but without the labour of the clergy, our children would have been lost. To the credit of the clergy it was, that, since 1870, not a single Catholic school had been given up. He was pleased to say that the laity were doing more now than heretofore to assist their clergy.

"Canon Lapôtre gave thanks in behalf of the **clergy.**

"Canon Hobson proposed the health of the Bishop, and spoke of his long work under Bishop Vaughan, whom he had succeeded.

"The Bishop briefly responded.

"Lord Clifford proposed the health of the community. His lordship said that he had had the pleasure of being among their friends from the time of their first arrival. He likened them to the chosen people coming into their own inheritance, or, according to more modern ideas, they might be compared to a colonial settlement, with which none would be more in sympathy than Englishmen. He then wished all happiness and prosperity to the Abbey, and would always be their firm friend to the best of his power.

"The Abbot ended by saying that he would always do all in his power to help the diocesan clergy, and trusted to see them often at the Abbey."

One of the earliest works undertaken by Abbot Boniface was to restore to its place of honour in the Abbey church the ancient statue of our Lady of Buckfast, of which mention has been made more than once in these pages, and this work of reparation is almost a landmark in our history.

Among the causes that provoked the insurrection in 1549 of the men of Devon and Cornwall, as declared by the insurgents themselves, one was the taking away from the churches of the statues of our Blessed Lady and the Saints by the Royal Commissioners. One of these, the image of our Lady, venerated in the church of Buckfast Abbey, was in part recovered by the monks some twenty years ago, and has since, under the care of Mr F. Walters, been completely restored and the recovered portion incorporated with the rest, yet so as to leave the marks of the sacrilegious destruction distinctly visible. It is 3 ft. 8 in. high, and represents the Blessed Virgin crowned, and with the Divine Child on her right arm. When the statue, or rather the fragment of it, was brought to light, the original colour of our Lady's azure mantle, studded with gold circles, and a broad band of gold down the fold of her robe, was still perfect, and has been accurately reproduced. To make reparation, in these happier times of Edward VII., for the outrage done to the Mother of God in the reign of Edward VI., the restored statue, a work of great beauty, was solemnly blessed and replaced in the Abbey temporary church by Abbot Boniface, on Sunday, Feast of our Lady Help of Christians, 24th May 1903.

South Devon was of old the heart of Mary's Dowry; in her honour were dedicated the abbeys of Buckfast and Buckland, and churches at Holne, Bickington, Totnes, Abbotskerswell, Chudleigh, Dartington, Denbury, Broadkempstone, St Mary Church, and many another. This it is that invests with special significance the unique ceremony at Buckfast Abbey, when, in the presence of a crowded congregation, amid the blaze of tapers, with the chant of hymns and the rites of the Church, our Blessed Lady's beautiful image, placed in a niche above an altar specially constructed for it, was solemnly blessed by the Abbot.

Dr Macnamara's generous gift was devoted to completing the west front of the Abbey, according to the simple but noble designs of Mr Walters. This new portion of the monastery was blessed by the Bishop of Plymouth, on St Joseph's Feast, 19th March 1904.

Abbot Natter's time of government only lasted a little over three years and a half. His zeal for monastic discipline and his devotedness to the welfare of his monastery were conspicuous. He had a deep and affectionate reverence for his Bishop. Beloved by his community and wonderfully popular among his neighbours, he seemed destined to enjoy a long and tranquil term of office. In the month of May he was elected Abbot-Visitor at the Provincial Chapter held at the monastery of Kain-la-Tombe, near Tournai, and was soon after directed by the Abbot-General to visit the monastery of Niño-Dios, in the Argentine Republic.

Leaving Buckfast on Monday, 23rd July, he stopped for a day at St Augustine's Abbey, Ramsgate, to take part in the festivities of the jubilee of that monastery. Thence he travelled to Paris to meet Abbot Lemoine, who was to discharge the duties of office of Visitor during his absence. From Paris he journeyed to Barcelona, where Dom Anscar Vonier, who was to be his companion, had arranged to meet him. They were to embark for Buenos Ayres on the *Sirio*. The *Sirio*, a vessel belonging to the Italian

General Navigation Company, was a steel screw steamer, of 2275 net tonnage, built in Glasgow by Messrs Napier in 1883. The Abbot and Dom Anscar went on board her on Friday, 3rd August. According to the Company's official statement, she had on board 60 first and second class passengers, 695 emigrants, and a crew of 127.

Right Reverend Dom Anscar Vonier, O.S.B., Abbot of Buckfast.
Elected 14th September 1906. Received the Abbatial Blessing from
the Bishop of Plymouth, 18th October 1906.

CHAPTER XXVIII

The wreck of the *Sirio*, 4th August 1906. Death of Abbot Boniface. Election of Abbot Anscar Vonier; his blessing and enthronement by the Bishop of Plymouth, 18th October 1906.

OUR Abbot was, according to his companion's account, quite as cheerful as was his wont during the last three or four days of his life. His conversation was chiefly on Buckfast and its community, on his plans and hopes for the welfare of his Abbey. The sea was calm and the voyage prosperous, until about three in the afternoon of the second day, when the ship struck on the rocks off Cape Palos, not far from Cartagena. Here we may best let Abbot Anscar give his account of his predecessor's last hour of life.

"I left Barcelona with Father Abbot on 3rd August, and as far as we could tell, the vessel seemed to be manœuvred all right, and nothing occurred till it struck the rocks the next afternoon, about three o'clock. I was in my cabin at the time. It was like a heavy grinding, and the impact was so great that it threw me on the floor. As soon as I realised what had happened, I hastened on deck to see the Abbot. I found him on deck with several hundred other passengers, but several of the first-class passengers never came on deck at all. I asked the Abbot what he thought of it. He said, with perfect equanimity: 'I don't think there is any danger, provided the people keep quiet.' We were in view of the coast, and just then a steamer was passing astern of us, and all on deck shouted themselves hoarse to draw her attention, but the steamer did not change its course. The shouting created a pandemonium, but the scene described in some newspapers, stating that arms and knives were used, had no existence. I know that many of the emigrants helped their companions to get into the boats that came later on. The Abbot smilingly said: 'Perhaps you will go down to the cabin and fetch our life-belts?' I rushed down, but could find only the Abbot's belt, which I brought up, and found the Abbot, with two bishops and two priests, on their knees preparing to die. One of the bishops gave general Absolution. I put the life-belt beside Father Abbot, but he did not take it at the moment. When, a second later, he turned round and said calmly, 'Where is my life-belt?' it had disappeared, and he quietly remarked, 'Someone has taken it.' Four or five minutes had passed since the ship struck, and she was still keeping the same position. Just then we felt the deck sinking under our feet, and understood it might be our last hour.

"I fell on my knees, asking the Abbot for Absolution, which he gave me, and I gave him Absolution. Then we embraced each other, and I said in French: 'Good-bye, Father Abbot, for it is the Will of God that we should die; we die happy, we have nothing to lose? He replied, 'Good-bye, Father Anscar,' with great tenderness, and I left him to go to the third-class passengers, in order to prepare them for death. I had hardly gone five or six steps when the sinking ship settled by the stern. Nearly all the first-class passengers, and a few hundred of the emigrants—for what reason I do not know—rushed towards the stern and sank with the ship. I was far enough away not to be carried down, but at the same time the *Sirio* lurched from left to right. This pitched me into the sea. As soon as I felt the water, I made an effort to get out, and succeeded, but how I cannot tell. The only thing I remember is that I clutched something, which I determined not to let go. Very soon I found myself on a part of the vessel that was still above water, with two or three hundred people. Every moment I expected a complete sinking of the ship, and I therefore availed myself of the time to prepare my companions for death, and I witnessed many heroic incidents of resignation to the Will of God with Christian hopefulness. However, the sea being very calm, the bow of the ship kept wedged between the rocks. I could see the rocks under water. The cries of the people, especially the women and children, were most pitiful. The ship's boats, as soon as they were put on the water, were filled with people and capsized, and this several times . . ." After relating how they were taken off by the fishing smack *Joven Miguel*, he continues: "I had not landed half an hour when I heard cries in the street that a Bishop (the Archbishop of Para) had just come ashore, so I ran to a house where he was, and he told me that he had been floating on the sea with his life-belt for four hours. Darkness was coming on when he hailed a passing steamer and was taken on board. He told me that after the sinking of the stern, he came to the surface with five or six others — among them Abbot Natter. Then he saw the Abbot for about a quarter of an hour clinging to a plank, till he was out of sight, and the last thing he saw was the Abbot placing his hand to his face as if to make the Sign of the Cross."—(*Tablet*, 8th September 1906.) The good Bishop wished to conceal awhile from Father Anscar the Abbot's death, lest he should be in his agitated state too much overpowered. He told others that he saw the Abbot's hold on the plank loosened, and that he immediately sank. An Austrian banker, employed in the Austrian consular service, was swimming towards land, and, as he related to Father Anscar, he heard the Abbot behind him praying aloud in English. They had become acquainted on board the *Sirio*, but the Austrian was himself too exhausted to render any assistance. Three days after the wreck, about 550 were known to have been rescued and 382 were reported missing. The brave captain of the *Joven Miguel*, revolver in hand, compelled his crew to stay by the *Sirio* as long as there was the chance of saving a single life. The Brazilian Archbishop of St Paul, who was drowned, gave his cross to be kissed by one of his diocesans, at the last moment, and met his death with heroic calmness, speaking words of comfort to those around him.

So swift and sudden was the last catastrophe that

our Abbot had not time, like his companion, to exercise his ministry on behalf of the passengers around him. Though calm, and resigned to die, yet there was a deep sadness in his last tender farewell that added to the greatness and merit of his sacrifice. His last ardent prayer, as we well know, was for his beloved community.

The grief and consternation of the monks at the first news of the shipwreck was aggravated by the painful suspense of the next few days. Very soon there was no room left for hope, and on the Wednesday after the death of the Abbot the first solemn Requiem was sung. All around the monastery there was bitter grief in every household, as if for the loss of a dear relative, and for weeks afterwards a stream of letters of condolence bore witness to the esteem and affection Abbot Boniface had inspired in all who had known him.

On the 21st of August, the Bishop of Plymouth sang a Requiem Mass at Buckfast for our beloved prelate. Abbot Bergh of Ramsgate, Mgr. Courtenay, Vicar-General of the diocese, with the Provost and the greater past of the Cathedral Chapter, many of the diocesan clergy, and the Cistercian Prior of Wood Barton, were present in the sanctuary. The church was densely crowded, and tears streamed down the faces of many as the solemn chant of the mass was sung by the monks. Very touchingly did Canon Keiley, who preached, allude to the call of our Lord to St Peter over the waters: "Come." That call Abbot Boniface heard in his hour of sacrifice, and obeyed it.

Thirty days have to pass from the death of one

of our Abbots to the election of his successor, and ten days more are allowed for possible appeals against the election. On the Feast of the Exaltation of the Holy Cross, Dom Anscar Vonier was elected to succeed Abbot Boniface Natter.

Dom Anscar was born at Ringschnaitt, in Wurtemberg, not far from the celebrated but now suppressed Benedictine Abbey of Ochsenhausen, on St Martin's day, 1875, and was christened Martin. He entered among the Buckfast *alumni* in 1888, at the age of thirteen, and was ordained priest at Buckfast on the 17th of December 1898, by Bishop Graham of Plymouth. In November 1905, he was sent from Buckfast to teach philosophy at S. Anselmo, in Rome, where he had taken his academical degree a few years before. Leaving Rome for Spain in July 1906, he joined his Abbot at Barcelona, and was shipwrecked with him on the 4th of August, as we have just related. His strenuous resistance to his own election, his attachment to regular observance, and his intellectual gifts, are a guarantee of future success in his office. His monastic patron, St Anscar (Oscar), Apostle of Sweden, entered the monastery of Old Corbie at the same age as Abbot Anscar's, when he came to Buckfast; both held the office of Master of the boys and teacher in the schools of the cloister. Abbot Anscar may be even the hundredth Abbot of Buckfast, for it existed before the days of Old Corbie or St Anscar.

On the 18th of October 1906, he was blessed and enthroned at Buckfast by Bishop Graham.

The eagerness to assist at the ceremony, and the intense emotion felt by those who had the good fortune to be present, were even greater that on the former occasion. Recent events were in everyone's thoughts, and it is no wonder that the features of the youthful Abbot were eagerly scanned as he passed down the church with his two assistants, giving his blessing to the people. The two assistant-abbots were those of Ampleforth and Caermaria, the Abbots of Erdington and Farnborough occupying the first stalls in choir. Other stalls were occupied by the Canons of Plymouth with the Provost and the Vicar-General, the Priors of Ramsgate and Woodbarton, and members of the secular and regular clergy. The scene was impressive and beautiful. About fifty of the diocesan clergy had come to honour the Abbey by their presence, and their trained voices had a noble effect at the singing of the Penitential Psalms and the Litany while the Abbot lay prostrate before the altar, and at the final " Te Deum." Among the laity, Lord Clifford alone, by his privilege as quasi-founder of the restored Abbey, occupied a stall in choir, being next to the Abbot of Erdington. Among the unseen influences that gladdened the hearts of the monks, the presence of their beloved and venerated Bishop was of the most powerful.

Canon Keily preached. He touched a chord that vibrated in the heart of every one of his hearers when he spoke of the election of Abbot Anscar at so early an age. Men might think he lacked the experience that could only come through age and sorrow, "But God had given him 'one crowded hour of glorious life,' in which had been focussed the experiences that made up a long life. He had been to the gates of death, and had returned, and if his heart had not grown, like the prophet's gourd, in a night, all lessons were lost, and the human heart could learn nothing."

Not a few Anglicans were present among the invited guests, and their kindly and sympathetic interest was an indication of the mighty change that has passed over England during the past fifty years.

Devonshire was as worthily represented by Lord Clifford, Lord and Lady Seaton, the Hon. Richard Dawson of Hólne Park, and many others, as by the De Nunants and De Helions in the days of Abbot Eustace, or by the Ordgars and Ordulphs in those of Abbot Ælfwine.

Dr Macnamara, to whom the latest addition to the Abbey buildings was due, could not be absent from such an occasion; and though it would be out of place to give the names of the 180 guests who sat down to luncheon after the ceremony, I must not omit Herr Vonier, the Abbot's brother.

Nor would it be to the purpose to go through the healths proposed and speeches made at luncheon, but a few sentences from the latter will not be superfluous.

The Abbot's speech was indeed worthy of the occasion. He professed his resolve to walk in the footsteps of him whose last blessing he had received on the deck of the sinking ship in the Mediterranean. Many hearts had gone out in sympathy to the monks in their great trial, and the hidden source of this sympathy had been a true appreciation of the vivifying principle of their own, as of every religious community. That principle was a firm faith in the supernatural, a realising by faith of things unseen, the faith that had built up all the old English abbeys, among which Buckfast alone had risen from its ashes. With all his might he would labour to uphold that high ideal which through weal and woe had been the strength of the Abbey. He had just received a telegram from Rome, conveying the Holy Father's blessing and felicitations. All knew that the Papacy was the strongest power on earth for the maintenance of the supernatural ideal. The present Pontiff had shown it in the tremendous sacrifice he had made in France sooner than give up one tittle of what his sense of duty forbade him to abandon. He (the Abbot) was about to propose the health of Pope Pius X. and King Edward, so he would wish to add a word on the latter subject. It was sweet to serve Almighty God under the English flag. (These words evoked loud applause.) Loyalty to the Holy See, loyalty to the King, loyalty to England, were blended together in one in the heart of a monk.

Most kind and genial was the speech of his Lordship the Bishop, as he expressed his delight at the choice of Abbot Anscar by the monks. He recalled with pleasure that from the first tonsure upwards he had conferred every grade in the priesthood on the new Abbot.

Lord Clifford spoke at length on the late Abbot Natter. He felt that there had been a special interposition of God's Providence, disposing that Abbot Natter's last days should be spent in conferring with his future successor on the interests of their monastery. They had all loved and revered

Abbot Boniface. Abbot Anscar was one of themselves, one whom they had known from childhood, and he felt assured of the future prosperity of the Abbey under his rule. So ended another memorable day for Buckfast Abbey.

SINK STONE OF LARGE PISCINA.

[*To face page* 254.

APPENDIX

HISTORICAL NOTES

Thorpe's translation of charter granted in the Exeter Shiremote
A.D. 1040 (*or earlier*).

Here is made known, in this writing, how the compacts were made at Exeter before Earl Godwine and before all the shire, betwixt Bishop Alfwold and the convent at Sherborne, and Care Toki's sons, concerning the land at Holcombe. That was, that they were agreed that the brothers should all go from the land save one who is named Ulf, to whom it was bequeathed; that he should have it for his day, and after his day the land should go as it stands, with meat and with men, without litigation and without contention, to the holy monastery at Sherborne.

Of this are witnesses: Godwine, Earl; and Alfwold, Bishop in Dorsetshire; and Lyfing, Bishop in the North; and Ælfwine, Abbot at Buckfast; and Sihtric, Abbot at Tavistock; and Odda, and Ælfric his brother, and Ordgar and his two brothers, Ælfgar and Escbern; and Dodda Child, and Alon, and Æthelmaer Cola's son, and Osmaer, and Leofwine, at Exeter; and Ælfweard Alfwold's son, and Wiking, and Ælfgar, at Minehead; and Wulfweard, at Winsham; and Hunewine Heca's son, and Ælfwig, at Haydon; and Godman, priest, and Lutsige, in Wight. And whoever will avert this, or think to withdraw it from the holy place, he shall be averted from God in domesday, and be cast down amid the boiling fire of hell torment, with Judas Christ's betrayer, ever eternally condemned, unless he here the more deeply make amends. Of these' writings there are two; one is at Sherborne, and the second at Crediton. One speaks for both.

II.

Sir Roger de Nunant's charter, granted to the monks of Buckfast about 1105; original now in the Abbey.

[The acquisition by Abbot Natter of the original of our earliest charter after the Norman Conquest, referred to in Chapter VI., is almost a landmark in our history. It is beautifully written, and as the writing was in all probability executed by the monks at Buckfast, it gives it an additional interest.

The list of witnesses is headed by the name of "Osbern Rufus, priest." As the knights whose names follow are for the greater part among the most distinguished of the lesser barons in our county, it is likely that there was some reason besides piety for giving the first place to a priest who was not an ecclesiastical dignity.

About the date which I have assigned to this charter as the probable one, died Bishop Osbern of Exeter, the brother of William Fitzosbern, Earl of Hereford, an intimate friend of the Conqueror, and one of his most valiant followers at the battle of Hastings. The Earl received extensive grants in the west. The brothers were near relatives of St Edward the Confessor, and Bishop Osbern had been the Confessor's chaplain. Osbern, the priest who held the place of honour among the knightly signatories, is almost certainly a relative of the Bishop of Exeter, perhaps his nephew. He may even have written the deed. Of course, it is not to be presumed that the noble knights were able to sign their names. The original charter is beautifully written. I have ventured to give my own translation.]

"Notum sit omnibus tam presentibus quam futuris, quod Ego, Rogerus de Nunant, pro salute animæ meæ et uxoris meæ Aliciæ, et liberorum meorum et pro animabus omnium antecessorum meorum et successorum meorum, dedi ecclesiæ de Bocfestria et monachis ibidem Deo servientibus, concessu Guidonis filii mei, et Henrici et ceterorum liberorum meorum in perpetuam elemosinam, solutam liberam et quietam ab omni exactione et servicio seculari, terram meam de Sideham, cum bosco et cum tota mea parte aque ex utraque parte, scilicet ex orientali parte vie que venit a veteri vado de Norbroc usque ad Niweforth in Derta, ut inde inveniant panem et vinum ad missas cantandas. Et ne perversorum hominum malignitate hec nostra cartula irritata cassetur, hanc ipsam sigilli mei munimine confirmo. Qui autem eam cassare presumpserit, maledictionens beate Dei genitricis Marie et meam non evadet. Sed qui cam ratam habuerint et firmam, ejusdem Virginis proteccione letentur. Libertate tamen retenta eundi et redeundi mihi et hominibus meis per viam de Norbroc ad Niwefort ad forum de Aspernetune et communione pasture quantum terra illa porrigitur. His testibus: Osberno rufo presbitero, Henrico de Nunant, Jordano de Hode, Willelmo Walense, Willelmo de Baumes, David-Rogero pe de levre. Willelmo Daco juniore et multis aliis."

Translation.

Be it known to all present and to come hereafter, that I, Roger de Nunant, for the welfare of my soul, and the souls of my wife Alice and my children, and for the souls of all my ancestors and my descendants, have given to the Church of Buckfast and to the monks that serve God there, all my land of Sideham, with the wood and all my portion of the water (the North Brook), on both sides; that is to say: eastwards from the road that cometh from the old ford of Northbrook,[1] as far as New Ford on the Dart; that they may therefrom find bread and wine for masses to be sung. And that this our charter be not made null and void by the iniquity of wicked men, I confirm it by the security of my seal. But whosoever shall presume to annul it shall not avoid the malediction of Blessed Mary, the Mother of God, nor mine. And may they who shall keep it firm and inviolate enjoy the protection of the same Blessed Virgin. The right of way, however, being reserved to me and

[1] *I.e.*, the road that crosses the brook at the Old Ford.

my men going and coming to and from Ashburton market by the way of Northbrook[1] to New Ford, with rights of sharing in the pasture, as far as the land aforesaid extends.

These are the witnesses: Osbern Rufus,[2] the priest, Henry de Nunant, Jordan de Hode, William de Walys, William de Beaumes, David Roger Pe-de-levre (*Pied-de-lièvre* = Harefoot), William Le Denys the younger, and many others.

III.

Abbots of Buckfast from the reign of Ethelred II. whose names have been preserved.

Those marked * are not absolutely certain, and the name of Bishop John Bothe is inserted only on the authority of Scipio Squier, the Devonshire antiquary. Only in a minority of cases has the date of institution been ascertainable; in the rest the date given is the earliest on which the name appears in authentic documents. The list is still very incomplete. Ælfwine was still living in 1066; then follows an interval of seventy-six years to Eustace, and then a gap of half a century to William I. Thenceforward the list seems fairly complete, but in the latter part of the fifteenth century there was a deplorable negligence in the custody of registers. With the exception of Bishop Bothe, whose whole career at Buckfast could not have exceeded two years, we have an interval of thirty-four years between Abbot Matthew and Abbot King.

A.D.		A.D.	
*994	Ælfsige.	1258	Durandus.
1040	Ælfwine.	1268	Henry.
1143	Eustace.	1272	Simon.
1196	William I.	1280	Robert.
1207	Nicholas.	1290	Peter II.
1225	Michael.	1316	Robert II.
1242	Peter I.	1327	Stephen I.
1246	William II.	1332	John I. (of Churchstowe).
1247	Howell.		
1257	William III.	1333	William IV. (Gifford).

[1] *I.e.*, the path along its banks.

[2] *I.e.*, the red-haired, or the ruddy. Perhaps a personal designation but afterwards a family name Rede.

HISTORY OF BUCKFAST ABBEY

A.D.
1348 Stephen II. (of Cornwall).
1349 Philip (Beaumont).
1358 Robert III. (Simons).
1395 William V. (Paderstow).
1400 William VI. (Slade).
1415 William VII. (Beaghe).
1432 Thomas (Rogger).
1440 John I. (Ffytchett).
1449 John II. (Matthew).
*1464 John III. (Bothe, afterwards Bishop of Exeter).
1483 John IV. (King).
1498 John V. (Rede).
*1500 Seinclere (Pomeroy).
1512 Alfred (Gill).
1525 John VI. (Rede).
      (Gabriel Donne, intruded in 1536, cannot be counted among our Abbots.)
1902 Boniface (Natter). Elected 19th November 1902. Confirmed 17th December 1902. Installed 14th January 1903. Received from the Bishop of Plymouth his abbatial blessing, and was enthroned in the Abbey Church, on the Feast of St Matthias, 24th February 1903. Perished in the wreck of the *Sirio*, 4th August 1906.
1906 Anscar Vonier. Elected 14th September 1906. Confirmed 31st September. Installed 9th October. Received the abbatial blessing and was enthroned by the Bishop of Plymouth, 18th October, Feast of St Luke, 1906.

Among the very numerous Anglo-Saxon Abbots from the western counties whose names appear in Wessex charters, are necessarily those of Buckfast. But as they do not hold the names of their monasteries, they cannot be identified without great difficulty.

IV.

The Arms of Buckfast Abbey.

These are given by Mr Brooking Rowe as—sable, a crozier in pale argent, the crook or, surmounted by a stag's head caboshed, of the second, horned gules. A sketch is given in Leland's *Collectanea*.

But in Carew's Scroll of Arms (Harleian MS. 2129 and 5871 in Brit. Mus.) they are twice given *azure* instead of *sable*. The authority of Sir George Carew, Earl of Totnes, is very great, and it is clear that there was some variation in use in the arms of our Abbey. Abbot Anscar has decided to |follow Carew's description. Lord Clifford has most kindly granted permission to the community to impale the arms of Clifford with their own.

V.

St Edmund's Church at Kingsbridge.

Kingsbridge forms part of Churchstow, one of the Abbey possessions in Saxon times. Even in those times it is not unlikely that it had its oratory, in addition to the parish church of Churchstow, for the use, at least on week-days, of a priest from the Abbey who would be there occasionally, or of the Abbot himself, and the labourers would hear mass there, though on Sundays and feast-days they would hear it in the parish church.

A substantial church, built by the monks of Buckfast, certainly existed at Kingsbridge in the thirteenth century, if not earlier. From W. Davies, Esq., of Kingsbridge, to whom I am much indebted, I learn that a document extant among the Kingsbridge Church records, contains an examination of witnesses before Bishop Stapeldon, A.D. 1309. The witnesses affirm that for sixty years at least before that date, a church had existed in Kingsbridge with all ecclesiastical rights save that of sepulture. This takes us back to at least A.D. 1250, possibly to an earlier date.

Either Howell or William (III.) was Abbot in 1250. The

Abbey was prosperous at that date, and it was a likely time for the monks, who were fond of building, to undertake the erection of a substantial church at Kingsbridge.

Now Mr Brooking Rowe has given, from Hawkin's *History of Kingsbridge*, an undated document which he says was written "probably late in the twelfth century." This is, of course, quite possible, but it is also possible that it belongs to the earlier half of the thirteenth. The latter part must have presented some difficulty to the transcriber, perhaps from the writing being decayed, though one can see, at least in part, what was intended. It is with the first lines that we are concerned, which are quite clear, and may be translated as follows :—

"Be it known to all, present and future, that I, M. (perhaps for Magister) de Littlecumba, Rector of the Church of Churchstow, have granted to the Abbot and Monks of Buckfast that they may build a church in honour of Blessed Edmund, King and Martyr, in their demesne, in the vill that is called Kingsbridge." This is clearly the church referred to in 1309. Now, as it is not possible that a church having all rights save that of sepulture could have remained unconsecrated for over a century and a half, and as a church whereof the principal walls remain standing would not be re-consecrated, what are we to say of the consecration of Kingsbridge Church by Bishop Stafford, on the 26th of August 1414? Clearly this: that at some date between 1309 and 1414, perhaps about 1400, in which the enterprising Abbot Slade entered on office, the church was so enlarged that the greater part of the walls were levelled to make a larger church. The parishioners in 1414 say that it had been built "long ago"; but they might well have thought ten years quite long enough to wait for the consecration. The style of the church would help to settle the question, though changes of style appear somewhat later in Devonshire churches than elsewhere.

VI.

Possessions of the Abbey at Buckfastleigh itself at the time of the Dissolution.

For the information contained in this note the writer is indebted to the kindness of E. F. Tanner, Esq., of Hawson

Court, Buckfastleigh, secretary to the Dartmoor Preservation Association.

The society in question is fortunate in having for its chairman Mr J. Brooking Rowe, to whom I am indebted for by far the greatest part of what is contained in the preceding pages. The first volume of the society's publications is of the greatest value, both for antiquarian research and as a defence of the rights of common, exercisable on Dartmoor. It contains an admirable historical introduction by Sir F. Pollock, a History of the Rights of Common upon the Forest of Dartmoor and the Commons of Devonshire, by Mr Percival Birkett, a Summary of Evidence for the said rights, and upwards of sixty pages of hitherto unpublished documents in support of the Summary. What is mainly of interest for the Abbey of Buckfast is the evidence, in the first place, in the reign of Henry VIII., that "John, Abbot of the Monastery and House of Our Blessed Lady of Buckfast," held in right of the said Monastery, South Holne Moor, Brent Moor, and Buckfast Moor.

Another document of great interest is a list of " Ye demeanys that belongyth to the Abbe of Buckfast . . . the whiche Sir Thomas Denys Knyght hath purchasyd of the Kyng. Here followith, the tennts namys that holdith the Demeanys and the rente of ev'y pcell thereof.

"Peter Rowland and Thomas Golde holdith a close called the brode furlong for . . . vj*li.*
The same Peter holdith a close called Byrcherd Parke for . . . . . xxxiii*s.* iiii*d.*
John Ferys, Thomas Styrges, and Thomas Bove holdith Howkemer wood and lower Byrgyer mede for . . . · . . iiij*li.*
Wyllym Langeworthye holdith the hier Byrgerd mede and Byrgerd Ball for . . xl. . . .
Thomas Bovey holdith Bremelby and Whaythill for . . . . . . iii*li.* vi*s.* viii*d.*
John Serell and John Goolde of Chageforde holdith a certen ground callyd betwene ii styles for vi*li.*
Robert Hamelyn holdith the Northwode and Henbery woode and Henbery downe for . vi*li.*
Wyllym Felbert holdith the daye house at Graunge

and a close callyd Langb ... and a lytell medowe for . . . . . iiii*li*.
Robert Bovey, James Madoke, Saund Skynner, and Walter Dollyng, they holdith the fysshin with c'tayne gardens for . . . vi*li*. xiij*s*. iii*d*.
John Dolling holdith the south pke for . lvi*s*. viii*d*.
Robert Bovey holdith Shippery parke for . . xii*s*.
John Chase holdith Laverens mede and c'tayne howeses in the Abbey for . iii*li*. vi*s*. viii*d*.
John Beryd at Stert holdith a medowe . vi*s*. viii*d*."

Almost all of these demesnes still bear the same names, and many of the families named therein are still living in the neighbourhood. Among the Abbey possessions was likewise that part of Dartmoor, as we have said, known as Buckfast Moor, the limits whereof are still marked out.

VII.

Some discoveries during excavations.

In the basement of the now-restored tower, formerly belonging to the master of the lay-brothers, and adjoining their quarters (the *cellarium*), a museum has been found of many hundreds of fragments of masonry, or other objects, discovered in the course of excavation. A large number of blue, yellow, and green encaustic tiles; a fragment of stained glass with the figure of a pelican; a "leaden" *bulla* of John XXII.; pieces of carved stone and statuary in every variety of style (from Early Norman to Late Perpendicular), coins, etc., are in the collection. Some of the objects form the illustrations to these pages; one deserves a special description, which I give in the words of a learned member of the Society of Antiquaries:—

"The French Benedictine monks, now at Buckfast in Devonshire, whilst digging out the foundations of the old Abbey church, came upon a circular-headed copper-gilt door of a small shrine, enriched with enamel, which, through the kindness of our Fellow, Mr Walters, is exhibited here to-night. It measures almost 4 ins. in height by 2½ ins. in width. Mr

Franks, C.B., and Mr Charles H. Read, F.S.A., say it was made in Limoges, and is of early thirteenth century manufacture. The design on the door is a gilt half figure of an angel issuing out of a white and blue cloud. The wings are erect and crossed in saltire over the head. The left hand is raised in prayer, and the right hand is hid by the keyhole. This keyhole Mr Franks believes to be as old as the rest of the shrine. The face of the angel is three-quarters shown. The nimbus is green. The background is blue, powdered with eleven roses. A perfect shrine, of the same date and ornamented with like roses and clouds, is in the possession of the Soc. Antiq., London. These enamelled reliquaries of Limoges are often called in inventories *Cofra Lemovicensis* or batent de Limoges. The British Museum and South Kensington Museum have several perfect examples, and in Laberte's *Handbook of the Arts of the Middle Ages* at least three are engraved."

VIII.

Holcombe Burnell, the home of Sir Thomas Denys.

The following interesting description of Holcombe Burnell, the home of the first lay proprietor of our Abbey, in whose family it remained for several generations, I owe to the kindness of a friend, Mr H. Hems of Exeter :—

"After getting clear of St Thomas, on the opposite bank of the Exe, it is an almost continuous ascent to Long Down (three miles), which is part, I believe, of Holcombe Burnell. The place consists, in the main, of a few small houses, standing on the right-hand side of the main road from Exeter. It faces a deep pitch of combe, wild and hilly. Here the road forks. Taking the highest, the right-hand one (the way to Tedburn-St-Mary), in a short space and upon the highest ground in the neighbourhood, a wood of considerable extent is reached (on the left). At its very commencement is a path which by tortuous windings leads right through to the other side, and communicates with a bridle road. Following its slight descent, the manor-house, now known as Holcombe Burton, is seen almost immediately, and the embattled western tower of the adjacent church of St John the Baptist. The farm is in the occupation of Mrs Sophia Channing. Hard by is a modern village school that jars on the medieval grouping of the surroundings.

"Although really nestled in a dell, the church and adjacent manor-house stand upon well-wooded high ground, and from the south side of the former there is an extensive view of the surrounding country.

"The house is of Tudor character. Its windows are low, square-headed, and divided by three stone mullions, with lead glazing. The brick chimneys are covered with ivy. The back faces a rather deep dingle. The original building appears to have extended still further westward, for some old oak panelling on the south end of that side, looking to the uninitiated like a blocked window, was once internal panelling, and indicates that part of the fabric has gone. The old brick boundary wall, separating the front garden, is original, and shows how an ancient brick wall appears that has never been re-pointed. It is as old as any of the brickwork at Hampton Court.

"The church is small; simply nave, chancel, north aisle, S.-W. porch, and low embattled western tower—a distinctly fifteenth-century edifice. There are indications of a much earlier building; the belfry windows are lancet ones. But oldest of all is the head to the south-west doorway, a small well-preserved specimen of good Norman. It shows three carved heads, one the keystone, the others terminals, with circular pateræ between. Part of the granite-coped fifteenth-century boundary wall remains, to the south of the church. The monolith octagonal shaft of the old cross still remains."

IX.

Abbot John Rede.

That our last pre-Reformation abbot was expelled to make room for Gabriel Donne is very probable from a letter, dated from Antwerp, 31st July, of Thomas Tebolde to the Archbishop of Canterbury, where he writes that "within these five or six weeks he (Donne) is come to England, and by Mr Secretary's help has obtained an Abbey of 1000 marks in the west country." Abbot Rede would naturally apply to the Bishop of Exeter for a benefice. A few months after the intrusion I find a John Rede vicar of Davidstowe in Cornwall.

INDEX OF NAMES OF PERSONS

(CHIEFLY WITH REFERENCE TO TIMES PRIOR TO
A.D. 1539)

	PAGE
ACTON, Philip	179
Adam of Bridestowe	124
Adam of Lidford	124
Ælfric, monk at Deerhurst	21
Ælfwine, Abbot	7, 19, 27
Ælfsige, Abbot	17
Æthelstan, King of England	4
Alan of Exeter	124
Albemarle, John de	85
Alfwold, Bishop	20
Allaria, Abbot	238
St Anscar	250
Anscar, Abbot (see Vonier)	
St Anselm, Archbishop	51
Arnold, Prior (see Guy)	
Ash, Robert	153
Audley, James and Thomas	227
Avery, William	210
Aylmer, Abbot	18
BARI, Comte de	225
Barlynch, John	153

INDEX OF NAMES OF PERSONS

	PAGE
Bathe, Walter de	83
Bauceyn, Stephen and Richard de	90-92
Baumeis, William de	42
Beaghe, William, Abbot	153, 170
Beaumont, Philip, Abbot	142
Beaumont, William	145
Bede, Venerable	14
Beornwyn, the Lady	8
Bergh, Thomas, Abbot	238, 249
St Bernard of Clairvaux	58
Birt, Don. Norbert	10
Blondy, Richard, Bishop	99
Bodmin, Prior of	238
Boniface, Abbot (see Natter)	
B. Boniface of Savoy, Abp.	91
Bothe, John, Bishop	175
Braose, William de	69
Braye, Lord	224
Brindle, Mgr.	225
Briteville, Guy de	83
Bronescombe, Walter, Bishop	97 *sqq.*
Brownlow, Bishop	225
Buckfast, Arnold and William	179
Budde, John and William	153
CANUTE (see Knut)	
Challons, Ralph de	83
Champernowne, Sir Philip	113
Chester, Walter	153
Chichester, family of X.	149
Clifford, the Dowager Lady	226
Clifford of Chudleigh, Lord	225, 235
Clifford, Rt. Rev. Bishop	225
Clinton, Lord	36

INDEX OF NAMES OF PERSONS

	PAGE
Coffin, Edmund	154
Cole, Philip	124
Courtenay, Hugh de	122
Courtenays (see Devon, Earl of)	
Cowle, John	210
DAVID the huntsman	42
Dawson, Hon. Richard	252
Davidson, J. B.	2, 3
Denbigh, Earl of	225
Denis, Stephen, Abbot	227
Denys, Sir Thomas	214
Denys, William le	42
Devon, Countess of	166
Devon, Edward, Earl of	164
Devon, Earl of	225
Dodda Child	35
Donne, Gabriel	195 *sqq.*
Dove, Richard	141
Doyge, John	210
Durand, Abbot	98
EDGAR, King	23
Edmonds, Canon	x
Ednoth, Bishop	17
Edward the First	107
EDWARD THE SEVENTH	240, 253
Erdington, Abbot of	235
Ethelmode, Bishop	2
B. Eugene III, Pope	57 *sqq.*
Eustace, Abbot	41, 47, 53
FERRERS, William de	85
Ffytchett, John, Abbot	173
Ffytchett, Sir Thomas	173

INDEX OF NAMES OF PERSONS

	PAGE
Finamore, William	85
Ford, Edmund, Abbot	235
Ford, John	181
Fougères, Ralph de	49
GASQUET, Aidan, Abbot	142, 235
Gifford, Walter	124
Gifford, William, Abbot	112, 124
Giffords	137
Godman the Priest	21
Gorwet, Richard	153
Graham, Rt. Rev. Charles, Bishop of Plymouth	225, 233, 249
Grandisson, John de, Bishop	132 *sqq.*
Guy, Arnold, Prior	188, 195, 209
Gyll, John, Abbot	186
Gyll, Thomas	186
Gyst, William	153
HAMELIN of Deandon	83
Hedley, Rt. Rev. Bishop	224
Helion, Sir Robert de	82 *sqq.*
Hems, Harry	x
Henry, Abbot	92, 98
Henry of Poundstock	98
Herries, Lord	224
Hingeston-Randolph, Rev. F. C.	140
Hode, John de	41
Howell, Abbot	89
Huddleston, Abbot	199
Hugh of Brent	124
Hunter-Blair, Rev. Sir David Oswald	238
INNOCENT III., Pope	66
KEAULA, Martin	88
Keily, Canon	251

INDEX OF NAMES OF PERSONS

	PAGE
King, John, Abbot	175
Knut	19, 23
Kulla, Hugh	88
LANE-FOX, G. S.	224
Lemoine, Abbot Leander	229
LEO XIII., POPE	237
Leofric, Bishop	28
Lilly, W. S.	224
Llandaff, Viscount	224
Lyfing, Bishop	19
MACNAMARA, Dr	239, 252
Manning, Cardinal	224
Marchant, Robert	154
Margaret, nun at Lacock	106
Martyn, John	154
Matthew, John, Abbot	154, 173
Matthews (see Llandaff)	
Michael, Abbot	78
Mivart, Dr St George	225
Molesworth, Sir Paul	225
More, Waryn de la	85
Muard, Père	221
NATTER, Boniface, Abbot	229 *sqq.*
Newman, Cardinal	224
Nicholas, Abbot	77
Norfolk, Duke of	177, 224
Nunant, Sir Roger de	38
Nunants, de	39-43
ODDA, Earl of Devon	21
Ordulf, Earl	22
Osbern	41

INDEX OF NAMES OF PERSONS

	PAGE
Patterson, Bishop	223
Paderstow, William, Abbot	153
Peter (I., II.), Abbots	78, 80, 89, 120, 127
Petre, Sir William	33, 201, *sqq.*
St Petrock	9, 10
Philip, Abbot	33
PIUS X., POPE	253
Pomeroy, Seinclere, Abbot	44, 80
Pomeroy, Sir William	101
QUIVIL, Bishop	117
REDE, John, Abbot	113, 187 *sqq.*
Reichel, Rev. O.	5
St Robert of Citeaux	225
Robert, Abbot	100, 107, 120, *sqq.*
Robinson, Mgr. Croke	236
Roddon, John	154
Rogger, Thomas, Abbot	172
Rowland, Stephen	153
B. SERLO, Abbot	58
Shapcott, William	210
Shilstone, John de	85
Simon, Abbot	105
Simons, Robert, Abbot	138
Slade, William, Abbot	173
Spitchwick, Michael de	83
Splatt, Richard	210
Stafford, Bishop	160
Stapeldon, Bishop	122
Staymbourne, John	179
Stele, Edward	153
Stephen, Abbot	133, 135
Stourton, John	153, 155
Sturgeon, John	154

INDEX OF NAMES OF PERSONS

	PAGE
TAYLOR, Richard	210
Theobald, Archbishop	62
St Thomas of Canterbury	62
St Thomas of Hereford	91
Tracy, Sir William de	64
Tyulla, Richard	102
ULLATHORNE, Archbishop	224
VALLETORTS	70, 85
Vaughan, Dom Jerome	225
Vaughan, Rt. Rev. William, Bishop of Plymouth	222, 225
Veysey, Bishop	223
B. Vitalis of Savigny	45 *sqq*
Vonier, Anscar, Abbot	245
WALSH, Hussey	224
Walter of Plympton	124
Walter of Totnes	124
Walters, Frederick	224
Walton, Miss	x
Ware, John, Bishop	144
Watts, John	153
Widworthy, Sir William de	112
William, Abbot	89
Woodbarton, Prior of	239
Worthy, Charles	ix

PRINTED BY OLIVER AND BOYD, EDINBURGH